"Effective homileticians are always treading on new terrain to plow groundbreaking pulpit pathways. In *Preaching Through Time*, Casey Barton skillfully reveals his reconstruction of homiletics vis-à-vis the lenses of anachronism and the drama of participation. This book will expand your homiletical horizons to see the preaching enterprise in fresh ways so that your listeners will zealously partake in God's drama of redeeming a fallen world and even take pleasure in the process as well."

—MATTHEW D. KIM
Associate Professor of Preaching and Ministry,
Gordon-Conwell Theological Seminary;
author of *Preaching with Cultural Intelligence:
Understanding the People Who Hear Our Sermons*

"How confident are we in preaching that the Spirit speaks now through ancient texts? Without marginalizing the need for careful exegesis, Barton denies that historical distance between ourselves and the biblical texts is an ugly ditch to be bridged. He compellingly calls us instead to homiletical practices consistent with the truth: by divine wisdom Scripture is inherently suited to empower the church in mission through time as we participate in the fulfillment of God's eschatological purposes."

—STEPHEN CHESTER
Professor of New Testament, North Park Theological Seminary

Preaching Through Time

Preaching Through Time

Anachronism as a Way Forward for Preaching

CASEY C. BARTON

Foreword by
Paul Scott Wilson

CASCADE *Books* • Eugene, Oregon

PREACHING THROUGH TIME
Anachronism as a Way Forward for Preaching

Copyright © 2017 Casey C. Barton. All rights reserved. Except for brief quotations in critical publications or reviews, no part of this book may be reproduced in any manner without prior written permission from the publisher. Write: Permissions, Wipf and Stock Publishers, 199 W. 8th Ave., Suite 3, Eugene, OR 97401.

Cascade Books
An Imprint of Wipf and Stock Publishers
199 W. 8th Ave., Suite 3
Eugene, OR 97401

www.wipfandstock.com

PAPERBACK ISBN: 978-1-4982-3464-1
HARDCOVER ISBN: 978-1-4982-3466-5
EBOOK ISBN: 978-1-4982-3465-8

Cataloguing-in-Publication data:

Names: Barton, Casey C. | Wilson, Paul Scott, 1949–, foreword.

Title: Preaching through time : anachronism as a way forward for preaching / Casey C. Barton ; foreword by Paul Scott wilson.

Description: Eugene, OR : Cascade Books, 2017 | Includes bibliographical references.

Identifiers: ISBN 978-1-4982-3464-1 (paperback) | ISBN 978-1-4982-3466-5 (hardcover) | ISBN 978-1-4982-3465-8 (ebook)

Subjects: LCSH: Preaching.

Classification: BV4211.2 .B25 2017 (print) | BV4211.2 .B25 (ebook)

Manufactured in the U.S.A.   JULY 26, 2017

Unless otherwise indicated, all Scripture quotations are from the ESV® Bible (The Holy Bible, English Standard Version®), copyright © 2001 by Crossway, a publishing ministry of Good News Publishers. Used by permission. All rights reserved.

Images from *Testament* are used by permission of the author, Douglas Rushkoff.

To those who have mentored me
in a love for the art and theology of preaching:
Preston Busch, Scott M. Gibson, and Paul Scott Wilson

And especially to those who have put up with me along the way:
first Sarah, then Eugene, and finally, Theo

I am God, and there is no other; I am God, and there is none like me, declaring the end from the beginning and from ancient times things not yet done, saying, "My counsel shall stand, and I will accomplish all my purpose."

—Isaiah 46:9–10

We speak about a theopoetic because the theme of divinity requires a dynamic and dramatic speech. Divinity has to do with the glory of God and the creature's participation in it. But this means participation in his life and activity and this is something other than passive mystical illumination or epiphanies of the sacred.

—Amos Niven Wilder, *Theopoetic*

Contents

Foreword by Paul Scott Wilson | ix

Introduction: Anachronism for Preaching: The Sermon In and Out of Time | 1
1. Hermeneutics and Their Homiletical Practices | 12
2. Practical Eschatology: Reclaiming Time for the Pulpit | 58
3. Now and Then: A Dramatic Organization of Time | 87
4. Anachronism: Traveling through Time | 111
5. The Anachronistic Sermon: Preaching Times Together | 163

Conclusions: Restoring Time to Our Preaching | 194

Appendix: Sermons Out of Time | 203
Bibliography | 227

Foreword

In February 2016, scientists celebrated the first evidence of gravitational waves in outer space. Einstein first predicted the existence of these waves more than one hundred years ago in his general theory of relativity, but it took this long to establish their existence. He theorized that gravity affects the shape of space and the flow of time, that time slows down as one approaches the speed of light, and that space is like a bed sheet with wrinkles in it. Kip Thorne, a scientist who spent his entire career trying to prove the existence of gravitational waves, sent an email on the occasion of the confirmed discovery, writing, "Until now, we scientists have only seen warped space-time when it's calm. It's as though we had only seen the ocean's surface on a calm day but had never seen it roiled in a storm, with crashing waves."[1] Such confirmation opens new dimensions of science and ways of conceiving the universe.

Homiletics is not quantum science, yet in his own way Casey Barton pioneers theory reconceiving the role of time and space for preaching. He invites preachers to explore whether in their representation of the Bible they are limited to then and now. Traditionally, preachers use a bridge between the biblical text and the present, between what a text meant and what it means. Each has its place. The bridges preachers generally build are limited to identity (what was then is the same now), analogy/simile/metaphor (what was then is like now in this particular regard), or allegory (then is really a code language for what we may unlock now). Of the three, the allegory bridge has been the most rickety, notably with biblical texts that have a plain meaning that is rejected in favor of a new set of imagined parallel

---

1. Overbye, "Gravitational Waves Detected," para. 11.

meanings, a process of interpretation known as allegoresis. Every detail has a corresponding connection in the new code. In Genesis 24, for instance, where Rebekah gets water for Abraham's servant and his camels, some fanciful preacher might suggest that the water of God's Word was intended for both the house of Israel and for those outside it. The advantage of the earlier two bridges is that the biblical text is safeguarded and preserved in faithful ways that resonate with apostolic and catholic faith, or the *fidei regula*.

Barton's study of time and space opens options for creative preachers who seek something other than a bridge. He offers anachronism, normally a literary device that juxtaposes things and people from different times and places. If one was using anachronism simply as a literary device, which is less than what Barton intends, a sermon on Luke 1:39 ("In those days Mary set out and went with haste" to see Elizabeth) might portray Mary putting on her Nike running shoes for the journey. A sermon on John 4:1–27, the woman at the well, might portray Jesus entering a roadside cafe where the woman is a waitress coming around with the menus and a pitcher of water. Anachronism is a form of temporal and spatial contradiction. What is presented cannot be because it belongs in another time or place. The root meaning of anachronism is "against" or "out of" time. Because our common notions of time and space are inseparable, anachronism is not limited to temporal matters.

Barton encourages preachers to think of anachronism as a defining feature of the whole sermon, not just a detail here or there that is placed in a time where it does not fit. He conceives of the entire sermon as a drama in which past, present, and future meet, where time and space become fluid, much as they are in many movies. Past time may still be represented as past, but it is nonetheless currently present, not cut off or remote. The future too can be simultaneously present, instead of being impossibly separate. Any place can be co-present with any other space (again, as in movies).

We tend to think of anachronism as something from the past put in the present, or something present put in the past. Barton encourages preachers to think of it also with regard to the future, especially the future present, God's eschatological promises fulfilled or being fulfilled. Each moment is open to the inbreaking of salvation. Traditional notions of sequential time or *chronos* give way to *kairos* time in which anything might happen in the presence of God. Anachronism is time viewed in part from God's perspective, a theological scaffold for God's saving acts.

WHAT PROBLEM MIGHT THIS FIX?

Is something broken that anachronism addresses? Anachronism is an alternative to the traditional sermonic concept of application. Application tends to put time in boxes and, some would say, thereby to distort it. Rudyard Kipling said, "East is east and West is west and never the two shall meet," and the same is true of time—past is past and present is present. This modern notion of time tends to be binary and prioritizes the present over the past. What matters most is now. God's character in the past tends to be suppressed in favor of how God's character is perceived in the present. In this modernist approach, the past is examined for propositional truths that are then brought forward through history and presented as universal or timeless truths in the present. In preaching, these truths are often stripped of their contexts, or the present context and worldviews are artificially imposed on the past. Information about God is the main focus, not a dynamic or experiential relationship with God. When information is prioritized over experience, listeners tend to become passive recipients who then still need to appropriate what is said for their own lives. Part of the purpose of preaching can be conceived as the breaking down of fixed barriers between then, now, and tomorrow.

Literary scholar Zhang Longxi, who is well versed in both Eastern and Western thought, is suspicious of the adequacy of history to recapture the past: "The past cannot be fully present in the historical account."[2] He adds, "Historical grounding turns out to be nothing more than constructing a context for a literary text out of other historical accounts, and the obvious circularity of such textual construction makes it difficult to substantiate any claim to historical truth or authenticity."[3] This line of thought has implications for preachers who may not have questioned the adequacy of historical, information-laden approaches to the biblical text. What history can do is give a reasonable approximation of what is known about the past, but on its own it may not be able to represent it well. The maxim for oral composition is show don't tell. If preaching on the wedding at Cana in John 2, it might be accurate historically to write an essay about the text in its historical setting. However, if a preacher were with words to paint a picture of the events, to communicate an experience complete with the smell of roast lamb cooking, the sounds of children playing to stringed musical instruments, and the bouquet of gallons of water turned to red wine, history might come to life. Another literary scholar, Hayden White, once argued that modern thought

2. Zhang, *Allegoresis*, 46.
3. Ibid., 57–58.

draws a false distinction between history and fiction or imagination.[4] Sometimes we get closer to history through drama, as seen for instance in the popular British fictional TV series *Downton Abbey*, where the period around World War I comes alive in ways that traditional history cannot capture.

Barton's notion of anachronism presents an alternative or postmodern understanding of time. Instead of time conceived as a series of fragments, with priority given to the present, anachronism envisions a continuum of time and space, where the common unifying element is the ongoing nurture of a loving God working out God's saving purposes for the world. God does this not least by conscripting Christ's followers in God's metadrama. Time represents both our distance from biblical texts and our connections to them, as Barton notes: "Time is our hermeneutic" (page 58). Instead of balancing or maintaining a tension between then and now, preaching generates a new moment of experience. That moment is in continuity with all other moments; there are no barriers between them, nor is one artificially cut off from others. The moment is nonetheless specific to the worship time and culture.

While Barton's notions of time and space may seem newfangled and out of the ordinary, they are rooted in the Bible, where he finds Paul and Luke enrolling the church in the past and the future, in medieval preaching and art, and in much contemporary film. Anachronism as Barton conceives it is not just an occasional literary device, like Peter after Jesus's arrest wearing sunglasses and a Red Sox cap turned backwards. Anachronism now becomes an extended experience, a drama, an extended metaphor that is performed and in which listeners participate, finding their God-intended roles in the world.

ANACHRONISM AS DRAMA

The imitational dimension of anachronism, that is, its ability to capture and represent life as it is lived, helps people find their own roles in the presented drama. The Bible guides the script and the focus on God invites the listeners to consider sermonic experience in terms of God's larger plans. These two dimensions, the imitational and the divine, build upon a series of interdisciplinary developments since the 1950s. The New Homiletic, which arose among other things alongside the school of thought known as the New Hermeneutic, strove for the recovery of plot, narrative, image, and metaphor for the pulpit over against excessive modernist dependence on reason

---

4. White, *Tropics of Discourse*, 98, 121.

and logic. Other movements were significant: the focus on the performative dimensions of language identified by J. L. Austin,[5] on theopoetics by Amos Wilder,[6] on Jesus's use of parables in biblical studies, on doctrine as a kind of grammar as argued by George Lindbeck,[7] on narrative theology and metaphor especially in the 1970s and 1980s, on the importance of "thick description"[8] in ethnography following the lead of Clifford Geertz,[9] and on theodrama following Hans Urs von Balthasar.[10]

Two scholars in theodrama offer insights that relate to what Barton conceives. Richard Heyduck writes,

> Christianity is best understood not as a system of knowledge or as a culture, but as an ongoing drama. Doctrine is that which tells the church how to live the drama. Doctrine shows us the plot, the setting and the *dramatis personae* ... The key reality is not what we know about God but that God is active in the world today (the main character in the play) and that God invites us to join in the mission (become actors in the play).[11]

Doctrines make sense for Heyduck not as free-floating propositions but in the context of "the (at least minimally) coordinated actions of others" in the historically conditioned particularity of a community of faith.[12]

Kevin J. Vanhoozer, in his *Drama of Doctrine: A Canonical Linguistic Approach to Christian Theology*, argues that "doctrine is direction for fitting participation in an ongoing drama of redemption."[13] Doctrine offers "something to be believed by us, done by us, felt by us. Doctrine directs disciples as they seek to orient themselves in the church and in the world vis-à-vis the truth, goodness, and beauty defined by Jesus Christ."[14] Such direction comes from the intersection of the biblical text itself, the Spirit, and the congregation. "The urgent question ... is whether genuine Christian community is received through apostolic witness—mediated by the

---

5. Austin, *How to Do Things*.
6. Wilder, *Theopoetic*.
7. Lindbeck, *The Nature of Doctrine*.
8. Thick description is the use of detailed narrative accounts to describe complex social events in their settings, thereby giving social researchers confidence to analyze and draw their conclusions.
9. Geertz, *The Interpretation of Cultures*.
10. Balthasar, *Theo-drama*.
11. Heyduck, *Recovery of Doctrine*, x.
12. Ibid., 101; 52–55.
13. Vanhoozer, *Drama of Doctrine*, 45.
14. Ibid., 82.

biblical text—or whether it is produced in and by the community's performance, a social construction."[15] The saying of something is one thing, the performance of it is something else. "Dramas are not devised primarily to convey information but to move us, to persuade us, to delight us, to purge us of unwanted feelings."[16] For Vanhoozer, "the Christian way is fundamentally *dramatic*. . . . It concerns the way of living truthfully."[17]

WHAT MIGHT SERMONS LOOK LIKE?

Drama takes preaching one step beyond narrative. What one finds in Barton's approach to anachronism is encouragement to preach in plotted ways, using narrative and other devices to enroll the congregants in a dramatic script. Preachers thereby teach, enculturate, and offer guidance for community involvement, identity and action within the overarching Christian story. The Triune God may be said to be the director. God is also the main character, since some of the focus is on highlighting God's action and direction in the biblical text and in the world, near and far.

In performance, the sermon causes things to happen. What the community performs is God's will. Earlier generations of preachers put their trust in universal principles, procedures, and propositions extracted from Scripture. What was disclosed to the congregation was an ongoing informational monologue about the text or God. In Barton's mode of preaching, as in much of the New Homiletic, sermons effect something. Preachers perform by the act of speaking, by reflecting, and by enrolling the congregation as active participants. Listeners' needs and feelings are anticipated. Preachers may offer people something to believe (e.g., Jesus Christ died for you), to experience (e.g., a fresh start in Christ), or to enact (e.g., a role in relationship to church and the world).

The sermon in Barton's hands is dynamic. It does not present timeless truths but represents the Bible as a script in which we may find our lives. The text is not objectified as something to be excavated and mined for ideas and experiences but is appreciated in itself as an organic, dynamic event out of which meaning grows and relationships form.

The preacher begins by looking for an issue or tension in the text that intersects with the lives of people today. There is no disconnection between past events and present. The present grows out of the past, and out of the future as well. Narrative is a key way in which most people experience reality.

15. Ibid., 170.
16. Ibid., 182.
17. Ibid., 15.

They organize their perceptions of reality along lines of plot and perceived intention (real or not). Once relationships in the sermon are established across time and space, the roles of today's participants become clear. The sermon is eventful and those moments are its meaning. It portrays people in relationship with each other and the Triune God. Meaning is a living process: the community performs God's word and will.

In Barton's thinking, anachronism, rather than bridging, is the main way of moving from text to sermon. The preacher conceives how the sermon might be presented as a drama, where the events portrayed might take place, and when. The plot or action can be conceived in separate acts, perhaps five as in Shakespeare, with the last act devoted to helping the congregation determine their own roles. The script is not separate from the congregants; it is their story and God's that is revealed. They have roles to play. Preachers need to think through anachronism so as to choose details and events that listeners will recognize and identify within their own lives. The sermon ceases to be conceived as a unit of meaning or a completed work. It is one performance in an ongoing drama, the meanings of which are to be found in it and beyond it, in living it out during the week.

The French literary scholar Roland Barthes once distinguished between a writerly text (*texte scriptible*) that readers write through interpreting it and a readerly text (*texte lisible*). The latter is located in the past and its meaning is representative and fixed. It gives the illusion of being open and transparent but leaves the readers outside of the production of meaning.[18] Perhaps the anachronistic sermon needs to be conceived less as a writerly text than as a *performerly* text that is perpetually present and that listeners help compose through enactment. The performerly text is participatory.

In the movie *Dead Poets Society*, the teacher, Mr. Keating (played by Robin Williams), recites a Whitman poem to his literature students titled "O Me! O Life!" with the last line, "The powerful play goes on, and you may contribute a verse." Keating asks his students, "What will your verse be?" Barton probably would have preachers ask their congregations, "What will your role be?"

OUTSTANDING ISSUES

What Barton achieves here is the beginning of a very important conversation. Many questions are answered, and others raised. For example, what are the drawbacks of anachronistic sermons? Like narrative sermons, might they work more readily with narrative or dramatic texts than for instance

18. Barthes, S/Z, 4–5.

with epistles? Do they demand too much art from the preacher? By contrast, the African American spiritual "There Is a Balm in Gilead" reminds us in its chorus, "If you cannot sing like angels, / if you cannot preach like Paul, / you can tell the love of Jesus, / and say he died for all." Just telling the simple story is enough. Is there anything inherent in the structure of an anachronistic sermon that encourages the gospel to be preached? Preaching is composed of both teaching, of which drama can be a form, and proclamation understood as direct loving speech from God. Is the latter still possible in an anachronistic sermon, or might the contrivance of dramatic structure get in the way? Might there be hybrid forms of anachronistic sermons, and if so, what would they look like? While questions like this may not find complete answers here, a foundation for answering them is laid. Readers, like Barton's participating listeners to sermons, are invited to bring their own anachronism practices to the table and engage in a pioneering conversation.

Scholars and preachers alike should be grateful to Barton for venturing into new homiletical ground where a revised theology of time and space are needed. Some scholars are now finding in the Bible something akin to what Barton wants to draw from it in sermons. Cheryl Bridges Johns puts the matter beautifully:

> The Bible becomes an icon or a portal wherein "light from the future streams into the present." As Steven Land has noted, the Bible creates a divine fusion of time. In this fusion of space and time the past draws near and the future bends toward the present. Reading the text is, therefore, an eschatological experience, a transtemporal journey that brings participants into the eternal presence of God. This space is thus sacramental, offering within its borders the efficacious power of transformation. It is abounding with real presence.[19]

At the very least, such poetic thoughts are an affirmation of the new perspectives Barton opens for preaching and the biblical nature of the challenge he brings.

Paul Scott Wilson
Professor of Homiletics
Emmanuel College of Victoria University
in the University of Toronto

---

19. Johns, "Transcripts," 163. She cites here Berdyaev, *Slavery and Freedom*, 261.

Introduction

Anachronism for Preaching
The Sermon In and Out of Time

IN THE PAGES THAT FOLLOW IT IS MY THESIS THAT THE SERMON CAN and must be more than a communication of good news to the people, it must invite participation in God's dramatic narrative that continuously unfolds in reality and through time. Anachronism, preaching together disparate moments of God's drama in a way that is timely, creates proclamation of God's gospel and invites God's people to participate in that gospel drama right now.

This project for me started with movies and ended (or, rather, it continues) in time. My final semester of seminary found me with an extra elective. Rather than taking another Hebrew exegesis course, or another semester of pastoral counseling (which, looking back, would have been the most practical decision), through the Boston Theological Institute I decided to travel into the city that last semester to take a class at Boston University from Bryan Stone called "Faith and Film." From the course description it sounded like the greatest semester ever devised. We would gather together as a class, watch movies, and discuss them in a theological context. And the class was everything I expected it to be. We watched great films, from classics to pop icons, and somehow found God speaking through the midst of it all. God met me during that time, but in a way that would become more than the watching and discussing of movies.

My pursuit of a theological education was fueled by my love of preaching and the desire to be a better preacher. Up until that point all of my electives in college and seminary had centered upon the pulpit. And so it was no surprise that the semester concluded for me with the question of what preachers could learn from the storytelling devices, styles, and processes employed by our time's biggest storytellers. If it was the preacher's call to tell the story, what could be gleaned from arguably the best (or at least the best grossing) storytellers who had sharpened their art for projection before the eyes of millions? This question for me became the catalyst of the next era of my life in education and ministry.

Over the next years of study I would pursue doctoral studies largely through the practice of preaching, reading homiletical, hermeneutical, and pop culture theology, learning cinema studies, and watching a ton of movies (maybe more than was actually justified as "homework"). Through this study my understanding of Christian faith shifted in some significant ways. My faith went from one that was primarily cognitive to one that is a living process and fundamentally participatory. Samuel Taylor Coleridge and Horace Bushnell got me out of my head and into the living of life. Additionally, my understanding of God's word shifted from one that is spatial (we exegete packets of information to distill timeless truths) to one that is entirely temporal (these things happened, and they continue to happen, *in time*). Theological dramatists such as Richard Heyduck, N. T. Wright, and Kevin Vanhoozer pulled me out of the audience and onto the stage. With these shifts, significantly, my concepts of preaching God's drama shifted as well. When explanation or application of the text on their own became flat or static, I came to understand my task to be the creation of a dynamic call to God's people to participate in the timely drama that they are indeed living in right now. All of this occurred with some significant speech from God through films such as *Magnolia* (1999), *Memento* (2000), *Signs* (2002), *Cold Mountain* (2003), and especially *Strictly Ballroom* (1992), *William Shakespeare's Romeo + Juliet* (1996), and *Moulin Rouge* (2001). These films, with others and alongside many homiletical conversation partners, shifted my thinking about homiletics. Our hermeneutic for preaching must be temporal rather than spatial. Our task is to wrinkle time rather than build hermeneutical bridges. All of these shifts, from the cognitive to the participatory, from the spatial and static to the eventful and timely, from application to active and ongoing participation, are apparent in the work that follows. Each is taken up in the development of anachronism as a theological and homiletical device. Bringing moments in time together *anachronistically* in the proclamation of the gospel is the timely way forward for the sermon today.

In the pages below I am seeking to do at least three things. First, I want to examine, and in some ways challenge, how my fellow preachers traditionally, and generally, answer the hermeneutical question that we face each week as we face the congregation of God's people. Second, I want to create and propose a theological starting point for a homiletic characterized by time rather than by space. Reasserting eschatology as central to all theology and adopting theological and hermeneutical constructs rooted in drama for preaching gets us here. Third, I want to engage in popular culture for more than mere sermon illustration. There is more to a film than how it can illustrate a particular text. In all of this it is my hope to invite participation in a discussion about preaching that will serve to make all of us called to the pulpit better proclaimers of the gospel of Christ.

CHALLENGING OUR HERMENEUTICAL STARTING POINTS

I began attending church late in high school. To this day I love that church and am grateful for people who invested in the life of a kid who caused them a lot of trouble. The sermons I heard at that church generally followed the same pattern Sunday after Sunday. They formulaically began with a topic and had five, or seven, or ten points with just as many texts to support them. This produced sermons with titles such as "Ten Ways to Improve Your Marriage" and "Improving Your Serve: Five Principles for Serving God and Others." There was never anything unbiblical about these sermons. But I do remember wondering if there was anything more to this story *of* Jesus than principles *about* Jesus. I went to bible college to learn to preach and pastor and learned how to explain, prove, and apply the text—all really good homiletical skills, essential for communication. But then other authors added to my homiletical thought in terms of narrative, story, experience, worlds, and especially the conceptualization of preaching as an art.

I've come to believe that one significant difference between these types of preaching has to do with how different preachers think of the nature of faith and in turn how they answer the hermeneutical question: What does this ancient text have to say to people who live thousands of years after it was written? Or, more simply, what am I supposed to say about this text this Sunday? A conceptualization of a more cognitive faith sees the preacher communicating cognitive principles, building his or her congregation's knowledge of God. A faith viewed as more experiential has the preacher seeking to create experiences of God for the church. A concept of faith as incongruent with the state of the world in which we live has the preacher creating a new world for the disciple of Jesus to live in.

What, though, if your concept of Christian faith is none of the above but is rather more akin to that of the Romantic theologians such as Coleridge and Bushnell: faith is a life and a living process? Or, what homiletical theology is available to the preacher whose life and living process has collided with dramatic theologians such as Wright, or Vanhoozer? What does the sermon look like and how is proclamation accomplished in the context of faith as life within a historical, ongoing drama that God is continually directing and in which we all play a continuing and essential role as principal characters? When the nature of faith shifts from more static to more dramatic, proclamation of that faith must shift as well, from more static to more dramatic.

This is what the anachronistic sermon seeks to accomplish. In the homiletic that follows I have sought to create a paradigm that in some ways stands alongside those that have come before, in other ways grows out of them, and in still others, one that hopefully stands on its own in its recovery of time and the creation of a sermon caught between past and future, between memory and hope. While challenging homiletical assumptions is a theme that runs throughout the whole of this work, chapter 1 especially surveys homiletical theories according to their hermeneutical commitments. What one finds when studying homiletical options is that many rely on a hermeneutical paradigm that inherently diminishes the temporality and historicity of the biblical drama, thereby misidentifying hermeneutical distance as spatial and in need of a bridge, rather than as temporal and in need of continued enactment. The whole of this work after this seeks to begin the shift to a more temporal hermeneutic and homiletic.

ANACHRONISM AND DRAMA: A HOMILETICAL STARTING POINT

Theologian Kevin Vanhoozer's canonical-linguistic theology proposes drama as the central organizing principle for theology, doctrine, and for Christian discipleship (chapter 3 will cover this dramatic theology in detail). An aspect of Vanhoozer's theology here that is in need of development is its growth into a practical theology. As my convictions about faith have turned more participatory than cognitive or experiential, and as preaching is my particular area of interest, what I have sought to accomplish in this work is to develop the practical theology of preaching within a dramatic theological context such as Vanhoozer's (and Wright's, and Heyduck's). This has entailed at least three moves for me: reclaiming time for theology and for preaching, organizing time through drama, and hermeneutically and theologically traveling through time with anachronism.

After the conclusions of chapter 1, that our current homiletical practices disjoint (or worse remove) time from preaching, I have found it necessary to reassert time and history as a viable concept and context for our theology and preaching. This is the subject of chapter 2. Eschatology is the frame of Christian theology that deals not merely with end time, but is the matrix for all of Christian time. Theology as eschatology sets all of our preaching within the inescapable context of time. This shifts our view of the text. Rather than pericopes of information in need of distillation into timeless packets ready to bridge the distance between the page and the congregation, the text is the historical accounting of God's eventful drama in and through time. Time becomes the essential distance from and inherent connection between the congregation and the story, simply because we are reading and living different moments in the same story. A purposeful eschatology reasserts time as essential for preaching.

Chapter 3 takes the time inherent in God's story and organizes it under the rubric of drama. Examining dramatic theological constructs helps the preacher to see the temporal continuity between then and now. Again, time is both our distance from and connection to the events recorded in text. What happens in one moment of the drama grows out of what came before and grows into all of the moments after. In this sense, God's people are connected temporally, and inseparably, to the entire story that has come before. A dramatic theology gives organization for the preacher seeking to preach the connection between God's work among God's people then, and God's work among God's people now.

Within the drama, a hermeneutical means for connecting moments in time is necessary. This is where we seek to answer the persistent hermeneutical question temporally. It is here that, looking for a means of time travel between the moment of the text and the moment of my congregation, that I have developed the theological device of anachronism which both elucidates the text for the church today while calling God's people to participate in God's drama right now. Theological anachronism is the hermeneutical means of moving from text to sermon, from then to now, in a dramatic, temporal, and creative manner that intrinsically calls for participation in the ongoing drama. Chapter 4 proposes, defines, and develops anachronism as a specifically theological and hermeneutical device for preaching, finding an artistic and theological thread for anachronistic communication running through Scripture, medieval theologies, and postmodern popular art and media.

Time, drama, and anachronism represent for me the proposal of a homiletical starting point for preaching today. Chapter 5 pulls together the threads of the whole into the beginning of an anachronistic homiletic that both communicates the story as it has come to us and calls the church to participate in the story now and into the future. Here, the theological and homiletical shifts I am proposing take on practical proclamation. Our homiletical process begins to shift from building hermeneutical bridges to enacting the drama; from creating outlines to scripting the sermon; from the goal of application to the call to participation; from illustrating to creating time and space artistically and anachronistically. This final chapter gives practical examples of anachronistic sermons and the Appendix presents some sermon manuscripts of preaching in a dramatic and anachronistic mode—my attempt to practice what I preach, or preach what I practice, if you will.

ENGAGING POPULAR CULTURE FOR PREACHING

In what follows I have attempted to engage with popular culture, especially with theology and film studies, at a level that is deeper than I have typically found in homiletical literature. Generally preachers have been happy to find in contemporary film (or music, or television, or most any other pop culture artifacts) a means for illustrating points or parts of the sermon. One question that presents itself, however, is whether there is something more that we as preachers can learn from filmmakers and the stories they work so artistically to create. In the pages that follow, and especially in chapters 4 and 5, I have attempted to engage purposefully with postmodern art in the form of the graphic novel and popular film in order to think through how these particular artists, in this case Douglas Rushkoff and Baz Luhrmann, can help preachers learn how to create art in our sermons. Indeed, Rushkoff, Luhrmann, and others live within and out of time and utilize anachronism as a matter of course in their arts.

The engagement with popular culture in the following study serves at least two distinct purposes. First, a study of these particular postmodern artists' manipulation and appropriation of time gives guidance to the preacher in creating the anachronistic sermon today. The preacher as dramatic artist can learn creativity in the craft as he or she takes in what these artists do in their hermeneutics with the manipulation of time. In what is the central task of preaching—the communication of an ancient story for contemporary life participation—non-preachers Rushkoff and Luhrmann are masters in their respective arts of graphic novel and film.

A second purpose here is to contribute something to the field described in various terms including "theology and popular culture" studies. In the conversation between theologians about the intersection of Christian theology and popular culture, including popular arts such as film, television, and music, the implications of theology's intersection with popular arts such as film and other media for the church's *practical theology* has been underdeveloped, and actually largely unaddressed. For instance, Robert Johnston's wonderful 2007 work, *Reframing Theology and Film*, sought to bring a summary to theology and film studies so far and to propose directions for moving forward in the discipline. While all of the essays in the book discuss the importance of film and theology studies, there is little insight or direction given to how these important studies have or might work their way out in the practical theology of the church. While practical theology was not the stated purpose of the book it seems to me a notable lacuna in the field on the whole. Practical theology is an understudied and just as important aspect of these disciplines. I am attempting to add a voice to the discussion.

On the other side of the conversation, preachers have generally not been willing to dive deep when it comes to these areas of investigation. When homileticians do seek to engage cultural arts such as film for preaching it is often done in the form of appropriating film for sermon illustration. This, however, can be done in ways that trivialize the work of art as a work of art, reducing the story told in a work of cinematic art to mere illustration of the story that the preacher is telling. The practice of using films as sermon illustration, while potentially pragmatically helpful, does not intrinsically work to aid the preacher in creating his or her own new work of art in the sermon. However, engaging in the arts as a means of first appreciating them as art, and then as conversation partners as we seek to create our own works of dramatic sermonic art by asking *how* these artists create, holds significant promise for the preacher who preaches within drama. The following aims at a deeper engagement with the arts for homiletical direction, contributing both to homiletical and theology-popular culture studies.

The impetus of such engagement for the preacher is potentially significant. Popular media plays a central role in the communication, shaping, and construction of values in our culture. Film and religion scholar Margaret Miles has asserted that somewhere along the way popular media such as contemporary film has supplanted the preacher in the pulpit as a primary voice shaping morals and values:

> "Congregations" became "audiences" as film created a new public sphere in which, under the guise of "entertainment," values are formulated, circulated, resisted, and negotiated. . . . The point of my study, then, is . . . to acknowledge that the representation and examination of values and moral commitments does not presently occur most pointedly in churches, synagogues, or mosques, but before the eyes of "congregations" in movie theaters. North Americans—even those with religious

affiliations—now gather about cinema and television screens rather than in churches to ponder the moral quandaries of American life.[1]

For Miles, films and other public media have shifted the locus of moral conversation to the theater rather than the sanctuary. Robert Jewett's study of film and theology stands in agreement with Miles. He observes that "many contemporary Americans are shaped much more decisively by popular culture than by their formal education or their religious training." For Jewett, films "are a primary arena for discovering and debating important moral, cultural, and religious issues" in contemporary North American culture.[2] Additionally, Bryan Stone emphasizes the value of looking to popular media as a means of understanding the "human predicament" and better interpreting the biblical text.[3] For Stone, films can be "regularly and quite amazingly a source of revelation about ourselves and our world. . . . The cinema reveals what we value as human beings, our hopes and our fears. It asks our deepest questions, expresses our mightiest rage, and reflects our most basic dreams."[4] Cinematic storytellers are telling the stories that shape people's lives at very deep levels. And they are doing it, in many ways, better than we are.

The point then is that if contemporary popular media has the effect that an increasing number of theology and pop culture authors are saying that it does—that is, to both reflect and shape deep, important values and morality in the culture in which the preacher lives—then it follows that the preacher may benefit from a sustained and serious study of this media. On one level, broadly the preacher can gain insight into the beliefs and values of the society through the behaviors, struggles, and conversations of that society played out on the screen. In this way the preacher better understands her or his listeners. Further, and potentially even more valuable, a study of just how film is so successful in creating and telling powerful stories for cultural appropriation will help the preacher to be a better storyteller, invested in the craft of preaching as a dramatic art form. I believe that the benefit of this type of study for homiletics, and for practical theologies in general, is potentially quite significant. Throughout the following pages, and especially in chapters 4 and 5, popular media is a significant conversation partner for my homiletic.

---

1. Miles, *Seeing and Believing*, 25.
2. Jewett, *Saint Paul at the Movies*, 6.
3. Stone, *Faith and Film*, 3.
4. Ibid., 4.

SOME DEFINITIONS

One final matter is to introduce and define some key terms that I work with in the following pages. Concepts such as *narrative, drama, metaphor, anachronism, allegory,* and *participation* deserve clarification from the start. All of these will factor into what follows.

Narrative and *drama* are related terms with at least one significant difference. Bordwell and Thompson, writing in terms of film theory, offer a succinct definition of narrative:

> We can consider a narrative to be *a chain of events in cause-effect relationship occurring in time and space.* A narrative is thus what we usually mean by the term *story.* . . . Typically, a narrative begins with one situation; a series of changes occurs according to a pattern of cause and effect; finally, a new situation arises that brings about the end of the narrative.[5]

The term *narrative* is now routinely used in both theological and homiletical studies. In the following pages I will generally consider narrative according to the definition above, with the added provision that narratives, as narratives, are not necessarily enacted. A story is told on the page or in words. Once the narrative is enacted or people are invited to enter into it in the manner of participating in metaphor, it becomes drama. Drama is the enactment of the story in and through time. In terms of the biblical narrative/drama, chapter 3 will make clear that I consider the biblical narrative to be dramatic, that is, it has been and continues to be enacted in the world in and through time. This enactment includes all of the past, the present, and the coming future.

Metaphor and *anachronism* are also interrelated terms. Relying on the Romantic theologians such as Bushnell and Coleridge, metaphor consists of the reconciliation of opposites. That is, when two or more contradictory images or statements are brought together a new image is created that "sparks" new meaning or understanding without destroying the images or statements from which it is formed. Perhaps the classic example of this is the statement "love is a red rose." Literally, love is not a rose, and neither is a rose love. None of it is necessarily red. Together, however, the contradictory images resonate with one another to produce a new image with greater feeling and understanding. The new image created requires participation in the image for the image to exist.

Anachronism, as I will use the term here, refers to a metaphor set in motion through time. While classic definitions of anachronism define

---

5. Bordwell and Thompson, *Film Art,* 69. Emphasis original.

it as anything that appears out of temporal sequence, often characterizing it as something in need of removal for rationality to prevail, I am proposing a more aesthetic, imaginative, and theological appropriation of anachronism as a temporal and theological device. Metaphor brings together different images, ideas, or emotions in order to create a new image and hence a new understanding as one participates in the language event. Similarly, anachronism brings together two disparate moments of time—past and present or present and future—and allows them to create a new moment of understanding and participation in the present moment. The new moment created requires participation in the moment for the moment to exist. Anachronism is not simply preaching the text with updated or contemporary imagery or language. Anachronism is, rather, the theological hermeneutic by which we enter into, participate in, and call for God's people to participate in the Christian drama across time. I will address this in depth in the pages that follow.

One important aspect of both metaphor and anachronism is that neither absorbs, erases, or eclipses the identities or meanings of the device's constituent parts. A distinction must be made here between metaphor or anachronism in this sense and the way in which *allegory* is sometimes used.[6] As David Bartlett points out, "Allegory . . . juxtaposes a narrative and another reality. This reality provides the real or hidden meaning for the allegory."[7] With allegory one or more entities comprising the allegory may be translated or eclipsed in the transaction, losing their identities in the process. When an allegory juxtaposes two images or times for the purpose of asserting one or the other's *real* or *hidden* meaning, unique identity has been overshadowed. While not discounting the importance of the category allegory for theology, anachronism as I am defining it is not allegory. In metaphor and anachronism I am asserting that the devices are such that both moments of the dynamic retain unique identities while coming together to create a new experience, understanding, or meaning in and for the present moment. I will develop anachronism in greater detail in the following chapters.

Participation in the overarching drama is that to which both the unfinished nature of the present drama and anachronism call the gospel's readers and sermon's hearers. In terms of the drama, as the present is seen as what it is, that is, the leading temporal edge of the past and ongoing drama, the follower of Christ is called by the very shape and reality of the drama to participate in its enactment. Christian faith, in this scheme, calls for active

---

6. See Bartlett's distinction between *allegory* and *allegoresis* in "Allegory, Allegoresis," 5–6.

7. Ibid., 5.

participation in the drama of which we are a part. Anachronism fosters participation in bringing moments of the drama together in a language event that calls for participation in the new moment created. To preach anachronistically is to preach the fluid continuity of time and God's work in the events throughout while inviting the hearers to join the action of God's presence in the now.

Preaching within the drama in which the church exists requires a theological means of holding times in tension and moving between times. Anachronism as a theological device, rooted in eschatology as biblical temporality and in drama as the organization of time, does just this. The homiletical task can invite participation in God's dramatic narrative that continuously unfolds in reality and through time. Within this drama anachronism exists as a powerful theological device with practical, communicative uses. In a unified vision of time in which moments are freed to be brought together in theological and aesthetic relationship, preaching can be cast as calling for participation in the life of the drama moving forward, with anachronism as the key theological concept put to practical purposes in proclaiming the gospel of Jesus Christ today.

1

Hermeneutics and Their Homiletical Practices

ONE PERENNIAL QUESTION PREACHERS FACE IS THE HERMENEUTIcal move from text to sermon. How does one communicate the contemporary relevance of a text written in a different time and place for a different people? Biblical scholar Krister Stendahl raised the question with a blunt and practical charm: "Do these old documents have any meaning for us—except as sources for our knowledge of a small segment of first-century life and thought, or as a means for a nostalgic Christianity? If they have meaning in the present tense and sense, on what ground do they have this meaning?"[1] Homiletician David Buttrick echoed Stendahl's observations: "How can words written in an earlier age to a different people have *anything* to say to us today in a twentieth-century time and place? How can words bridge time?"[2] The question that stands at the base of all of our preaching, and as a result affects and shapes all preaching, is that of how one gets from text to sermon.

What does the text have to say to us today? Harry Emerson Fosdick commented on the practice of not moving from past text to God's gospel work now when he said, "Only the preacher . . . proceeds still upon the idea that folk come to church desperately anxious to find out what happened to the Jebusites."[3] To preach the gospel necessitates the translation of the gospel across time. All of our preaching, if it aims for a people's participation in the gospel, must be more than recitation of what the text says; it must be

---

1. Stendahl, "Biblical Theology, Contemporary," 435.
2. Buttrick, *Homiletic*, 264. Emphasis original.
3. Fosdick, *Living of These Days*, 92.

bold proclamation of what God is doing now rooted in the ongoing drama of what God has done. Getting from one to the other (or, holding them in tension), rather, is the business of engaging the hermeneutical question.

This hermeneutical question stands at the base of homiletical practice, and the manner in which the preacher engages it ultimately leads her or him to a particular homiletical theology. Essentially, how one accomplishes the hermeneutical task has determinative effect for the shape, goal, and outcome of one's sermon. Contemporary preaching has generally followed what might be labeled a *meant/means* framework, or a bridge paradigm, in the move from text to sermon.[4] This approach seeks first to understand what the text *meant* in its original setting. A bridge—for instance a propositional truth or experience of the text—is then created and inserted as a theological and communicative aid, and stands as the hermeneutical move that makes the text mean today. This framework for preaching may be labeled *bi-focal*, as it seeks to keep both the Bible and today in focus in interpreting the text and delivering the sermon.

While theologians and preachers have built different bridges with which one may cross what is perceived as a distance between text and us, there is at least one quality of this bi-focal framework that is consistent. In its conception and execution the bi-focal framework is spatial. That is, the distance between the text and today is, at least in concept and practice, viewed as a spatial distance between two places or, at times, between two worlds.[5] While this has been a helpful way of conceptualizing the hermeneutical task, a spatial focus in constructing hermeneutical bridges and preaching sermons effectively eclipses the real nature of the distance between then and now: time.

Essentially, there are not two separate spaces in which God works— one in which he appeared to Moses and Pharaoh or to Paul and Barnabas, and another in which we live. More starkly one might say that there are not two worlds—one in which Christ visits and shares God's grace and another into which that grace must be imported. The two points of the hermeneutical question, ultimately, do not have to do with variants on a theme of spatial distance. They have to do with the work of God in and through time—seeing God at work in time and space then, anticipating and identifying God at work in time and space right now.

The hermeneutical paradigms and their homiletical expressions shared below are, at their core, spatial responses to a temporal question.

---

4. See Farley, *Practicing Gospel*, 71–106, and Lash, "What Might Martyrdom Mean?"

5. The spatial quality of this homiletic is apparent in Stott's title, *Between Two Worlds*, and in the cover art of Farris's *Preaching That Matters*.

While each represents an important and potentially effective manner of preaching the gospel of Christ, the practical eclipse of the nature of both the moment of the text and the moment of today as eventful moments in time, with eventful moments in time and God between them, in each homiletical practice has the potential to obscure the nature of the text and of now as *events in time*. It is my assertion, below and in the following chapters, that to reframe the hermeneutical question as distinctly temporal, which is what it organically is, both animates the eventful work of God in all moments (then, now, future, and in between), and recenters the goal of preaching as a call to participation in God's gospel drama in the world today. Ultimately this is what an anachronistic and dramatic homiletic accomplishes.

Here we will explore the bi-focal hermeneutic as expressed in contemporary homiletics. Over the past century or so homiletical theory has generally availed itself of four ways of constructing this meant/means bridge: propositional, experiential, post-liberal, and theological. Each can produce a wonderful expression of the gospel for the church. However, with their spatial emphases each contributes to the disjointedness of biblical temporality and diminishes a goal of gospel-drama participation. Before engaging with the homiletical theologies directly, however, it will be a benefit to sort through the bi-focal hermeneutic that underpins contemporary homiletical practice. Within this context for contemporary preaching the following chapters will pursue an inherently temporal hermeneutic that leads to a homiletical practice distinctly rooted in the drama of God's gospel in the world today.

A HERMENEUTICAL CONTEXT FOR PREACHING: THE BI-FOCAL FRAMEWORK

Preachers in the twenty-first century find themselves within theological and homiletical contexts shaped by a modern historical consciousness that effects an intellectual, and traditionally and conceptually spatial, gap between the biblical text and the present. The theological and communicative goals become bridging this gap and homiletical practices (which are more than methods) become expressions in practical theology of the hermeneutical thought supporting them. The predominant hermeneutical means of bridging this gap for contemporary preachers have largely appropriated this modern framework in the bi-focal or bridge paradigm. In different homiletical approaches the bridge is constructed of different materials yet the overall framework and process is similar.

Time and Modernity: Privileging the Present

Many contemporary approaches to preaching operate within a hermeneutical framework made possible by modern historical-critical approaches to the biblical text shaped by the historical consciousness of the Enlightenment and post-Enlightenment eras. This historical consciousness identifies differences between life in the present and life as portrayed in the biblical text. David Schnasa Jacobsen sums up this dynamic in the phrase, "that was then, this is now," evidencing a view of the two moments as inherently and qualitatively different.[6] This critical distance has provided both benefits and costs for contemporary interpretation and functions to frame the key hermeneutical question for most preaching today.

Critical interpretive approaches to the biblical text were developed to a greater extent, along with the historical consciousness that has animated them, beginning in the Renaissance and through the Enlightenment and Modernity.[7] Prior to the Enlightenment time was generally viewed and lived as a unity, largely in the moment with only a vague sense of the differentness of the past.[8] The seeds of a modern critical approach to the Bible are evident as early as the Renaissance. "A new sense of the past" began to develop in the fifteenth and sixteenth centuries, as artists and scholars of the time began to define their own moment in history as a Renaissance and in contrast to what they were first to term the Middle or Dark Ages.[9] Peter Burke describes this movement in historical consciousness: "Like a new nation, the humanists in particular constructed a collective identity by contrasting themselves with the 'other' ... In short, the humanists considered the past (ancient and medieval) to be different in quality from the present, rather than more and more of the same thing."[10] Rather than viewing themselves in continuity with the past, a consciousness developed in which the present was defined as over and against the past. The past itself was divided into different eras and attitudes toward these different moments were divided as well. A view of a divisible present and past replaced a view of historical continuity.[11]

---

6. Jacobsen, *Preaching in the New Creation*, 3.

7. For more thorough discussions of the progression of thought throughout the Enlightenment and Modernity, see Krentz, *The Historical-Critical Method*; Frei, *The Eclipse of Biblical Narrative*; Grant and Tracy, *A Short History of the Interpretation of the Bible*; Thiselton, *The Two Horizons*; and McGrath, *The Genesis of Doctrine*.

8. See especially Frei, *Eclipse of Biblical Narrative*, 1–50; Auerbach, *Mimesis*, 143–73; Kolve, *Play Called Corpus Christi*, 101–23.

9. Burke, "Sense of Anachronism," 157.

10. Ibid., 157–58.

11. Krentz, *Historical-Critical Method*, 7.

One further characteristic of this modern perspective of time and history has been a general privileging of the present over and against the past. Richard Middleton and Brian Walsh describe this characteristic of modern culture as a foundational myth of progress. Since the fifteenth century, Western civilization has built for itself an overarching narrative of hard work and progress that separates past from present as present progresses into an increasingly bright and better future. This narrative is built on at least three modern developments, each nearly unarguable lynchpins of Western civilization. First, the scientific revolution of the sixteenth and seventeenth centuries granted insight and understanding into the workings of nature and humanity unlike any discipline prior. Second, with scientific knowledge of the world's workings, technological advances of the eighteenth century and following catalyzed the Industrial Revolution and imparted to humanity a mastery over the environment. Third, economic growth and the production of wealth followed in Western culture. In many ways, economic growth has been viewed as the motivating reason for scientific and technological advancement.[12] As the present has carried on a perpetual sense of progress often viewed as qualitatively different than (and in many ways superior to) life in the past, a sense of division between times and a superiority of the present is detectable in the modern West.

In terms of hermeneutics and biblical studies, the rise of this historical consciousness granted interpreters a different vantage point from which to view the past. A divisibility of history opened up a gap in historical consciousness that, once experienced, allowed one to view the past in a new light. This provided many positive gains for biblical interpretation. The rise of text criticism helped provide for more reliable texts, what Edgar Krentz calls "the basis of all historical work."[13] To be sure, historical-critical work has made possible nearly all critical research tools, from grammars to commentaries which have served to prevent a collapsing of past and present.[14] Krentz argues, for instance, that the historical-critical method both affirms "the continuity of biblical revelation with our time" and preserves the Bible's differentness:

> Historical criticism makes the gap between us and the biblical world as wide as it actually is, forces us to face the peculiarity and particularity of the texts in their world, and confronts us

---

12. Middleton and Walsh, *Truth Is Stranger*, 13–22.
13. Krentz, *Historical-Critical Method*, 24–25.
14. Ibid., 63.

with the Jesus who is the challenge to all cultures and securities of our world. Historical study prevents too rapid modernizing.[15]

There is continuity and distance inherent in a historical-critical study of the Bible.

It is this recognition of difference between the present and the past that prompts the identification of the past's strangeness, leads to the hermeneutical question posed by Stendahl above, and sets up the bi-focal framework for preaching discussed below. In light of historical consciousness, a means for navigating a distance between the pastness of the text and present knowledge and experience was needed—what might the biblical text mean in the present?

N. T. Wright observes two broad manners in which scholars after the Enlightenment have approached the text.[16] One approach is a hard skepticism, rejecting the historical sense of Scripture altogether, "calling the veracity of Christianity as a whole into question."[17] A second option preserves the meaningfulness of the text and engages in the exploration of the historical/literal sense of the text in order to find some universal or timeless meaning in it. This approach hopes to "refresh areas of contemporary life that the literal sense," in its historical setting (or, strangeness), may not reach. Wright notes that "what then emerges is a timeless message, a timeless truth, or a timeless call to decision."[18] The goal is to assert a present meaningfulness of

---

15. Ibid., 65.

16. It is important to note that Wright also acknowledges and utilizes other critical approaches to the text, such as literary criticism and theological approaches. Wright, *New Testament*, 26–28. Buttrick also identifies two similar approaches to the text: "As a result, historical-critical method split—for some it was based on radical skepticism; for others it was dedicated to confirming the truth of the Bible." Buttrick, *Captive Voice*, 13.

17. Wright, *New Testament*, 20. Emblematic of this approach is Benedict Spinoza (1632–77). Robert Grant has summarized Spinoza as concluding, "The divorce of theology from philosophy [Spinoza's goal] results in the abandonment of theology by any intelligent person" (*Short History of Biblical Interpretation*, 107). See also Krentz, *Historical-Critical Method*, 13–14.

18. Ibid. David Friedrich Strauss (1808–74), for instance, denied historicity for events such as miracles and the resurrection, yet "he tried to save the *eternal truths* contained in the historically dubious materials through the concept of myth." Krentz, *Historical-Critical Method*, 21–22. Emphasis mine. A twentieth-century variation is the work of Rudolf Bultmann (1884–1976), whose program of demythologization sought to strip mythological aspects from the biblical text, peeling away "false scandals" of a mythological worldview in order to get to the "real scandal" of Jesus Christ. For Bultmann, the *kerygma* is recontextualized as it is experienced existentially across time in new historically contingent moments. Bultmann, *Jesus Christ and Mythology*. I call it a variation, as one might argue that Bultmann's program is not so much after a *timeless* kerygma, as the kerygma is experienced anew in each new existential moment/context. As the *historical* context is removed in order to re-contextualize in any number of

the biblical message in view of the historical consciousness and questions effected by Modernity. Some of these will be addressed below in relation to homiletical programs. It is notable that in these modern directions for hermeneutical enquiry the removal of time is central. On the one hand these hermeneutics move away from time by rejecting the historical claim of the Bible's distinctly eventful story, or on the other in the practice of abstracting truths from the temporally developed and conditioned story that are *timeless*, that is, considered true yet abstracted from their temporal context.

This, then, broadly sets up a predominant hermeneutical framework for preaching as one approaches twentieth- and twenty-first-century preaching. The preacher is faced with a theological situation in which a historical consciousness effects an intellectual gap between the moments of the biblical text and the present. The hermeneutical task set before the preacher in this context has largely been to bridge the gap between past text and present life. This sets up the meant/means hermeneutical framework and the bi-focal paradigm for homiletical practice.

A Hermeneutic That Builds Bridges

Stendahl recognized the nature of the hermeneutical question after Modernity as consisting of two independent and sequential tasks: description and translation. He observed that since the seventeenth century there had been tension between the contemporary and the biblical but it was not until after the rise of historical criticism that this was fully recognized as a disparity between "two centuries with drastically different modes of thought," and hence the increasing need for translation from one epistemological moment to another.[19] In large part the modern hermeneutical task has been to navigate the distance between text and contemporary moment by working with the text in terms of what the text *meant* back then and then what the text now *means*.[20] This hermeneutical framework finds practical expression in bi-focal homiletical theologies, that is, in homiletical theologies in which the preacher seeks to work with both the textual and present poles in a critical manner.

In this bridge framework the interpreter first engages in the exegetical task of understanding what the text meant to its original readers and in its

---

other temporal moments, however, there is a sense in which it is timeless, or ahistorical. Stendahl describes Bultmann's program as "radically ahistorical" ("Biblical Theology, Contemporary," 427–28).

19. Stendahl, "Biblical Theology, Contemporary," 422.

20. Ibid., 419–20.

original context—the descriptive task. Once the text is described, the interpreter then confronts the task of translating this description into meaning for application in the present—the normative task.[21] This hermeneutical framework poses challenges for proclamation in the church. For instance, Gustav Brøndsted posed questions of biblical proclamation as follows:

> The two world views and the two languages are expressions, not only of past and present, but, wherever the gospel is preached, of a tension in which we live day by day. It is as men of the present that we are confronted with the traditional proclamation of the gospel and stand within it. The questions press upon us and show us the duality of the world in which we as Christians live, the duality of the position in which we as theologians find ourselves, as those who proclaim the apostolic gospel and participate in the contemporary culture pattern. Two world views, two languages. Is there any bridge between them? Is it possible to speak of the one in the language of the other?[22]

While Brøndsted is not entirely hopeful in his outlook for this task ("Like continental land masses the two worlds inevitably drift apart. Every bridge breaks."), it is just this task that has comprised the primary hermeneutical work of contemporary homiletics.[23]

In preaching these dual tasks are decisively wed. Stendahl recognized the bi-focal nature of preaching by casting the preacher as a "bilingual translator" who distinguishes modes of thought and language intrinsic to the biblical text and then "translates" this language into contemporary idiom relevant to contemporary life.[24] In addition to this image of translator, the bi-focal task of preaching has been cast variously as building a bridge between past and present;[25] as standing between the ancient "world" of the text and the contemporary "world" of the listener;[26] and as holding in tension the two "poles" of text and contemporary moment,[27] among others.

---

21. For Stendahl the descriptive and normative tasks are separate—biblical theology is centrally concerned with the task of description, leaving the overcoming of distance to the systematic or practical theologian. This divided paradigm has been challenged, however. See Ollenburger, "What Krister Stendahl 'Meant'"; Schüssler Fiorenza, *Revelation*; and Lash "What Martyrdom Might Mean."

22. Brøndsted, "Two World Concepts," 218.

23. Ibid., 221.

24. Stendahl, "Biblical Theology, Contemporary," 430.

25. See the Brøndsted extract above. Also, Farley expresses the task as building a bridge, though challenges the framework itself. Farley, *Practicing Gospel*, 73.

26. Stott, *Between Two Worlds*.

27. See Allmen, *Preaching and Congregation*, 20–31.

However it is formulated, the task is largely the same: to proclaim an ancient text as meaningful or authoritative in the present. Theologian Edward Farley observes that this bi-focal paradigm is so ingrained in present-day homiletical structures that it is now rarely reflected upon critically.[28]

BRIDGING TIME WITH WORDS: CONTEMPORARY HOMILETICAL THEOLOGIES

While this hermeneutical framework has been foundational for many different contemporary homiletical theories the overall framework and process is similar. A number of frameworks for classifying homiletical methods currently exist in the preaching literature.[29] The approach here asks how homiletical theories navigate the temporal distance between text and sermon.[30] Or, how do preachers treat time in moving from the text to contemporary sermon? At least four broad means of navigating the distance emerge.[31] Time, which is the actual distance between text and today, is traded for a spatial conception of the task in each of the models. Ultimately the time between then and now is treated in a "timeless" manner. What follows provides an overview of these four approaches through representative preachers in each perspective.

Cognitive Hermeneutics and Propositional Preaching: A Move outside of Time

A traditional strand of homiletical practice has sought to move from past text to present experience through a move outside of time, distilling "eternal," or "timeless" statements of truth. In this homiletic the preacher reformulates the content of the Bible into propositional statements offered

---

28. Farley, *Practicing Gospel*, 72.

29. Jensen, *Telling the Story*, organizes contemporary preaching according to its goal—as didactic preaching, proclamatory preaching, or story preaching. Rose, *Sharing the Word*, groups homiletical approaches according to their "voices": traditional, kerygmatic, transformational, and marginal. Achtemeier's typology finds its structure, at least in part, in relation to the sermon's handling of the hermeneutical task as outlined above. She identifies four types of preaching operative in North American pulpits: propositional, thematic, creational or creative, and experimental. Achtemeier, "The Artful Dialogue."

30. This is akin to McKim's study of how preachers use Scripture: *The Bible in Theology and Preaching*.

31. This organizational rationale is not itself perfect, as these homiletical approaches are not monolithic but diverse.

primarily for cognitive reception. The historically contingent aspects of the text may be undervalued in favor of the intrinsic and non-temporal propositional content that is true for all people in all places in all times. This restatement of the truth component of the text is seen as at once biblical in that it arises from the text (and is hence authoritative), and immediately relevant in that it is given in the contemporary idiom. The "timeless truths" formulated from the text are understood as the text's intrinsic meaning, universal and non-perspectival. It is these propositions, either stated non-perspectivally or "reclothed" in contemporary idiom, that become authoritative and meaningful.

James T. Cleland: A Cognitive-Propositional Bridge

James T. Cleland (1908–74) described all preaching as bi-focal at its best.[32] For Cleland the task of preaching did not revolve around a single pole (either past biblical text or contemporary situation), which would be circular. Rather, preaching is elliptical, containing two poles: "the historic faith and the present day."[33] Both poles are indispensable as "together they form the Word of God."[34] The task of Cleland's homiletic is to bring the two together in order that God's word might be heard.

In his 1953 lectures on preaching Cleland outlined his view of the preacher's task and formulated a methodology for accomplishing the task.[35] The Bible, Cleland stated, contains the word of God, which is essentially the activity of God in seeking to reconcile humanity to himself.[36] God's word is confined in temporal and material facts: "The eternal Word of God is always cabined, cribbed and confined by the temporal and material facts in which it reveals itself. The temporal conditions the eternal; it conceals the Word as well as reveals it; it mumbles or stammers or mispronounces the Word."[37] Cleland says that it is this hidden, contextual nature of the word of God in the text that obscures its eternal truth and real significance from the contemporary reader. The eternal truth, then, must be liberated from its contextual bonds.

---

32. Others representing this approach include Andrew Blackwood and Ilion T. Jones. See Blackwood, *Preaching from the Bible*; Blackwood, *The Preparation of Sermons*; Jones, *Principles and Practice of Preaching*.

33. Cleland, *Preaching to Be Understood*, 43.

34. Ibid.

35. Cleland, *The True and Lively Word*.

36. Ibid., 23–25.

37. Ibid., 30.

Cleland is more specific as he describes how the preacher might approach the task of finding this eternal truth. Consciously bi-focal in keeping both text and listener in mind in the preparation of the sermon, the preacher has recourse to "three complementary ways of tearing the truth out of the text."[38] These activities include a study of the text in its original language or multiple translations; exegesis, that is, "a critical analysis of the selected verses in their geographical, historical and cultural settings, with special attention paid to the author's purpose" and exposition, "the elucidation of the spiritual principle in the passage as it is determined by the exegesis."[39] These activities together propel the preacher through a three-step process for constructing the sermon, first aiming at finding the word of God within the text. Cleland describes the work as to "first discern and then discount the local and temporal, so that what is eternal, and therefore permanent, may stand alone."[40] Once this universal word is de-contextualized, the direction of sermon preparation is reversed as the preacher must recontextualize the word in the present-day world of the listener: "So the preparer of the sermon, at this point, has to reverse his field. He has been pulling the eternal out of the temporary; now he must do the opposite. He must insert the timeless word into time—his time, their time, contemporary time. He must surround the World-view with the twentieth-century, in his parish. He must paint the Word with local colour."[41] This second step is essential to the preaching process as it is not enough to "free [the Word] from its ancient historical trappings. . . . We must re-clothe it for today."[42] The final step in preparing the sermon is to find contemporary words in which to communicate the recontextualized truth in the present.

In Cleland's later work he formulates the task similarly and more starkly propositional. The process is marked by formulating a series of propositions—a textual proposition, what the text said to its original hearers; an eternal proposition, true for all people in all times in all places; and a final proposition, which is the eternal proposition "incarnate."[43] The formula for preparing a sermon is given: "Investigation, or exegesis, deals with the *then*; interpretation, or exposition, deals with the *always*; application deals with the *now*. And the result? The Word of God is preached."[44]

38. Ibid., 72.
39. Ibid.
40. Ibid., 73.
41. Ibid., 74.
42. Ibid., 75.
43. Cleland, *Preaching to Be Understood*, 73, 77.
44. Ibid.

Observations

In a cognitive-propositional approach events described in the text hold value for the timeless, propositional truths that they may contain.[45] Cleland's cognition-focused approach uses the text as a repository of propositional truth. The act of freeing this cognitive information from its contingent, temporally conditioned form and stating it as a proposition bridges the distance between text and sermon. There is first a move outside of time (a *timeless* truth) then a translation of the atemporal statement for the present moment. Cleland's homiletic overtly engages in "tearing the truth out of the text," and then translating this truth into "eternal" statements of propositional truth.[46] After a move outside of spatio-temporal reality, the propositions are inserted back into time. The historically contingent nature of the text is, in many ways, undervalued as it is treated as an object from which to gain cognitive knowledge about God in the present. Past events cease to be events and are treated as objects. As past is viewed as confining God's word it becomes undesirable and discardable. Further, future finds little place in a paradigm that deals with only two moments—past and present. In a cognitive-propositional homiletic eschatology becomes difficult to maintain and time is, at best, disjointed. Propositional statements of truth are not, in themselves, problematic. However, when the past is devalued against the present, something of the text's nature as recalling past historical events is lost.

Experiential Hermeneutics and the New Homiletic: Creating Present Experience

In part as a response to the type of cognitive homiletics described above, H. Grady Davis's assertion that form and substance coexist, neither discardable, prompted a movement of homiletical theory in the direction of what would eventually become known as the New Homiletic. The New Homiletic would move away from a focus on timeless, cognitive truths, toward an emphasis on preaching as creating a present experience. This vein of homiletical theology is now extensive, having produced diverse styles and methodologies since the seminal texts were published. Looking back at the New Homiletic in 1997 Eugene Lowry recalled a number of homiletical approaches

---

45. Dulles, *Models of Revelation*, 45.
46. Cleland, *True and Lively Word*, 72.

it prompted, such as inductive movement,[47] story sermons,[48] narrative sermons,[49] trans-conscious African American sermons,[50] phenomenological movement,[51] and conversational-episodal sermons,[52] among others.[53] This diversity makes speaking of the New Homiletic monolithically, in many ways, impossible. For instance, while much of the New Homiletic emphasis on experience can be traced back to the theology of the New Hermeneutic, the writings of Henry Mitchell[54] and David Buttrick,[55] for instance, do not fall so cleanly into this category. What follows is first a broad overview of the New Homiletic's origins and context followed by a discussion of two of its practitioners, Eugene Lowry and David Buttrick. The goal in discussing Lowry and Buttrick will not be to provide a complete inquiry into their respective homiletics. Rather, the discussion will be framed by their hermeneutical approaches in moving from past text to present sermon. I have chosen Lowry and Buttrick in order to present them as examples of homiletical theories based upon the common thread throughout the field, the creation of an experience.

---

47. Craddock, *As One without Authority*; Craddock, *Preaching*.

48. For example, Steimle, Niedenthal, and Rice, *Preaching the Story*; Jensen, *Telling the Story*; Jensen, *Thinking in Story*; Williams, "Preaching as Storytelling"; Williams, *Friends for Life*.

49. See especially Lowry, *The Homiletical Plot*; Lowry, *Doing Time in the Pulpit*; Lowry, *How to Preach a Parable*.

50. Mitchell, *The Recovery of Preaching*; McClain, *Come Sunday*; and Crawford, *The Hum*.

51. See Buttrick, *Homiletic*.

52. See Rose, *Sharing the Word*.

53. Lowry, *The Sermon*. Other ways to classify movements in the New Homiletic have been promoted, notably Eslinger, *The Web of Preaching*, a reworking of his earlier *A New Hearing*.

54. Mitchell discusses the New Hermeneutic and concludes that "our Black ancestors knew and followed these rules long before the Germans spelled out the new hermeneutic" (*Black Preaching*, 10). Mitchell's emphasis on experience comes more from a tradition of African American preaching and a desire to preach holistically to both mind and emotions. Also, a shared cultural identity militates against the existentialism of the New Homiletic. Mitchell, *Celebration and Experience in Preaching*.

55. Buttrick's approach relies on phenomenology and emphasizes shared congregational consciousness as opposed to the existentialism of the New Hermeneutic. *Homiletic*, 5–20.

The New Homiletic: Origins and Context

It was Davis's *Design for Preaching* in 1958,[56] along with David Randolph's *Renewal of Preaching* in 1969,[57] Fred Craddock's *As One without Authority* in 1971,[58] and the development of the New Hermeneutic school in theology, that signaled a turn in homiletical thought that eschewed rationalistic, propositional models in favor of an understanding of preaching as "event."[59] Randolph described the eventful nature of this new movement: "A new preaching is coming to birth in the travail of our times . . . preaching is being rejected as a habit and affirmed as a happening. The definition of preaching which is dawning on these horizons may be stated this way: *Preaching is the event in which the biblical text is interpreted in order that its meaning will come to expression in the concrete situation of the hearers.*"[60] It is the sermon's eventfulness that bridges temporal and experiential distance between past text and contemporary moment.

While quite diverse it is the quality of preaching as present event that ties together the New Homiletic. In their summary, Reid, Bullock, and Fleer describe the collective unity of the preachers in this stream as marked by "the creation of an experience in which both speaker and audience are co-participants in an event of understanding."[61] David Lose notes that "the New Homiletic's experiential approach understands truth not as information to be grasped but as an event to be experienced . . . such sermons seek to create an encounter between listener and Word."[62] John McClure describes the imaginative and symbolic quality of New Homiletic preaching: "[These preachers] strive to discover life symbols by creating new metaphoric juxtapositions and reversals and by unfolding the inner narratives of traditions, persons, and communities. They search for insight into the nature of reality and God by journeying outside the lines of formal logic, exploring imaginative (not imaginary) cognitive paradigms."[63] The experiential quality is evident in Randolph's homiletical theory where "preaching is understood not as the packaging of a product, but as the evocation of an event," and the

---

56. Davis, *Design for Preaching*.

57. Randolph, *The Renewal of Preaching*.

58. Craddock, *As One without Authority*.

59. McClure, under the rubric of "ontological reason," also cites the theologies of Paul Tillich, H. Richard Niebuhr, and Reinhold Niebuhr, as foundational for experiential homiletics. McClure, *Other-wise Preaching*, 75–76.

60. Randolph, *Renewal of Preaching*, 1. Emphasis original.

61. Reid, Bullock, and Fleer, "Creation of an Experience," 1.

62. Lose, "Whither Hence, New Homiletic?," 256.

63. McClure, *Other-wise Preaching*, 78.

operative question asked of the sermon is not what it says, but "what does the sermon do?"[64] This, in particular, is in contrast to a more cognitively focused homiletic.

Lose posits at least three cultural and theological developments occurring around the time of the New Homiletic's beginnings that served to make the movement possible and shape its development. The first factor is the development of "a more holistic sense of preaching," as preaching began to "accent the affective, as well as rational, elements of the sermon and thereby bridge a perceived gap between head and heart, mind and body, and intellect and emotions."[65] In this emphasis on experience the sermon moves away from a propositional transfer of information. Craddock emphasized the power of words as more than vehicles of informational content: "Certainly the content of communication is important, but it is in *speaking* words that an event occurs which transcends the informational dimension of the transaction. Something happens, involving at least two people, because spoken words effect participation and community."[66] Through a renewed sense of the power of words this more holistic sense of preaching aims at the creation of an event.

The second factor contributing to the New Homiletic's rise is the development of an increasing recognition of the literary character of the Bible. Whereas in an earlier cognitive-centered homiletical approach texts were de-contextualized and recontextualized regardless of literary context or genre, the relation of form and content was now recognized to a greater degree. It was here that Davis's *Design for Preaching* became increasingly influential with his call for a sermon to be the organic outgrowth of its generative idea: "The thought generates the sermon, and the sermon embodies the thought, thus creating not a mechanism but an organism."[67] Amos Wilder highlighted the importance of the Bible's literary forms for interpretation.[68] For Randolph, this meant that the homiletical forms most consistent with the "fundamental appeal of the kerygma" and with the shape of the text

---

64. Randolph, *Renewal of Preaching*, 19. Emphasis original.

65. Lose, "Whither Hence, New Homiletic?," 257.

66. Craddock, *As One without Authority*, 27–28. Emphasis original. Lucy Rose proposes that it is an emphasis on the power of language that achieves this experiential quality (*Sharing the Word*, 67).

67. Davis, *Design for Preaching*, 22.

68. Wilder, *Early Christian Rhetoric*. Lose, citing Long's *Literary Forms*, notes that Wilder's attention to literary forms has had influence in both the early and later stages of the New Homiletic ("Whither Hence, New Homiletic?," 257). Though not strictly within the New Homiletic, an emphasis on literary forms of the biblical text is also present in Graves, *The Sermon as Symphony*, and in Greidanus, *The Modern Preacher*.

tend towards parable, biography, autobiography, dialogue, examples, and authentication by existence.[69]

A final factor that facilitated the growth of much of the New Homiletic, according to Lose, is the theological development of the New Hermeneutic. The New Hermeneutic approached the hermeneutical task with the goal of bringing the gospel to expression in the lives of contemporary readers. Seizing on the notion that language does more than describe or reflect reality, but rather names and therefore creates reality, theologians such as Gerhard Ebeling and Ernst Fuchs promoted the nature of language as performative.[70] That is to say, language is inherently eventful: "To understand a word—any word[—]one pays attention to what it does."[71] When it comes to the Bible, then, it must be observed that its language is not static but is continually effecting a response from its readers/listeners. Lose observes that "recognizing the inherently dynamic content of words sets up an organic relationship between the text and the interpreter that inevitably leads to proclamation."[72] In proclamation an event is created in which preacher and listener are brought into contact with the Word, which demands participation and effects a response in the moment of interaction. The sermonic event brings to expression an experience of the gospel in the present moment of the listener, and as such it is precisely this experience which moves the preacher across the hermeneutical gap.

Lose notes that the implications of the New Hermentutic's observations for preaching are numerous. Significantly, it provided the preacher an organic manner of moving from past text to present sermon:

> Ebeling and Fuchs not only reinvigorated the preacher's view of the sermon as "eventful," however, they also placed in the preacher's hands the means by which to move confidently from ancient text to contemporary sermon so as to bridge the historical gap between writing and hearing and mediate the present eventfulness of the gospel. Further, by their focus on the present-day reception of the gospel as an "event," they helped redefine truth in experiential rather than cognitive terms, a move that prompted the turn away from propositionalist notions of doctrine and preaching.[73]

---

69. Randolph, *Renewal of Preaching*, 58–73.

70. Lose, "Whither Hence, New Homiletic?," 259. Ebeling and Fuchs were drawing on Heiddeggar as well as J. L. Austin.

71. Ibid.

72. Ibid.

73. Ibid., 260.

Practically, this is evident in Randolph's description of the new task for biblical criticism set by the New Hermeneutic, and its effect for preaching:

> [This new task is] not just to see the establishment of the text in its "pastness" as an end in itself, but to visualize the written text as a point in a moving line which reaches backward and forward in time and by this means to understand it in the present.... A criticism which seeks only to establish the text in its pastness is untrue both to the text and to the preacher, and for the same reason: the text is part of a speech event which can never be hermetically sealed off from the present.[74]

The written text intersects the present moment and it is in the interaction that a speech event is realized and an experience of the text is created. It is the sermon's experiential quality, in which the preacher mediates "the present eventfulness of the gospel," that both allows the homiletician to overcome the hermeneutical divide and characterizes the New Homiletic. These qualities find expression in the homiletic of Eugene Lowry.

Eugene Lowry: Sermon Time Orders Experience

In Lowry's *Homiletical Plot* the reader is asked to lay aside traditional notions of sermonic form as he casts homiletical theory in distinctly temporal terms.[75] Rather than a doctrinal lecture constructed to convey information Lowry contends that the sermon, at its best, "is an *event-in-time*, a narrative art form akin more to a play or a novel in shape than to a book."[76] It is this quality of the sermon as event, having as its goal the *occurrence* of the word in human experience, that serves to overcome the hermeneutical gap—the gospel comes to expression as it is experienced narratively as present event.

Lowry begins with issues of form and distinguishes the direction of his homiletic from that which has come before. Sermons are most often conceived of in terms of propositions related logically in outline form. Lowry dissents: "But a sermon is not a logical assemblage; a sermon is an event-in-time which follows the logic born of the communication interaction between preacher and congregation. To organize on the basis of the logic of ideational ingredients is to miss altogether the dynamics of the communicational reality."[77] These "dynamics of the communicational

---

74. Randolph, *Renewal of Preaching*, 37–38.
75. Lowry, *Homiletical Plot*, xix.
76. Ibid., xx. Emphasis original.
77. Ibid., 8.

reality" in the interaction between preacher and listener are what shape the sermon. Rather than constructing an outline to order ideas Lowry seeks a structure that orders experience.[78] His emphasis on the ordering of experience leads Lowry to largely reject propositional ideas as ineffectual for working in time. Propositional statements are at best "no more than dead skeletons of what once was lived experience," and at worst "propositional thought . . . distorts and even reforms the experiential meaning so that it is scarcely recognizable."[79]

To view the sermon as essentially an organic ordering of experience rather than a wooden construction Lowry requires a new image for preaching. It is here that Lowry turns to narrative plot. According to Lowry, the plot begins as a "homiletical bind," something that seems unresolved. This "disequilibrium" becomes the generative idea that gives the sermon its power to unfold towards resolution in light of the gospel.[80] This movement from disequilibrium to resolution should be the characteristic shape of the sermon, indeed, of every sermon.[81] In trading ideas for experience the goal of such a homiletical structure inevitably changes as well. While an idea-based homiletic sought to convey understanding, an ordering of experience seeks to create a "happening," an experience of good news in the homiletical moment.[82]

Lowry identifies five stages of his homiletical plot that facilitate the experience of the gospel: (1) upsetting the equilibrium, (2) analyzing the discrepancy, (3) disclosing the clue to resolution, (4) experiencing the gospel, and (5) anticipating the consequences. The first three stages, says Lowry, are salient in setting the stage for the gospel, "so that when the gospel is then proclaimed it is *effective*—that is, it *does* what it says, and *is* that to which it refers."[83] Once the resolution to the human condition is exposed and the gospel is experienced, Lowry moves to "anticipating the consequences." This final move visualizes a new future and asks, "What—in light of this intersection of human condition with the gospel—can be expected, should be done, or is now possible?"[84] The experience effects an opportunity for change.

---

78. Lowry, *Doing Time*, 8.
79. Ibid., 79–80.
80. Lowry, *Homiletical Plot*, 12.
81. Ibid., 13. Lowry does discuss variety of sermon form (ibid., 90–95).
82. Lowry, *Doing Time*, 27.
83. Lowry, *Homiletical Plot*, 77. Emphasis original.
84. Ibid., 80.

David Buttrick: Naming God in Human Consciousness

David Buttrick's homiletic proposes a phenomenological approach to the preaching task. Buttrick laments the loss of confidence in language, especially in the church, and seeks to rehabilitate its use in showing its power in naming the world and telling stories. Stories "conjoin in consciousness to tell us who we are and where we are in the world: *Stories give identity*."[85] Preaching, then, has the power to "rename the world 'God's world' with metaphorical power, and can change identity by incorporating all our stories into 'God's story.' Preaching constructs in consciousness a 'faith-world' related to God."[86] There is no objective stance for the preacher in this context as all stand within the faith-story of a "being-saved community." What defines the present time in Christian faith is that we are included in this "being-saved community in an unfolding story related to the Living Symbol, Jesus Christ."[87] Through preaching identity is conferred and the story is told. God is boldly named into the world.[88]

While the purpose here is not to provide a full treatment of Buttrick's homiletic, a discussion of his hermeneutic in moving between past text and present sermon is relevant.[89] Buttrick employs what he calls a "double hermeneutic." The preacher encounters the symbols of early Christian communities in biblical texts, and he or she encounters them in a specific context. Buttrick refers to this context as our "*being-saved*-in-the-world." He goes on to say,

> After all, Christ is good news of our salvation and not merely idle information about past-tense history. Thus, age on age, the particular shape of being-saved-in-the-world will interpret Christ in ever-new ways. While Jesus Christ may well be said to be the same "yesterday, today, and forever," our grasp of being-saved changes as in every era different dominations are named and different liberations dreamed. The texts we study are not locked up tight in a vault labeled "Original Meaning," but articulate differently as the situation of the being-saved community is reshaped.[90]

85. Buttrick, *Homiletic*, 10. Emphasis original.
86. Ibid., 11.
87. Ibid., 16.
88. Ibid., 19.
89. For fuller overviews of Buttrick's *Homiletic*, see Long, "The Significance of David Buttrick's Homiletic," and McClure's section on "Buttrick and phenomenological reason" in *Other-wise Preaching*. Both offer helpful critiques.
90. Buttrick, *Homiletic*, 259. Emphasis original.

He summarizes, saying that there is a twofold task for preaching: "*We interpret revelation in light of being-saved, and we grasp being-saved in view of revelation.*"[91]

In light of the nature of Christ and the being-saved community's changing context Buttrick finds fault with preaching that involves a subject-object split.[92] In asking how to move to sermon, then, he attempts to avoid static "perennials" that would mire the hermeneutical and homiletical process. He critiques three different proposed bridges between text and sermon: perennial truth, human experience, and faith experience.[93] Common to all three is that each bridge is ultimately inadequate in the job it seeks to accomplish: moving from text to sermon.[94]

Dismissing each of these options, Buttrick asks if there is a perennial at all. He first suggests that preachers look for a "theological field delineated by the text" rather than simple parallels between the text and the present. This leads the conversation to the interaction of a being-saved community and revelation of God. In this context the perennial needed is one that is both constant and changing. A structure of human consciousness, as opposed to the content of consciousness at any given point in time, is the changing constant. Buttrick explains,

> The world in consciousness is ever-changing, mysteries of being human are variously understood, the shape of the being-saved community—not to mention images of salvation—may be different, even the ways in which we grasp symbols of revelation may alter from age to age. . . . Nevertheless the *structure* of Christian consciousness is similar in every age. Thus we may avoid having to posit a fixed-truth gospel or a constant human experience, neither of which may be maintained against the fact of a changing consciousness.[95]

Rather than objectifying meaning in truths or experiences Buttrick would seek to bring meaning to expression in human consciousness. The texts/symbols may remain the same, but consciousness' meaning making of them

---

91. Ibid., 261. Emphasis original.

92. Ibid., 262.

93. The first two are approximate to the cognitive-propositional and many aspects of the experiential bridges presented above. The third is more difficult to locate with reference to the above approaches, but is in some ways similar to Paul Scott Wilson's emphasis on the structure of the gospel, discussed below.

94. One might point out Buttrick's seeming exaggeration in regard to these homiletical views. Specifically, a valid question emerges as to whether there is really no truth or value in any of these manners of approaching the text homiletically.

95. Buttrick, *Homiletic*, 269.

changes from age to age. In this sense, meaning occurs in front of the text in the interaction between interpreter (or, the being-saved community) and text.[96] Buttrick notes, "We are suggesting that the *reality* of God-with-us now is the proper focus of our preaching."[97]

When it comes to preaching then, Buttrick asks just what it is that the preacher is aiming to gain from a text and he suggests a "world of meaning through the words."[98] One may be able to discern a text's intending and hermeneutical consciousness. The direction of intent today is the proximate direction of the text's intending. The hermeneutical consciousness gives clues to the "hermeneutical field out of which the writer writes."[99] The sermon will rely on these to cross the temporal gap, that is, to determine the answer to the question "what does the text prompt us to preach now?"[100]

Elsewhere Buttrick moves more explicitly in the direction of Edward Farley and others in terms of the locus of preaching: text or gospel?[101] He asks, "Do we preach to study particular, peculiar biblical passages, or is preaching a theological endeavor that seeks to make sense of life now in view of God's graciousness in Jesus Christ?"[102] Buttrick goes on to note that "the result of the assumption—namely, that every little swatch of scripture contains some sort of Word of God—is that preachers and teachers squeeze moral or spiritual meanings out of disparate passages, apparently under the illusion that any and every bit of scriptural writing contains a magic God-message."[103] Rather than vesting meaning in each individual text Buttrick states that "the Bible offers meaning by handing out a story with a beginning and an end and, in between, a narrative understanding of how God may interface with our sinful humanity."[104]

Observations

Preaching in the New Homiletic sets itself apart from traditional cognitive-propositional models. One unique aspect is the notion of experience or

---

96. See Jacobsen, "Homiletical Exegesis," 459, and Bartlett, *Between the Bible and the Church*, 37–72.
97. Buttrick, *Captive Voice*, 11.
98. Buttrick, *Homiletic*, 276.
99. Ibid.
100. Ibid., 273.
101. Farley, *Practicing Gospel*, 71–92.
102. Buttrick, *Captive Voice*, 11.
103. Buttrick, *Homiletic*, 16.
104. Buttrick, *Captive Voice*, 17.

event as that which makes the past text meaningful in the present moment. Preachers intersect Scripture and human experience in such a way that the gospel might be experienced in the present moment. In such a schema, the biblical text can be valued as a catalyst for experience in the present. It is this experiential bridge, or present event, that moves the preacher from text to sermon. Whereas in a cognitive approach Christianity became a matter of acquiring knowledge about God, in much of the New Homiletic Christianity is something more dynamic, occurring on experiential and not merely cognitive levels. All of these qualities have added dramatically to the robust nature of contemporary preaching. Lowry and Buttrick exemplify these qualities and have added to the depth of contemporary homiletics in valuable ways. However, the New Homiletic, with its present-centered hermeneutic, still does not hold past and present in tension. Rather, experience in the present is privileged over the present experience's connection to past event. In addition to alienating past this can result in a displacement of the future aspect of Christian faith.

In the New Homiletic the biblical text may be treated as a catalyst for universal (in the sense that experiences are assumed to be effected for all listening) human experiences in the present moment. Charles Campbell has been critical specifically of the narrative preachers in the New Homiletic, such as Lowry, for their emphasis on experience: "The emphasis on experience brings with it the danger of theological 'relationalism'—a relationalism that dares to make no claims for God apart from the experience of human beings. Human experience becomes the focus of the sermon, rather than God in Jesus Christ, whose identity is rendered in the biblical narrative."[105] The experience that becomes the locus of meaning is present human experience, seemingly disconnected from the real eventful and temporal human experience of the past recorded in the eventful nature of the text. The person and work of Christ in the historically unique and distinctive events narrated in the gospels, for instance, are translated into *a personal experience of Christ in the present*. The eventful nature of the present is preserved at the expense of the dynamic eventfulness of the past.

Further, for the preacher to be able to mediate this experience universally to a gathered congregation is hopeful, at best. McClure critiques many of the experiential preachers for assuming that their congregations are homogenous unities in which experience can be mediated uniformly.[106] Lose observes that this elevation of present experience is similar to

---

105. Campbell, *Preaching Jesus*, 141–42.

106. McClure, *Other-wise Preaching*, 81. Rose makes similar charges regarding the universalizing of experience (*Sharing the Word*, 78–81).

the cognitive-propositional approach in its "timeless" quality: "Preaching is thus still essentially a matter of transmission, if not of the timeless cognitive truths of the Old Homiletic, then of the timeless (in that they are always existential) experiential events of the New."[107] What one ends up with is a gospel that may be experienced in any present moment but that requires little or no actual historical or temporal connection. The past, in such a construct, is simply treated as a catalyst for personal experience in the present.

While some New Homiletic approaches tend to begin with the past and then move away from it, the dynamic is somewhat different for Buttrick. Buttrick is intensely concerned with the text's interaction with the world today. He insists, "Must preaching be past tense, or do we preach standing before a present-day, active God of our lives? We are not suggesting that Christ is not a crucial, indeed *the* crucial disclosure of God. But we are suggesting that the *reality* of God-with-us now is the proper focus of our preaching."[108] Buttrick's homiletic views meaning as happening "in front of," or with the "audience of the text," and as such, there is a continuing historical contingency to meaning that is exerted in each new moment that the gospel is experienced.[109] When it comes to the historical anchoring of the text in real event behind the text Buttrick is less enthusiastic, speaking of revelation as symbol rather than as occurring in real historical time.[110]

When time and history is proposed as vehicle for God's revelation Buttrick is reductionistic in referring only to the salvation-history school of theology, which sought to objectively recount acts of God in historical events. For Buttrick, revelation comes to expression in human consciousness through language, symbols, and stories: "If we begin to think of revelation in relation to symbols, myths, and rituals that are given to social consciousness, we will take a turn toward mysteries of language and, thus, toward a renewed theology of the Word."[111]

While Buttrick's discomfort with the salvation-history school and his difficulty with an "objective" accounting of historical facts is acknowledged, it is important to note that there has been more than this one attempt to anchor revelation in history. Retaining a high critique of the salvation-history school, theologians such as Stendahl, Wolfhart Pannenberg, and N. T. Wright have sought to formulate a theology for revelation in history.[112]

---

107. Lose, "Whither Hence, New Homiletic?," 261.

108. Buttrick, *Captive Voice*, 11.

109. Jacobsen, "Homiletical Exegesis," 459–60.

110. Buttrick, *Homiletic*, 113.

111. Ibid., 116.

112. The salvation-history approach has been critiqued by other theologians who

One might not fully abandon history as a category for revelation, or as an important hermeneutical dialogue partner. The biblical writers were conspicuously interested in real-world events. Wright addresses the event-laden nature of the biblical writings. Speaking of the stories told in first-century Judaism and early Christianity surrounding the person of Jesus, he notes that these stories were intimately involved with real history: "For [these writers] the place where Israel's god had acted decisively for the salvation of the world was not in their taking pen and ink to write the gospels, but in their god's taking flesh and blood to die on a cross." The gospel writers' work is to be seen as "derivative from and dependent upon that fact."[113] Buttrick is correct that a focus on the Bible in order to proclaim a past-tense faith, or to elevate the text itself beyond its place, is in many ways a defective proclamation. Simultaneously, however, one senses a loss in terms of time, history, and events as real events in Buttrick's phenomenological swing the other direction. When he asks, "Must preaching be past tense, or do we preach standing before a present-day, active God of our lives?" one might ask why preaching cannot be both.[114] Can both past and present tenses be

---

retain a commitment to history as mode of God's revelation, and there are other formulations of revelation as history. Notably, see discussions of Wolfhart Pannenberg in Krentz, *Historical-Critical Method*, 81–82, and in Thiselton, *Two Horizons*, 74–84; Dulles, *Models of Revelation*, 58–60; and Pannenberg's own essay, "The Revelation of God in Jesus of Nazareth." The inadequacy of the salvation-history approach within biblical theology was recognized by Stendahl, who judged it as highly inconsistent ("Biblical Theology, Contemporary," 428). Wright, a New Testament theologian with commitments to the historical nature of Christianity, critiques the salvation-history school and goes on to formulate new approaches to Christianity and history. Among Wright's difficulties with the salvation-history school, he rejects a view of biblical authority based on an account that supposedly comes closest to objective facts. If this were the case, any new discovery of ancient documents that were shown to be somehow closer would then necessarily supplant the New Testament account. Further, the salvation-history school's insistence that it is God's mighty acts that are divine revelation, and not the biblical text, cuts against "the Protestant insistence on the text itself as being divine revelation." These do not serve as justification for ignoring the historical question, however. For Wright's own part, he embarks on a public study of New Testament theology seeking to hold in tension history, normative theology, and contemporary meaning, proposing a dramatic model for biblical authority. Wright's historical approach is set within an epistemological system that he labels "critical realism," which is inherently relational in the interaction of knower and object, and which decisively sets his project apart from the salvation-history or biblical theology school. See *New Testament*, 16, 21, 30–80 (on critical realism and theories of knowledge) and 81–120 (on history and the New Testament); Wright, "How Can the Bible Be Authoritative?" Wright continues in subsequent volumes of the series, *Jesus and the Victory of God* and *The Resurrection of the Son of God*.

113. Wright, *New Testament*, 23, 41.

114. Buttrick, *Captive Voice*, 11.

held in a more holistic tension? Indeed, we do stand before a present-day, living and active God in the here and now. And so did the authors of the texts we now experience. Christian faith is past tense in the sense that it is intimately and inextricably linked to past tense events that have constituted and continue to form the faith. The *perfect tense* in Greek serves as helpful here—a completed past event or action with continuing consequences—as opposed to (or in tension with) a static or repeating *punctiliar* view of moments.[115]

Postliberal Preaching: Other-Worldly Hermeneutics

The postliberal project in theology has arisen out of the theology of Karl Barth and has largely rested on Hans Frei's observations about the nature of post-Enlightenment biblical criticism and George Lindbeck's regarding the nature of doctrine.[116] In postliberal theology the changes brought about by Modernity included what Frei referred to as the "great reversal" of biblical hermeneutics in which the interpreter wrested authority away from the text, and the biblical narrative was no longer free to remain a unified whole that rendered reality. Gary Dorrien summarizes the founding argument: "Modern conservative and liberal approaches to the Bible both undermine the authority of scripture by locating the meaning of biblical teaching in some doctrine or worldview that is held to be more foundational than scripture itself."[117] The modern method of reading the text is misguided at its core as it eclipses the narrative nature and function of the text. In response, postliberal theologies have sought to undo, in a certain sense, what had been reversed in Modernity. A postliberal approach seeks to allow the biblical narrative, as narrative, to project a world, and through that world's events to render the unique identity of its central character Jesus Christ.[118] In hermeneutical and temporal terms, the postliberal approach removes both the past event and present moment into another reality that the reader or listener must enter into (from her or his own reality) and then recognize as reality as it really

---

115. Stendahl comments, "The church lives, not only by the aorist of the Holy Spirit, but by the perfect tense as the Greeks understood it: an action which is completed and the effects of which are still with us" ("Biblical Theology, Contemporary," 428).

116. Dorrien, "Third Way in Theology?," 16.

117. Ibid., 17.

118. This is a broad summary of postliberal theology. A fuller account is accessible in Frei's and Lindbeck's texts cited above, as well as in Frei, *The Identity of Jesus Christ*, and the first half especially of Campbell, *Preaching Jesus*. See also Placher, "Postliberal Theology."

is. The hermeneutical move is not so much one across time as it is a move outside of normal spatio-temporal reality.

Homiletically, there have been a handful of attempts at appropriating a postliberal theology.[119] The two under study here, Mark Ellingsen and Charles Campbell, attempt to avoid methodologies that translate meaning from the text into some other mode or category.[120] In each homiletical theory one sees the directionality of hermeneutical flow change so that it is ultimately the biblical "world" that overcomes the contemporary "world" of the reader/hearer. As such, the direction of movement between the two poles of the bi-focal paradigm is, for the postliberals, reversed.

Mark Ellingsen: Preaching a Literary World

Karl Barth wrote that what one encounters in the Bible is a "strange new world."[121] Ellingsen observes that this biblical world "seems so foreign, so inimical to the world as we know it, that the critical consciousness implanted in our psyche by Western technological culture leads us to wonder if the events it reports are really true or meaningful for us in the late twentieth century."[122] It is in the context of this discrepancy that contemporary preaching occurs. Ellingsen critiques past attempts to overcome this distance, such as propositional preaching that is a product of the church's attempt to confront scientific and critical historical thinking. The three-point form of preaching "abandons the biblical world and its literary forms. Instead of an actual presentation of that world, one receives from this model sermons 'about biblical topics.'"[123] Similarly, Ellingsen labels sermons allegory where "an effort is made to get behind what the biblical text literally says in order to discern what it really means."[124] These homiletical approaches translate the text into "categories of some other conceptual system," such as human experience. Texts then "are emptied of their own reality and treated only as symbolic expressions of a deeper truth."[125] Alternatively, the theological and homiletical task must be to re-present this strange biblical world in its

---

119. See also Eslinger, *Narrative and Imagination*; and more recently, the collection of essays in Green and Pasquarello, *Narrative Reading, Narrative Preaching*, may be considered to a greater or lesser extent postliberal.

120. Ellingsen, *The Integrity of Biblical Narrative*; Campbell, *Preaching Jesus*.

121. Barth, *Word of God*, 28–50, cited in Ellingsen, *Integrity of Biblical Narrative*, 18.

122. Ellingsen, *Integrity of Biblical Narrative*, 18.

123. Ibid., 18–19.

124. Ibid., 11.

125. Ibid.

fullness: "the task of preaching is to tell the Bible's stories about that world," not to fit its stories into a modern version of the world.[126]

For Ellingsen, because of a modern critical consciousness the historicity of the biblical accounts can no longer be asserted in an intellectually credible manner. Instead, he opts to view the nature of the biblical narrative as primarily literary by presenting the text as a complete narrative world that cannot, because of its quality as literature and not history, be critiqued by modern science or critical history. This does not necessarily mean that he views the stories as "untrue," but that he views historical questions as of secondary importance. By viewing the Bible as exclusively literary Ellingsen hopes to avoid the uncertainty in interpretation that comes with affirming that it is historically referential. Through a reliance on American New Criticism he seeks to arrive at a text's "normative, literal meaning . . . not contingent upon the interpreter's perspectives."[127] Ellingsen removes the narratives from historical-critical scrutiny by casting the Bible as history-*like* literature, or "realistic narrative." This is the Bible's "narrative unity."[128]

The homiletical effect of viewing the Bible as a "realistic narrative" is that "an attempt should be made via these texts to draw hearers or readers into the biblical world, to identify one's contemporaries and their situation with the original audience or authors of the texts."[129] With Frei, Ellingsen affirms that the biblical world becomes the real world, "the world in which we should really live."[130] The claim of the biblical world on the reader or listener is "tyrannical," and "intends to overcome the reality of readers."[131] This plays out practically for Ellingsen in literally identifying his listeners as the characters in the text: "It is not sufficient to say that we are like Peter, Matthew, or John, and so we ought to start living like them."[132] Instead, the preacher must cast the listener *as* Peter, Matthew, or John. Only when the listener sees him or herself as the character, and within the biblical world —"these stories are about us"—has the sermon accomplished its task.[133]

Ellingsen, then, is concerned to protect the integrity of the Bible's narrative world by casting it as primarily literary. It is a world that, precisely because it is literary in character, is untouched by modern science

126. Ibid., 19.
127. Ibid., 28–29.
128. Ibid., 21.
129. Ibid., 22.
130. Ibid., 44.
131. Ibid.
132. Ibid., 46.
133. Ibid., 43.

and historical criticism and which allows Ellingsen to avoid questions of historicity.[134] The biblical world is so compelling that the bridge builds itself:

> Insofar as the literary style of the biblical accounts is somewhat akin to that of a realistic novel, it should follow that the biblical text would present us with a world. And the world it presents can be identified as the world of God's interactions with God's people through Jesus Christ. That is so compelling a world that if it is presented in our preaching with the same flair and power in which it was written, then its meaning for our lives takes care of itself. For the compelling character of that world presented by the biblical text is an objective literary fact, not just a confession of faith.[135]

The gulf between text and sermon is overcome as the Bible is allowed to project this literary world; the listeners to the sermon are drawn out of their worlds into it and become its characters as the biblical world absorbs their own reality. Temporally, the move is outside of time so that time cannot affect the literary character of the story. Both the past and present in this scheme are absorbed into an other reality.

Charles Campbell: The World Absorbed

Campbell's homiletical project, while in places significantly divergent from Ellingsen's, also relies primarily on Frei's hermeneutical system. Campbell's emphasis is for preacher to present the unsubstitutable character of Jesus Christ as rendered through the events described in just these texts. Campbell devotes a chapter in his study to those specifically narrative homileticians in the New Homiletic who have relied on the two world paradigm in such a way as to accept the hermeneutical reversal Frei identified. His insistence on Christology as central to preaching relies on the proper identification of the biblical world as the real world that absorbs the contemporary world.

Campbell is not as occupied as Ellingsen with the issue of historicity, only discussing history or historicity with regards to Frei's approach to faith and history.[136] While not outright rejecting some sort of historicity of the biblical narrative Frei thought it a fruitless endeavor to attempt to prove the biblical narrative as historically referential. Instead, he sought to interpret the Bible from a literary standpoint, an "internal logic of Christian belief

---

134. Ibid., 46.
135. Ibid., 36.
136. Campbell, *Preaching Jesus*, 9–28.

through a literary analysis of the gospel narratives."[137] In this sense, while the unique event of the resurrection cannot be proven historically, it cannot be denied according to the internal logic of Christian faith, that is, the resurrection is logically necessary to the literary structure of the New Testament. For Frei, and hence for Campbell, the Bible does not *mean* because the events it depicts have historical referents, though they may. The Bible's meaning arises from studying it as a thoroughly consistent literary work.

In addressing the two-worlds paradigm as operative specifically in New Homiletic narrative homileticians Campbell makes the observation that "there has been too little careful discussion about how these 'two stories' are brought together—or about whether this framework is the best way to pose the issue."[138] In an effort to examine this critical lacuna Campbell looks to some of the central figures of the New Homiletic's narrative school, critiquing the way these categories function within their systems. In each case Campbell asserts that the particular homiletician comes down on the inappropriate side of Frei's "great reversal" in hermeneutics: The directional flow begins with universal human experience and then seeks to conform the particular Christian story to these broader categories. In Campbell's analysis, and speaking in terms of Frei's theology, for these preachers "the world absorbs the biblical story, rather than the biblical story absorbing the world."[139] Campbell concludes his critique with the statement, "In narrative homiletics, as represented by Lowry, Rice, Craddock, and Steimle, the 'great reversal' of liberal theology continues in subtle and not-so-subtle ways. The world absorbs the Bible, rather than Scripture absorbing the world; Christology becomes the function of an independently generated soteriology."[140] Campbell's critique addresses the traditional direction of enquiry in the bi-focal paradigm.

Although Campbell questioned whether the bi-focal framework was the best way to posit the question he does not move outside of it. He only insists that the flow must be reversed—that the preacher must begin with the biblical world, giving the biblical story priority over the contemporary world, and thus the biblical world absorbs the listener's. Campbell characterizes the sermon as an interpretive performance of Scripture, "an embodiment of God's reign after the pattern of Jesus."[141] The goal of preaching is the creation of the Christian community through teaching the community's

---

137. Ibid., 18.
138. Ibid., 147.
139. Ibid.
140. Ibid., 165.
141. Ibid., 216.

distinctive language and practices.¹⁴² This occurs, however, as Campbell is concerned to draw the listener into the biblical world and for that world to overcome his or her own. Much like Ellingsen, then, the temporal move from past to present becomes a move to an atemporal reality, where both past and present are marginalized.

Observations

Both Ellingsen and Campbell provide valuable homiletical insight, especially in terms of preaching and narrative, the centrality of the person and work of Jesus Christ to the homiletical task, and an offered critique and corrective to some New Homiletic directions. Campbell's emphasis on the identity of Jesus Christ and critique of those who make Jesus into a model preacher rather than the one preached, adds a necessary voice to contemporary homiletical theory.¹⁴³ However, there are observations to be made regarding the postliberal treatment of time.

The postliberal approach critiques the direction of hermeneutical enquiry of other bi-focal approaches and seeks to reverse the direction of hermeneutical flow. The postliberal formulation prioritizes the past moment, or text, over the present, making its "other world" normative for today. However, this past moment is dehistoricized, moved outside of time, inasmuch as it is removed into a realm of otherness. The past and present are then effectively treated as otherworldly and outside of time. This devalues both the past and present historical moments of the preaching equation by removing the biblical text into an "other," ahistorical reality, and then ushering listeners into that world which subsequently consumes their real, lived-in realities.¹⁴⁴ This biblical world is not necessarily identified with a historical or temporal reality. The world posited in a postliberal model seemingly exists in some other spatio-temporal reality. Both Ellingsen and Campbell remove the biblical narrative into a realm of otherness where it remains ahistorical and untouched by historical criticism.¹⁴⁵

---

142. Ibid., 232.
143. Ibid., 178–80.
144. Lose, "Narrative and Proclamation," 7.
145. Krentz offers a stinging critique of the refusal to use historical criticism: "To refuse to use historical criticism in the face of the Bible's claim [to historical truth] would deny that the history told is true history, make impossible intellectual demands on faith, and separate history from the Bible that stresses its importance. It would be a form of the docetic heresy" (*Historical-Critical Method*, 63).

Ellingsen claims the Bible as yielding a literary world that is tyrannical in seeking to overcome the actual realities of those who enter. In the sermon Ellingsen proposes that listeners should be cast as the characters in the text, that is they become Peter, John, Ezekiel. In this paradigm, however, listeners in the homiletical setting lose their own identities in becoming someone else. Ellingsen dehistoricizes the biblical text by claiming it as an other world, and dehistoricizes the present moment as it is overcome by and absorbed into this other reality. Not only is the listener's personal history displaced but also his or her identity as this other reality absorbs the actual temporal and historical one in which the listener lives.

While Campbell in many ways diverges from Ellingsen, a similar dehistoricization is evident in his homiletic.[146] For Campbell, the biblical narrative yields the story that readers/listeners enter into and that then absorbs their reality. He critiques contemporary narrative homiletical approaches for the direction of homiletical flow—"the world absorbs the Bible, rather than Scripture absorbing the world."[147] But again Scripture is described as something that exists on a different spatio-temporal plane from the actual historical world. In such a hermeneutical and homiletical project both poles of the hermeneutical process are devalued as the Bible takes on a functional "otherness," and an ahistorical reality absorbs the actual world and temporal moment in which the reader or listener exists. Neither Ellingsen nor Campbell holds time in tension, as an other time overcomes and absorbs actual time, resulting in a functional timelessness. Time is removed as temporal and hermeneutical distances are overcome through time's removal.

Theology and Theological Preaching: A Tensive Hermeneutic

In addition to the propositional, experiential, and postliberal homiletical appropriations of time, another stream exists in which one sees time beginning to be held in tension. David Bartlett takes a hermeneutical approach that assigns value to perspectives that find meaning behind, in, or in front of the biblical text, attempting to hold in tension the viewpoints of each approach's emphasis. Others take a more distinctively theological approach in holding past and present together, finding a theological commonality between the text and the present. This turn to a theological commonality can be found in the writings of a growing number of homileticians, including

---

146. Campbell critiques Ellingsen in many areas. See *Preaching Jesus*, 180–86.
147. Ibid., 165.

H. Grady Davis,[148] Bryan Chapell,[149] and Stephen Farris,[150] among others.[151] Paul Scott Wilson moves from text to sermon by holding past and present in theological tension.[152] It is the consistent movement of the gospel from trouble to grace that provides a theological commonality operative both in the text and today. Wilson develops this further with his discussion of "fusion."

David Bartlett: Standing Next to the Text

David Bartlett looks at approaches to the biblical text in recent biblical, hermeneutical, literary, and homiletical scholarship.[153] He examines where different approaches to the text locate meaning, bringing into focus perceived loci of meaning based on the interpreter's conversation with the text rather than placing the text in a strict subject-object or historical-critical relationship with the interpreter. His focal question is, "Where does meaning reside in the present?" He presents three alternatives to traditional hermeneutical approaches, each incorporating a temporal distinction.

First, some interpreters are concerned with the "world" that the text projects, or the "world in front of the text." These hermeneutical approaches can be more interested in the narrative world that the text creates than in the historical and societal context in which the text was created.[154] Literary crit-

148. While Davis is closely linked with the foundations of the New Homiletic, his writings on the *tense* of preaching describe a theological movement from text to sermon as he emphasizes an inherently common theological situation operative both then and now. Davis discusses a commonality in anthropology, harmartiology, and Christology in the past text and present theology. He places the subjects into a theological category of "other" in saying that Christ's "eternity transcends all the mutations of time, cancels all tenses except the *now* of God" (*Design for Preaching*, 207).

149. Chapell's homiletic rests on theological grounds in aiming to identify commonality between text and today in the shared fallen condition of humanity and God's subsequent act of redemption. See his *Christ-Centered Preaching*. See also Wilson, *Preaching and Homiletical Theory*, 13–14, 102–3.

150. Farris poses an even greater theological commonality in emphasizing commonality over difference. Common theological conditions are posed in terms of ecclesiology, theology proper, anthropology, and revelation (Scripture). Farris's method of bridging is analogy, similar to Wilson's described here. Farris, *Preaching That Matters*, 7–10.

151. Farley takes a decisively theological approach to homiletics, though he disavows the bridge paradigm. Farley, *Practicing Gospel*, 71–92.

152. In positioning his approach as theological Wilson also locates himself within a tradition of theological preaching. Wilson, *Preaching and Homiletical Theory*, 74–86.

153. Bartlett, *Between the Bible and the Church*.

154. Ibid., 40. Bartlett relies on Ricoeur for this distinction.

icism in a variety of forms (new, narrative, and reader-response criticisms) and canonical criticism fall into this category. A second stream sets the locus of meaning within the "world behind the text," or, the ancient sociological world that gave rise to the writing of the text. For these approaches "the biblical texts are clues to the complicated social world that lies behind those texts."[155] Bartlett lays out different ways in particular of doing this social and social scientific research. What each share, however, is a commitment to reading the text as a window to that societal situation which stands behind and gave rise to the text as received. A third set of interpreters attends to "the world we bring to the text," and how the commitments readers bring with them to texts serve to inevitably affect interpretations. Bartlett notes that this group is largely comprised of liberation readings of the text and includes Latin American, Feminist, and African American readings.

In light of these particular stances toward the Bible's various "worlds," Bartlett revisits the task of historical criticism and its relevance for homiletics today. While the above hermeneutics find meaning in the world projected by the text into the present, the complex societal interrelationships extant at the time of the text's writing, or in what the reader may have to say to the text now, Bartlett looks for a space to retain historical-critical commitments. All of these approaches are valuable for Bartlett and he holds them in a sort of interpretive tension. While not ready to abandon Stendahl's hermeneutical formulation altogether he does understand critiques of the historical-critical method brought by the newer formulations.[156] However, whatever might be wrong with the historical-critical method and Stendahl's formulation of it, Bartlett observes that in the present it is not a serious possibility to abandon historical-criticism.[157] He notes that, "we can broaden the method, enrich its nuances and variety, but we cannot really escape the method without escaping history."[158] Further, Bartlett points to the Incarnation, saying that "to affirm the Incarnation is to acknowledge history, and to acknowledge history is to admit the validity of many of the old historical questions."[159] Christianity occurs in the world, and as such, is intimately tied to eventful time and history.

In many ways Bartlett retains commitments of a traditional historical-critical hermeneutic while allowing for a more dynamic hermeneutical system in the critical addition of newer hermeneutical approaches. In this

155. Ibid., 73.
156. Ibid., 139.
157. Krentz makes a similar point (*Historical-Critical Method*, 63).
158. Bartlett, *Between the Bible and the Church*, 143.
159. Ibid.

way Bartlett is able to hold in tension interpretative and homiletical commitments to past and present.

Paul Scott Wilson: Theological Deep Structure

A dual process moves Paul Scott Wilson from text to sermon. First, the identification of "concerns of the text" and their transposed analogues for today provide bridges that move from text to sermon. Second, these concerns are set within the theological movement of the gospel from law to gospel, trouble to grace. This "deep theological structure" shapes the sermon in such a way that the gospel will always be preached for today.[160] Additionally, a discussion of Wilson's concept of "fusion" as one means of making an ancient text present will highlight the extent to which he holds times in tension.

Wilson's primary approach in moving from the text to today holds the two moments in tension. His process rests on imagination and metaphor with insights gleaned from the nineteenth-century poet and philosopher Samuel Taylor Coleridge. For Coleridge imagination functioned as the "reconciliation of opposites," that is "the bringing together of two ideas that might not otherwise be connected and developing the creative energy that they generate."[161] Wilson images this with an old hand cranked generator with wires attached to both positive and negative poles. As the handle is cranked, and the wires are brought closer together, a spark would jump from one wire to the other. This is, Wilson says, like imagination: "The spark of imagination happens when two ideas that seem to have no apparent connection . . . are brought together."[162] The two opposites are not reconciled in a neutralizing sense. Rather, the two images or ideas are brought together to create new meaning. This is a relational view of language.[163]

The process of allowing imagination to spark between opposites helps Wilson move from text to sermon. He does this by identifying "concerns of the text," and then "concerns of the sermon." Concerns of the text refers to "each and every idea with which a biblical text is legitimately concerned."[164] A second category, concerns of the sermon, is set up to keep the contem-

---

160. Wilson's later works more fully integrate these processes than his earlier *Imagination of the Heart*. See Wilson, *The Four Pages of the Sermon*, and Wilson, *The Practice of Preaching*.

161. Wilson, *Imagination of the Heart*, 32.

162. Ibid., 34.

163. Ibid., 36.

164. Ibid., 71.

porary situation related to the text and yet unique in itself. Statements on this side of the equation represent "a transposed version of a concern of the text, generalizing textual details in order to speak to our situation."[165] Sufficient distance is kept between these two poles in order to allow the spark of imagination to jump between them. In this way both the textual and contemporary moments are held in tension and remain in tact with neither collapsing into the other. A new, timely, imaginative meaning is created in the creative interaction between the two.

In identifying concerns of the text, each represents a complete thought and is listed individually. The goal and effect of this process is "to dislodge ideas from the text in order that they may be heard anew for the first time."[166] Wilson provides examples from Isaiah 6:1–13, such as "King Uzziah died," "The country was in mourning," "Isaiah had a vision."[167] Once the text is broken down in this manner each statement is transposed into a concern of the sermon. These contemporary statements are evaluated as true statements of either how one experiences the world or how one understands it theologically. Wilson continues with Isaiah 6 as an example:

> Text: King Uzziah died.
> Sermon: Many die today. Or: Rulers die; or: Earthly powers pass away.
>
> Text: The country was in mourning.
> Sermon: Many are in mourning. Or: Our nations mourn; or: The world lacks direction.
>
> Text: Isaiah had a vision.
> Sermon: Christ is our vision. Or: We have no visions. Or: God is absent to us.[168]

This process of transposition has as its goal "moving the ideas through a time-change."[169] Much preaching, according to Wilson, lacks imagination because it fails to establish the polarity between the text and today, and the two moments become either isolated from each other or blurred together.

The transposition process finds its sermonic structure in a second aspect of Wilson's homiletic. The inherent gospel movement from trouble to grace animates the sermon with the very theological movement of the gospel. Wilson contends that sermons should operate from a "deep theological

---

165. Ibid., 86.
166. Ibid., 77.
167. Wilson, *Practice of Preaching*, 62.
168. Ibid., 73.
169. Wilson, *Imagination of the Heart*, 88.

structure" which serves as a type of grammar for the preacher's work. For Wilson the core of homiletical activity centers upon the gospel—the consistency of God in moving the human condition from judgment to forgiveness, or trouble to grace, sets the transposed concerns within their proper theological and homiletical framework.

Wilson discusses sermon form as existing at two levels, surface and deep structures: "Surface structure includes the sermon body, introduction, and conclusion, as well as issues of sermon genre. Deep structure is like grammar in language; it has to do with theological issues such as what it means to preach the gospel. Does the gospel also have structure that relates to its meaning, content, and effect? If so, does some of that structure need to be implemented in a sermon in order to communicate the content?"[170]

The deep theological structure that Wilson seeks allows the sermon to preach the gospel rather than merely communicate a text. For Wilson, "the gospel has identifiable content and shape and many biblical texts do not necessarily contain it in isolation, thus texts must be treated in a manner that leads to it."[171] Texts point to the gospel, says Wilson, and it is in the preaching of the gospel that the church finds its calling and purpose: "If there is to be any hope for the church in the future, it will arise from being faithful to its calling to preach and thereby live the gospel. The church has no other reason to exist and all else flows from it."[172]

Seeking to provide a corrective Wilson suggests that what is needed is a theological deep structure, or theological grammar, that is conducive to preaching the gospel. He begins with the observation that there is a movement inherent in the gospel which can be described as having a polar quality, moving between "sin and redemption, judgment and atonement, trouble and grace, cross and empty tomb, old age and new creation." Wilson elaborates: "The movement from one to the other is the signature movement of the gospel. Here we claim that trouble and grace are the basic grammar of the gospel, the basic structure that facilitates communication of the gospel. When the gospel provides the intentional deep grammar of the sermon, the sermon is better able to proclaim it."[173] The gospel, then, has an intrinsic form that centers upon the movement of events surrounding the life, crucifixion, resurrection, and ascension of Jesus Christ. Wilson describes

---

170. Wilson, *Practice of Preaching*, 131.

171. Ibid., 157. This is a departure from *Imagination of the Heart*; see 109-10, "Every text contains law and gospel, judgment and grace."

172. Wilson, *Practice of Preaching*, 158. In this regard Wilson finds much of the preaching of the church to be lacking, as "the gospel is not a dominant factor in most sermons" (ibid., 159).

173. Ibid., 160.

the gospel's form as moving "from trouble to grace, from Good Friday to Easter. It may be told and retold in many different ways—from the various perspectives offered by countless individual biblical texts and doctrines—but the basic story, the underlying movement, the final outcome remains the same."[174]

The gospel's form makes claims upon the sermon and Wilson suggests that the sermon should make its movement in the gospel direction from trouble to grace. Regardless of whatever other surface structures are at work in the sermon, functioning from a deeper theological level the movement from trouble to grace serves as a theological norm for the sermon.[175] Wilson envisions the sermon as being comprised of two theological parts: "The first part is trouble and serves to make listeners aware of their or others' sin (vertical) or brokenness and suffering (horizontal). It represents the old order and puts the burden on humanity to change. The second part is grace and declares that God accepts the burden for that change in and through Jesus Christ. The cross, in being proclaimed, makes a difference, brings in the new age."[176] The sermon does not do away with trouble but places trouble in proper perspective alongside grace so that the two are presented in tension with grace being "the dominant note because it is God's final word."[177]

Wilson's own homiletical proposal follows this structure, presenting the gospel in "four pages." Once the preacher views the sermon consisting of two roughly equal parts, trouble and grace, each of these parts is again divided so that the preacher moves through four phases of the sermon: trouble in the text, trouble in our situation/world, grace in the text, grace in our situation/world.[178] It is here that the theological commitment to the gospel is linked with the process of transposition above. Concerns of the text and of the sermon are evaluated for theological potential as either trouble or grace and thus find their places on the appropriate "page" of the sermon.[179] The movement in time inherent in the transposition process is set within the theological gospel movement from trouble to grace.

Wilson delves deeper into the tension extant between the biblical text and the contemporary moment as he discusses the deliberate use of what he terms "fusion" in the sermon. Fusion is "a process, first of the preacher

---

174. Ibid., 162.

175. Ibid., 163–64, 173. Wilson provides one notable exception in the "single exposition/application format," which does not lend itself well to a trouble/grace movement (ibid., 164).

176. Ibid., 173–74.

177. Ibid., 174.

178. Ibid. See also, Wilson, *Four Pages of the Sermon*.

179. Ibid., 63.

finding the people's story in the biblical story and second of the congregation recognizing their faith story in it. Fusion has to do with finding and being found by God."[180] It functions in a deeper way than when the preacher draws a simile or analogy between the text and the listeners' lives. Fusion, at its foundation based upon metaphor, does more. Listeners will enter into the biblical story, participate in it and experience their reflection there. This type of preaching is found in any tradition where "the Bible is read with some common understanding that this is about you, this is your story, you are being addressed by God, you are in this story."[181] Wilson goes on to identify a key characteristic of fusion as then and now merging together:

> Every preacher uses simile, metaphor, and analogy to establish parallels between then and now, but not every preacher establishes identity between then and now such that they merge into each other. Fusion is not the simple blending of then and now, although that comes close. What distinguishes fusion is degree and intensity: the result is not a point of comparison but a union of identity. Our own reflection is found in the biblical text, and biblical types are found for today. The focus of fusion is theology, matters of faith, Israel as church. Fusion as we are using it is finding our reflection in the biblical text in terms of God.[182]

What Wilson describes here is a holding of times, of moments in the overarching drama, together in tension in order for the contemporary listener to participate in the biblical drama. It is a tensive relationship with active engagement.

Observations

Bartlett and Wilson both hold hermeneutical and homiletical aspects of temporality in tension. Bartlett values the different, newer approaches to biblical criticism, and in the end he finds an irreducible place for time and history in the discussion: "The historical-critical method still helps our preaching because we are still historical people."[183] In light of this, Bartlett poses questions for biblical scholars from the perspective of homileticians and he notes the importance of paying "attention to not only the history of the text, but the history behind the text." He says, "When we preach, we want

---

180. Wilson, *Broken Words*, 80.
181. Ibid., 81.
182. Ibid., 82.
183. Bartlett, *Between the Bible and the Church*, 151.

to be able to talk about what God does in the world, not just what God does in the story."[184] History is not the final arbiter of faith, but Bartlett notes that "Scripture makes claims about what the real God does in the real world," and interest in this may be "part of a perfectly legitimate intuition that the God of creation needs to act in the world and not just between the covers of a book, however central that book may be to our faith."[185] For Bartlett, then, because the church exists in a temporal-historical reality, and it is in that very reality that the biblical text claims God has acted and continues to act, the assertion of history is not easily given up.

For Wilson, identifying statements of trouble and grace in the text and then, by way of imagination and metaphor, in the contemporary moment keeps the preacher in the movement of trouble to grace as he or she moves from text to sermon. Statements of trouble and grace give the preacher gospel-shaped pegs upon which to hang the sermon. It is this theological movement from trouble to grace, since it is the shape of the gospel, which allows Wilson's four-page homiletic to navigate the journey between text and sermon. He makes this tension even clearer in his discussion of fusion in which the "story of people in the biblical text becomes the story of the listeners through the two being brought together with the temporal and cultural gap between them dissolved."[186] In this way Wilson holds both similarity and difference, past and present, in a unique and imaginative tension.

Of the approaches presented above Wilson most of all, with his reliance on Coleridge, purposefully attempts to hold both the present and past poles of the equation in tension, allowing both to keep their unique identities. Further, for Wilson more than for any of the other preachers above, these poles are identified with moments in time. It is alongside this stream of thought that I will develop drama and anachronism as theological matrix and movement across time. That is, the purposeful bringing together of two moments of time for the goal of participation in the gospel drama. Anachronism differs from Wilson's approach, however, in that it is an explicitly temporal device that includes a tensive relationship with future time in addition to past and present, thereby paying deliberate attention to preaching's eschatological context. I will develop this more fully in the following chapters.

---

184. Ibid., 156.
185. Ibid., 158.
186. Wilson, "Fusion," 188.

SPACE AND TIME: DO OUR MODELS SERVE OUR GOALS?

An investigation into various homiletics and their underlying hermeneutics reveals potential dangers in the way that a modern understanding of time minimizes the dynamic, temporal, and eventful nature of the biblical drama. The predominant homiletical models evidence risks inherent in Modernity's disjointed temporality for preaching. In what follows I hope to affirm the importance of the meaning of the text today, something that stands as a goal for each of the homiletics above. A focus on the text's meaning today, and not merely what the text may have meant in another historical era or as a historical lesson, has been one of most important goals and achievements in communicating the gospel for contemporary homiletical movements. Each of the homiletical projects discussed above represents a potentially valuable path to preaching the gospel. But do our current models best serve our goals? Christian proclamation, and faith in general, disconnected from or atomizing history and time becomes defective. In the following pages I will propose a correction to a modern view of time in our hermeneutics for preaching by holding times in tension , past, present, and future. This connects Christian faith to its historical and eventful roots while organically calling the hearer to participation in what God is actively doing in this moment of that drama.

A disjointed practice of time is evident in our dominant avenues of moving from text to sermon. This disjointed temporality disconnects people living now from the eventfulness of the gospel, both then and now. What follows are potential downsides of a disjointed temporality for preaching and ultimately for the faith it produces. How well do our practices serve our goals?

A Disjointed Temporality Fails to Preserve the Past Event as Event

The bi-focal approach at work in Stendahl's interpretative framework, both in its formulation of the interpretive task and in its appropriation in particular homiletical approaches, has intrinsic potential to move too quickly from the historical contingency of biblical texts by objectifying them in order to extract universalized, or non-temporal, meaning for communication across time. Historical work may be done in conjunction with a text but often for the purpose of moving beyond the contingent historical nature of the text's meaning to "an ultimate truth which is beyond space and time, outside history altogether."[187] It is this ultimate truth, rising above historical contingencies, that is then applicable to all and which can then be used, recontextualized, appropriated, or preached today. This is then viewed as, as Wright notes, "the real fruit that emerges when the outer skin of historical circumstance is peeled away." Problems arise, however, when one asks if there is something lost in the peeling process. Wright identifies the issue: "The skin does not peel away so cleanly. . . . We may justifiably suspect that quite a lot of fruit has been thrown away, still sticking to the discarded skin."[188]

Lash further contends that Stendahl's framework itself objectifies the text in order to extract meaning, largely ignoring the temporal and eventful nature of the poles of the framework.[189] Once past events are objectified in this way, as Julian Hartt notes, "the past as a scientific isolate has been lifted out of that continuity in which alone historical events are real."[190] This distinctively modern treatment of time as divisible and translatable, new since the Enlightenment, pays little attention to past event as an event in time and as a result historical events of the text in some sense cease to be real *historical events*.[191] The process can move from past to present without the important step of preserving the past as a historical moment. In the homiletical practices above the past moment is in many ways eclipsed by a translation into timeless terms, an emphasis on one's present experience of the text, or a translation of the text and reader into another spatio-temporal reality.[192]

187. Wright, *New Testament*, 20.
188. Ibid.
189. Lash, "What Martyrdom Might Mean," 21.
190. Hartt, *Christian Critique of American Culture*, 276.
191. Genre considerations must influence this discussion. For instance, genres such as Wisdom, Poetry, or Apocalyptic do not necessarily claim to represent historical events, yet they do arise out of a historical context. Vanhoozer's discussion of genre's relation to canonical practices is helpful here (*Drama of Doctrine*, 216).
192. Reasons for the move from the past pole of the equation are diverse. Jacobsen, relying on Dulles's *Models of Revelation*, proposes that in one's theology of revelation, that is, "what a preacher thinks God is up to in preaching," one finds the path from text to sermon. As different theologies of revelation are operative in the above homiletical models, their relative emphases on the location of meaning are understandable. Specifically, a cognitive-propositional approach locates revelation as doctrine, having a clear emphasis on revelation in propositional form. The experiential homiletic correlates proximately with a theology of revelation as "inner experience." Wilson's homiletic fits as revelation in history. A postliberal homiletic operates out of a "dialectical presence," in which "matters deemed external to the text are no longer the focus." Homileticians such as Buttrick and Farley seem to operate out of a view of revelation as "new awareness," in which meaning is mediated through symbols that restructure experience. My

A Disjointed Temporality Breaks a Temporal/Absolute Dialectic

A modern temporality, with an emphasis on the divisibility of times and the priority of the present, tends toward a devaluation of the past, which then leads toward a breakdown of a temporal/absolute dialectic inherent to Christianity that must be held in tension. In the context of eschatology Jürgen Moltmann makes the assertion that in Christian faith concrete history intersects with the absolute in an irreducible way:

> Christian theology speaks of God with respect to the concrete, specific, and contingent history, which is told and witnessed to in the biblical writings. It speaks of the "God of Abraham, Isaac, and Jacob," of the "Father of Jesus Christ," and unites language about God with the memory of historical persons. It speaks of the God of the Exodus (in the first commandment) and of the God "that raised from the dead Jesus our Lord" (Rom. 4,24) and links language about God to the memory of historical events. It ties the memory of unique historical persons and unique historical events to language about God, the one, singular God and Lord of all men and all things. Thus it merges with the specific historical recollection a universal and absolute claim.[193]

Moltmann goes on to say that when this unity is broken Christianity disintegrates into either atheism or anthropology.[194] Erich Auerbach describes a similar dialectic inherent in the Christian faith evident especially up to the medieval period between the sublime and the everyday. This blending of the sublime and the everyday in the church's medieval history is a function of the church's Christology, as the sublime and the lowly were ultimately merged in Christ.[195] This theological view of time and space is rooted in the biblical text, as Moltmann notes, and is an integral piece of Christian faith and theology.

A translation of the text, without holding past and present in tension, treats the text as valuable for the timeless proposition it yields, or the perpetually present experience it produces, or the other spatio-temporal reality it unlocks. In these programs one does not necessarily experience the Absolute in historical time, as Moltmann argues is the case theologically.

---

particular commitments are more historical, though not exclusively so. See Jacobsen, "Homiletical Exegesis," especially 459–61.

193. Moltmann, "Theology as Eschatology," 1–2.
194. Ibid. For Moltmann, this unity has already broken down in modern theologies.
195. Auerbach, *Mimesis*, 151, 159.

Krentz points out that "to detach the Bible's contents from history is to deny the very nature of the Scriptures and the Gospel they proclaim."[196] Auerbach observes that when doctrine becomes severed from the particular stories in which it is embodied, what is left is "disembodied image."[197] Inasmuch as a text's meaning is transferred into a timeless principal, or into a perpetually present experience, or into an other world, a temporal/absolute dialectic may be ignored and what is preached is then not the fullness of the text (or of the gospel), but something less.

A Disjointed Temporality Flattens a Pan-temporal Conversation

The historically contingent nature of the biblical writings cannot so easily be translated into universal categories, or into an other world, without breaking our connection in the present to our faith community of the past or to what God is doing in the future. If meaning is entrenched in history there is a sense in which to move to the present without holding the past event in tension in some ways silences the voices of the original faith communities that produced the texts. Bartlett writes that such historical questions are eminent for theology and homiletics on the basis of the Great Commandment. Loving God and loving neighbor are pan-temporal activities that encompass neighbors across time: "The neighbors we love are not only those from other places; they are those from other times." He goes on to say, "The Yahwist and Mark are our neighbors in the communion of saints, and simply to use them as mirrors for ourselves or as excuses for our own creative ingenuity is to violate our Christian commitment. Cross-culturalism is not just synchronic; it is diachronic, too. We are called to love the community that shaped the Psalms and the community that read the Pastoral Epistles, even if they are very different from ourselves. We are commanded to love them enough to seek to understand them."[198] Too quick a move from contingent texts to universal meaning or experience breaks a temporal-communal quality of Christian faith, in a sense marginalizing authors and/or historical interpretive communities.

---

196. Krentz, *Historical-Critical Method*, 66.
197. Auerbach, *Mimesis*, 15–16.
198. Bartlett, *Between the Bible and the Church*, 143.

A Disjointed Temporality Eclipses a Future Tense of Christian Eschatology

The bi-focal paradigm deals hermeneutically and homiletically with just the two moments of past text and present moment. As such, an expression of the eschatological framework so important in the New Testament is, in many ways, made difficult. When only past and present are heard the future tense of Christianity loses a voice. Eclipsing this future tense of God's gospel drama leaves an interpretation of the present and the past incomplete, as it is the end of a story that holds it together and effects the meaning of the whole. An approach that seeks to hold modes of time—past, present, and future—in tension would be closer to presenting a biblical eschatology that unifies all of time and transforms time by prompting Christian community and discipleship right now. Chapter 2 will take an extended journey into eschatology, its relative absence from modern preaching, and its necessity for a dramatic and participatory homiletic.

A Disjointed Temporality Militates Against a View of God at Work in the World

Lose makes the compelling case in reviewing the postliberal approach that the direction of movement in Campbell's homiletic in calling the sermonic listener from his or her own world into the biblical reality is "diametrically opposed to God's movement in the Incarnation."[199] He goes on to say, "Most simply put, when the fourth evangelist climaxes his mighty hymn to God's Word, he does not conclude, 'And the Word created a new world and invited us into it,' but rather, 'And the Word became flesh and dwelt among us' ... We believe that it was, precisely, *for us and for our salvation* that Christ came down from heaven."[200] The direction of the Incarnation is always from God to the world, "simply because it is *in* the world which God created through the Word that God works salvation for the world *in and through* the Word made flesh."[201] In a postliberal homiletic, which removes the text and the listener to a dehistoricized reality, the work of God is no longer in this world. It is only in the narrative which renders the person of Christ that God is accessible. Lose goes on to observe that in the postliberal approach "neither word nor sacrament nor church has this ability [to render Christ],

---

199. Lose, "Narrative and Proclamation," 8.
200. Ibid. Emphasis original.
201. Ibid., 9. Emphasis original.

only narrative. Ultimately, the hearer is confronted with the startling possibility that *God is at work in no other place outside of the narrative!*"[202]

Although Lose's observations are directed towards the postliberal homiletic, his critique addresses both the timeless truths of the propositional approach and creation of present experience in the New Homiletic. Treating the poles of the hermeneutical equation as objects of extractable meaning rather than as moments of human existence in the one world that God created can locate God's action somewhere outside of creation. This breaks a temporal and narrative continuity present in the Christian faith. In Christian faith, which confesses God as intimately involved in creation, preeminently in the Incarnation, it is decidedly odd to hear language affirming the existence of "two worlds," a biblical and a contemporary, that is, one in which God works and another in which we live and into which God's works must be imported.[203]

CONCLUSIONS

In contemporary homiletical theories, and in the hermeneutic that underpins them, the issue of disjointed time becomes readily apparent in the hermeneutical task as applied to preaching. With Stendahl, preachers in the present ask weekly, "Do these old documents have any meaning for us . . . in the present tense and sense?"[204] How does one maneuver the temporal distance between a first-century text (or older) and a twenty-first-century life? Contemporary homiletics addresses this question most readily with a reliance on distinctively modern views of time which hold time and history as divisible, the present as superior to the past, and a diminished emphasis on the future. While modern thought has contributed greatly to the evolution of Western knowledge, there is a certain loss apparent in a hermeneutic and homiletic that fails to hold time in a continuous tension. A hermeneutic centered upon this divisibility, and the homiletic that arises from it, finds itself disjointed and divided from the eventfulness of the history recounted in the biblical text. As such, there is potential for a loss of the eventful nature of God at work in the world.

202. Ibid., 8. Emphasis original.

203. It should be noted that not all of the above approaches end up bracketing God's action from the world. Wilson's homiletic, for instance, deliberately seeks to escape this. *The Four Pages of the Sermon* challenges the preacher to name God in the world boldly (199). One might also point to Buttrick's homiletic as naming God in the world. This phenomenological naming and shaping in human consciousness is, however, divergent from my proposal for a more historically attuned homiletic. Buttrick, *Homiletic*, 5–20.

204. Stendahl, "Biblical Theology, Contemporary," 420.

Over the past century homiletical practice has in one way or another moved outside of time attempting to proclaim the gospel in this time. However, one question that presents itself is whether our hermeneutical models have served our homiletical practices and goals as well as they could. Wright summarizes a hermeneutical process that moves outside of time, even if to then recontextualize for the present, saying that it is a process "which ultimately seems to be illegitimate: that one attempts, as it were, to boil off certain timeless truths, models, or challenges into a sort of ethereal realm which is not anything immediately to do with space-time reality in order then to carry them across from the first century to any other given century and re-liquify them . . . making them relevant to a new situation."[205] The critique applies to the experiential and postliberal homiletics as much as it does to the cognitive-propositional; each projects a less-than-robust appropriation of time.

Contemporary preaching as sketched above has, in most instances, the good goal of proclaiming the gospel of Jesus Christ (and, the overall relation of God to God's people) to an audience thousands of years removed from the event/s. The practices we utilize to achieve these goals have at their core a reliance upon hermeneutical programs that employ a disjointed temporality for their processes. However, temporality in our hermeneutical process and homiletical practice can be united in such a way that addresses the above concerns, respects the eventfulness of the text, and helps call disciples to participation in the ongoing drama of God's work in the world today.

In the following chapters I will present a hermeneutical process that preserves a historical-temporal unity through the proposal of a dramatic framework. I will then develop a practical homiletic out of this dramatic hermeneutic. This dramatic hermeneutical framework and homiletical practice holds together the pastness of the biblical text with the present life situation of the preacher and congregation as the church continues to perform the ongoing drama into God's future. One important theological device for preaching within this framework is anachronism, bringing together two separate moments of the drama, past and present or present and future, in a temporal metaphor that creates a new moment of experience and understanding without destroying the identities of the original moments. This dramatic approach to time and to preaching holds time in tension, provides the preacher a means to move through it, and will occupy the remainder of this project. The following chapter will reassert eschatology as a means for unifying time across its modes, and then chapter 3 will propose drama as an organizing framework for unified time.

205. Wright, "How Can the Bible Be Authoritative?," 13.

2

Practical Eschatology
Reclaiming Time for the Pulpit

WHILE EACH HOMILETICAL THEOLOGY IN CHAPTER 1 PRESENTS A potentially valuable means for communicating the gospel in a present context, one thread that runs through them all, to one degree or another, is the atomization of time. Truth (even expressed propositionally) is not, indeed, timeless. It is expressed and experienced within a temporal context, is shaped by the moment in time in which it occurs, and is inherently connected to each moment that came before and each moment that will come after. Truth has an eventful impetus, and propositions disconnected from their eventfulness in time are only half-truths. Human experience is experienced in a continuity of time, each moment evolving from and dependent upon the moments that came before and each leading to experiences in every moment that will come after. We do not experience God in a present temporal isolation apart from God's past presence or God's coming future. Calling congregations into other worlds tends toward a devaluation of this world and a dehistoricization of time altogether. Theological patterns in preaching begin to hold time in greater tension yet still have the potential towards spatial hermeneutics which break time apart rather than keep it in continuity. Homiletical theologies that move outside of time in various manners and degrees disrupt the temporal flow of reality. We need a theology that sees the distance between then and now as what it is: the distance of time. Time is both the distance from and connection to the text. Time is our hermeneutic.

We are both separated from and connected to the past and future by time; time is simultaneously theological distance and unity. Time is the path we may look back upon to make sense of the past from which we've come and it is the road out ahead of us upon which the horizon of God's future is presently becoming reality. Time as theological distance and unity between now and the eventful text addresses the disjointedness apparent in current hermeneutical and homiletical approaches: preserving past events as events, recognizing a temporal/absolute dialectic, holding on to the robust nature of faith as a pan-temporal conversation, honestly looking to God's past and future as direction for the present, and declaring that God is at work in this world.

This chapter and the next provide a temporal hermeneutical framework for preaching through, first, a reassertion of eschatology as the theology that unifies all of time, and then by bringing the homiletical project under the overarching matrix of God's drama in the world. A homiletic, and the hermeneutic underpinning it, that links God's people in the present to God's people in the past and then calls for present participation in God's work into God's future must be able to hold modes of time together. In God's story, eschatology (by which I mean the theological framework of God's time especially evident in the New Testament and not necessarily the specific details or interpretations relating to "end times") holds in unity the three modes of time now viewed as separable and separated: past, present, future. Eschatology preserves this unity of past, present, and future, connecting us to the drama of God's people through all of time. Jürgen Moltmann's eschatological theology provides a good beginning place for exploring eschatology's tension, unity, and transformation of time, providing the foundation for a temporal and dramatic hermeneutic that unifies past, present, and future and links us to the text. Eschatology unifies time and unifies our preaching.

For Moltmann, God's very real future continually, in every moment, makes its way into the present and becomes the past experience of God's future with humanity. This tensive formulation of time's unity reverses time's direction as we tend to conceptualize it (time moves out of the future, rather than out of the past). This eschatological theology presents a fresh perspective on the past and present by granting temporal priority to the future as mode of God's being. With a strong emphasis on an anticipation of the coming of God this eschatological theology makes the future reality of God's promises tangible today in God's proleptic event, Jesus Christ. Moltmann thereby unites all modes of time in the moment and person of Jesus and in the gospel that proclaims God's presence in history. Memory (of God's work in the past) and hope (the anticipation of future promises made real and tangible in history) in the drama of Christianity are both unified and in tension, binding the present moment between past and future and calling the disciple to participate with God now. This eschatology holds promise for a homiletic that calls God's people to participate in God's gospel drama today.

THE ESCHATOLOGICAL TENSION OF TIME

The historical consciousness gifted to the contemporary interpreter by the Enlightenment and Modernity gives the preacher necessary exegetical tools with which to interpret the text in the present and gives us an essential vantage point so that we may avoid over-identification with the past. As Krentz says (in a rather spatial metaphor), the historical consciousness "makes the gap between us and the biblical world as wide as it really is."[1] There are essential benefits in recognizing differentness in time. However, a consequence of an overweening Modernity has been to undervalue the future, in terms of a biblical eschatology which accounts for all of time in a unified manner, as we seek an understanding of the meaning of our present and past. Apart from a tensive relationship between temporal modes certain theological questions go unanswered.

No Answers without an End

For Jürgen Moltmann, Modernity has brought with it theology's near abandonment of a future-looking eschatology. This eclipse is as true in practical theologies as it is in other theological endeavors and it affects a disunity of all times. Eschatology, however, is a theology that accounts for time, God's time for God's creation. Because all of humanity has a shared future in the hope of a second Advent, Christianity must rediscover the place of the future in its temporal cosmology. Without an articulated eschatology there is a brokenness in the tenses of time and humanity is left without hope in attempting to address the two most pressing questions of our existence: Is God present in the misery of our history? And what is humanity's identity in light of God's presence, or indeed God's absence? There are no adequate answers to these questions without a connection to history's end in God's kingdom. A contemporary homiletic must connect to the past text and God's future hope in the present. We may do this through a rediscovered

---

1. Krentz, *Historical-Critical Method*, 65.

eschatology that unifies and transforms all moments of time in the central person and work of Christ.

Abandoning a Future Theology

Stendahl laments that in post-Enlightenment theological approaches "biblical eschatology—i.e. the matrix of NT thought—was taken care of in a 'last chapter' of systematic theology dealing with the 'last things.'"[2] In Modernity eschatology, which in the past served as a central unifying doctrine as the Christian theology of all of time (not merely future time), has been transformed in significant ways.[3] In his 1968 essay "Hope and History," Moltmann identified two modern experiences that have contributed to what he labels "a new challenge to theology."[4] The first deals with the tendency of Christian theologies to abandon eschatology: "In the past two centuries, a Christian faith in God without hope for the future of the world has called forth a secular hope for the future of the world without faith in God.... We have arrived at a moment in history that provokes the question: Should there now be a parting of the ways in history, so that faith aligns itself with the past and unfaith with the future?"[5] The consequence of a modern tendency to atomize time, prevalent to varying degrees in the hermeneutics and homiletics of chapter 1, is clear in this observation. Unlinking modes of time in some sort of timelessness, whatever form that timelessness takes, poses the possibility of a future unlinked from God. Moltmann names this "the deep schism of the modern age," and sees its outworking as the tension between a past Enlightenment theism and an atheism brought about by the church's messianic hopes being misplaced in the modern era.

A second experience Moltmann points to as a challenge for contemporary theology is the emergence for the first time in history of what he refers to as "one world." The future of the world's people is now bound up together as humanity has developed the ability to destroy itself. He writes, "Therefore, today even the historical future will not be the continuation of the past but something new. In the past, human beings had histories in the plural but no common history in the singular. Today we have pasts in the plural: each people, each culture, each religion has its own past. But since in

---

2. Stendahl's framework does not overtly seek to correct this loss ("Biblical Theology, Contemporary," 435). See also Heyduck, *Recovery of Doctrine*, 149.

3. See Dunn, *Theology of Paul*, especially 466-92; Sampley, *Walking Between the Times*, 7-24; and Hays, *Moral Vision*, 16-46.

4. Moltmann, "Hope and History," 369.

5. Ibid. 369-70.

the future we will either perish together or survive in a new community, we have a future *only in the singular*."[6] Moltmann suggests that the movement of history is "beginning to reach the universal horizon of eschatology,"[7] or, that all of time is being unified in a shared future.

Both of these experiences of life in the modern world expose fissures in the relative stasis of contemporary theology. Tensions between theism and atheism, historical interpretation and modern understanding, mythological and demythologized worldviews, and theological and anthropological emphases in the theological endeavor come to the forefront. As a result, the underlying dialectical unity traditionally recognized in the Christian drama—"the tension between the historical and the absolute"—becomes increasingly difficult to maintain.[8] This breakdown becomes relevant to the preaching task as God becomes progressively separated from God's work in and through time. For Moltmann this is a problem that strikes at the heart of Christian faith:

> As long as the dialectical unity of particular history and special historical mediation with the universally relevant that pertains directly to everyone can be retained, that is, as long as the unity of Jesus with God and of God with Jesus can be retained, Christianity is alive. As soon as the dialectical unity between history and the absolute is broken, Christianity disintegrates. One can no longer become certain of God and salvation through Jesus and identify Jesus with that which pertains to every man.[9]

In the modern era this dialectical unity is broken. We have sought God's presence in realms of timelessness and outside history rather than in real historical moments and events.[10] With this disintegration between God and time two particular questions arise for the project of Christian theology that can only be answered with a reassertion of future eschatology, an assertion of God at work in and through a unity of time, past, present, and future. The questions are evident in our practical preaching as well. First, how can one claim that God exists in the shadow of history's tragedies? This is the theodicy question.[11] Secondly, who are we as human beings in the world? This is the question of human identity. For theologians and preachers, these questions demand answers tethered to the real presence of God in time. Answers

6. Ibid., 370. Emphasis original.
7. Ibid.
8. Moltmann, "Theology as Eschatology," 2.
9. Ibid.
10. Ibid.
11. Ibid., 3–4.

that propose God outside of time or as the ground of human experience fall short. Eschatology unifies time and answers these questions.

Eschatology's Necessity: God in the World

Answering the question that asks for a justification of God in the world must deal with the observation that in a modern understanding of history the temporal and absolute have separated. This separation, primarily, is why one sees a move outside of time into timeless space or inner experience in contemporary homiletical projects. However, Moltmann asserts that the character of Christianity at its core is marked by its historical quality, observing that in Christian faith concrete history inseparably intersects the universal and absolute:

> Christian theology speaks of God with respect to the concrete, specific, and contingent history, which is told and witnessed to in the biblical writings. It speaks of the "God of Abraham, Isaac, and Jacob," of the "Father of Jesus Christ," and unites language about God with the memory of historical persons. It speaks of the God of the Exodus (in the first commandment) and of the God "that raised from the dead Jesus our Lord" (Rom. 4,24) and links language about God to the memory of historical events. It ties the memory of unique historical persons and unique historical events to language about God, the one, singular God and Lord of all men and all things. Thus it merges with the specific historical recollection a universal and absolute claim.[12]

Moltmann proposes that there exists a correlative relationship: as long as the unity between particular history and dogmatic theology, or, the unity of "Jesus with God and of God with Jesus," remains intact, Christianity continues. However, if history is separated from the absolute, the languages with which Christian theology once spoke of God become increasingly meaningless as Christian tradition descends "into mere historical recollection and the absolute is grasped in new forms of experiencing absolute questionableness or certainty."[13] In our thinking or speaking of God, God becomes more relegated to the past and no present or future exist with him. In practical theology, God becomes relegated to a space outside of time—a propositional truth, a personal experience, an other world. Moltmann's is a

---

12. Ibid., 1–2.
13. Ibid., 2.

move away from a perceived timelessness toward an anticipation of God in all of time.

The status of Christian theology in the present cultural milieu is that unity between history and transcendence has disintegrated.[14] Moltmann comments that the forms with which Christianity was once communicated are no longer accepted. The impetus for this shift in worldview has been the Enlightenment with its greater emphasis on science and human progress than on faith and the transcendent. A. J. Conyers reflects on the process of conceiving history in the current situation:

> Science replaces metaphysics, and the older theology, as a means of comprehending existence. Just as the former systems of knowledge attempted to free man from the caprice of a transcendent unknown, the knowledge of history liberates him from the immanent chaos of revolutionary change. Thus he is made free from that which makes history historic—the unknowable and often cataclysmic future.[15]

For Conyers, following Moltmann, the contemporary theological project in the wake of the Enlightenment has been an exercise in attempting historical control. Moltmann concludes, "The theistic explanation of the world does not satisfy the man who no longer *in theoria* seeks for the ground of all transient things, but who wants to understand them in order to own them and to change them. The modern understanding of the world has no longer contemplative but operative character. Explanation of the world no longer looks for the eternal truth of transient things, but is explanation for the purpose of practical change."[16] The modern theological project pursues understanding for the sake of practical control.

While the modern project in theology, and modern hermeneutics and homiletics with it, has de-emphasized the eternal in favor of the human, it has not adequately addressed the fundamental question that the premodern worldview sought to answer: "Behind the theistic-metaphysical world view . . . lies a real plight of man and a real initiative to overcome it as well. The plight underlying theistic world explanation is the theodicy question: the question of the justification of God in the world, the question of the glory of God that fills all the lands, the question of a world which is the reflection of his divinity and which therein finds permanence against nothingness and chaos and thus is just. *Si Deus, unde malum?*"[17] Does God exist

---

14. Ibid.
15. Conyers, *God, Hope, and History*, 60.
16. Moltmann, "Theology as Eschatology," 2–3.
17. Ibid., 3–4.

here and now? Does God exist in and interact with God's people *in time*? And if God does, does this involvement in time make sense of the world and humanity's place in it? Finding God in propositions, experiences, or in other worlds, that is, finding God outside of time, does not fully answer these fundamental questions. What is needed is a theology that unifies time and that finds God at work within the eventful nature of the world in and through time. Humanity needs a proclamation that can name God in the world right now, connected to what has come before and to what is coming from God's future. Eschatology does this.

Eschatology links past, present, and future with the presence of God in a very real way. And the eschatological nature of all theology must characterize our hermeneutic and the homiletic that accompanies it. It is in the *timeliness* and eventful nature (rather than timelessness) of the gospel that these old documents hold meaning for us today in any real sense. Rather than in some way moving outside of time in order to find meaning in the text for the church, the preacher must connect the congregation to God in time.

Eschatology's Necessity: Human Identity

In addition to moving God outside of the misery of the world in proposition, experience, or other-worldliness, a disunity of time leaves humanity adrift in terms of our own identity in relation to God: Who are we and what is our place in the world? After cosmological proofs no longer provided sufficient answers to humanity's place in the world, modern psychological, moral, and existential proofs for God's existence grew in prominence. In this context the question of human identity resulted in the recasting of theology as anthropology. Moltmann observes, "As ground of the world, God's divinity could not be demonstrated to man, who becomes more and more the Lord of the world, but rather as the ground and primal situation of *human existence*. Banished from cosmology by natural science, theology now became anthropology."[18]

The underlying question that theology as anthropology highlights yet does not answer is the identity question, "the question of the justification of groundless and unstable human existence before God and of the justification of God in view of the existence dependent on him." In the shift to modern theologies, humanity assumed the place of God as the temporal center of the universe. While we have existed through history and in the world God has been pushed outside of it (into propositions, experiences, and other

18. Ibid., 5.

worlds for example) in many ways inaccessible in and through time. When no answer to the identity question is found in God in the world atheism is triggered as identity becomes anthropocentric, rather than theocentric.[19]

With the theological project turning decisively anthropological, "God could no longer be demonstrated as ground and Lord of the world, he was now understood as transcendent ground of one's being in the world. Here, man's soul, his spirituality, subjectivity, personality, or selfhood became the real referent of theological thought."[20] The end result of God's removal in and through time leaves modern theology without a theological answer to the intertwined theodicy and identity questions.[21] The drama of God as creator of, and at work in, the world is damaged without a biblical eschatology to hold times together in tension.

Abandoning the Future in Preaching

Indeed, the atomization of time with the loss of a coherent eschatology is observable in contemporary homiletics. The relative lack of homiletical materials dealing with eschatology bears out this point for preaching theology.[22] John McClure connects the eclipse of eschatology in contemporary pulpits to the rise of Modernity and modern science, especially since the 1920s. Remarking on the development of biblical criticism and scientific reasoning in the late eighteenth to early nineteenth centuries, McClure states, "Biblical criticism discredited traditional understandings of biblical apocalyptic."[23] He goes on to say, "It is the fundamental argument of those who distrust all forms of future eschatology that contemporary experience simply does not sustain the preaching and teaching of interventionist or 'supernaturalist' views of the future. The uncritical supernaturalism or postmillennialist and premillennialist eschatologies is not possible in a modern scientific milieu. These eschatological systems are charged with 'precritical biblicism and antiquated supernaturalism.'"[24] What the preacher trades for a seeming credibility in a modern context,

19. Ibid., 6.
20. Moltmann, "Hope and History," 374.
21. Ibid.
22. While there are texts addressing apocalyptic texts for preaching (see Jacobsen, *New Creation*; Jones and Sumney, *Preaching Apocalyptic Texts*), eschatology as a theological paradigm found in New Testament/Pauline theology and addressed to preaching is scarce in the literature, though not entirely absent. Thompson and Long serve as relative exceptions here: Thompson, *Preaching Like Paul*; Long, "The Life to Come."
23. McClure, "Preaching, Eschatology and World View."
24. Ibid., 4.

however, leaves unaddressed an aspect of temporality that, embedded in Christianity's founding texts, has historically driven the drama of Christian faith and action forward. In Modernity's rejection of apocalyptic, for better or for worse, we have also in many ways abandoned the eschatological theology that gives Christian faith its framework for proclaiming God in the world in and through time. Without future promise in addition to past memory the fullness of Christian proclamation becomes difficult to find. This leaves one with unanswered questions: Where is God in the world? Who are we in this economy of things?

In a modern view of time a clear distinction is evident between natural and supernatural, a distinction not as readily present in either premodern or postmodern thought as such a dichotomy is more often held in tension. However, the modern view has not always been the predominant view and at least in some corners of hermeneutics and biblical studies the sentiment is changing. Nineteenth-century theologian and pastor Horace Bushnell, for instance, held nature and the supernatural in radical tension with one another. For him, natural and supernatural, faith and rationality, were not opposites but interpenetrating modes of revelation of the same God.[25] In more contemporary terms N. T. Wright, whose project seeks to draw together elements of traditional study with postmodern considerations, notes, "I hope it is also clear that, just as I reject the subjective/objective distinction, so I reject the nature/supernature distinction which is equally a product of Enlightenment thinking."[26] Echoing sentiments from theologians such as Wolfhart Pannenberg and Moltmann, homiletician Paul Scott Wilson seeks a revival of future eschatology in the pulpit, noting that "life as we know it is like a book; how it ends affects the whole and implies the beginning. Each part connects with the beginning and leads to the end."[27] The drama's ending (or, in Christianity's case, new beginning) affects all parts of the whole.

Thomas Long simultaneously declares that eschatology is of central importance for the Christian pulpit and registers his dissatisfaction with how contemporary homiletics have integrated the theology. Long labels eschatology from the pulpit a "corrupt and neglected category" and sees it as distorted in three strands—futuristic (often fundamentalist), realized, and

---

25. Bushnell does not fall so cleanly into the category of "premodern" or "precritical," though he also cannot be painted as a Modern. See "The Reason of Faith." See also Bushnell, *Nature and the Supernatural*.

26. Wright, *New Testament*, 97.

27. Wilson, *Broken Words*, 152. For a treatment of this aspect of Pannenberg and Moltmann, see Krentz's discussion of "criticism and eschatology," in *Historical-Critical Method*, 81–84.

demythologized types.[28] In terms of temporality these modes of adopting eschatology in the pulpit all fail to hold past, present, and future in tension. Futuristic eschatology elevates the future over and often against the past and present, adopting an escapist tone in the process. A realized eschatology redefines future as past, thus diminishing the actual future aspect of the drama. A demythologized approach moves outside of time into universal narratives or categories. None of these approaches proclaims a dynamic theology of God at work in and through all tenses of time.

The marks of an unanswerable theodicy and anthropological theology are evident in the homiletical endeavors outlined in chapter one. Escaping the question of God's justification in the world, the propositional project removes God to timeless truth. Yet so-called timeless principles fall when trying to actually assert the presence of God in a world that can only be experienced in time. The postliberal formulation answers humanity's questions by asserting God's presence and humanity's identity, yet that presence and identity exist somewhere outside of this actual world where we actually exist. Further, to focus on personal and present experience, as with much of the New Homiletic, embraces theology as anthropology, grounding God's presence and justification in one's own experience of God. This leaves unlatched the important dialectical unity of God with history; the sacred and the profane.

Eschatology brings the historical and absolute back together in order to assert God's presence in time—from future into the present, which becomes our shared past together and with God. A homiletic that rethinks God in the world, finding human identity within the ground of God's presence, will embrace eschatology as the theology that unifies time and makes the drama of God's people, recorded in our authoritative texts, meaningful for life in the world right now and into our shared future. This is the goal of an anachronistic homiletic: to embrace God's *timeliness*, asserting his presence in all moments of the drama of his presence with his people. If it is the atomization of time and the absence of a future hope that has disconnected much of modern Christianity from temporal and historical moorings, and as such broken the intersection of the absolute with history, then it is at least partially the reassertion of biblical eschatology that will reconnect contemporary preaching and faith to the drama of God's work with God's people throughout all of time. Time is both our distance from and the connection to the text. In a postmodern milieu, however, this eschatology will look different than it has in the past.

---

28. Long, "Preaching God's Future," 196.

THE ESCHATOLOGICAL UNITY OF TIME

Eschatology is the theology within our systems that addresses both the tension and unity of all time. As Paul Wilson observes, every story has an ending and often it is the ending that changes one's reading of the narrative's entirety, unifying the whole together. Eschatology accounts for how the drama of humanity is finally renewed before the God who is in the world, and for how all time before that end is to be interpreted and experienced. Eschatology establishes the unity of all time in the Christian story. Moltmann acknowledges that a return to a theological situation similar to what existed prior to modern theological shifts is unrecoverable. Indeed, such a backwards shift is undesirable. However, in light of unanswered questions in Modernity a way forward is necessary. It is untenable to do theology in terms that exclude revelation's historical character or remove the meaning of revelation to an other realm. An eschatology that unifies time, as Moltmann conceptualizes it, recognizes God's presence as in the future, a future that already exists but is not yet experienced fully by the whole of God's people. This future kingdom continually moves into the present and becomes reality. His proposal posits a move toward that which has historically been central in all of Christian theology: "In view of the ambivalence of theology as cosmology and of theology as anthropology we are referred back to the question of the origin of Christian theology in the New Testament. All New Testament theologies, in view of the Christ event, speak of God eschatologically."[29] All theology is to be done in light of God's coming future, which grants significance to time spent "this side of the end, in history" and unifies times, past, present, and future.

> From first to last, and not merely in the epilogue, Christianity is eschatology, is hope, forward looking and forward moving, and therefore also revolutionizing and transforming the present. The eschatological is not one element *of* Christianity, but it is the medium of Christian faith as such, the key in which everything in it is set, the glow that suffuses everything here in the dawn of an expected new day.[30]

As central to all Christian faith eschatology is, in Moltmann's view, the means by which contemporary theology may overcome a temporality that has been divided in the modern era: "In the modern dissent between historical and dogmatic theology, between Christian tradition and present absoluteness, eschatological theology offers itself exegetically as well

---

29. Moltmann, "Theology as Eschatology," 6.
30. Moltmann, *Theology of Hope*, 15–16.

as systematically as new possibility to think together God and history, the kingdom and Jesus, salvation and the cross, life and resurrection, the concrete and the universal."[31] Homiletically, eschatology reconnects the Church with the past of God's people in the present as we continually experience the coming of God from God's future. We then, as in our shared past, presently engage in the mission and calling that carries God's drama into that future.

Christian eschatology neither necessitates an apocalyptic vision of the world, nor is it a personal or private illumination of existence. Rather, for Moltmann, Christian eschatology is "the horizon of expectation for a world transforming initiative through which 'the renewal of the world is anticipated in this age in a certain sense.'"[32] This eschatology is centrally christological. For preaching, eschatology links all of time together in God's drama in the world today, allowing the preacher to move through time as she or he names God in the world now. We see this unity of time in understanding the future as the mode of God's being, anticipation of God now, and in Christ who is the prolepsis of God's kingdom.

Future as Mode of God's Being

Moltmann contrasts his own eschatology with that of other twentieth-century theologians who would transpose eschatology into either time or eternity.[33] God continually enters reality from God's future mode of being in every moment of time. In this way all of time is connected in the person and work of Christ. This unified temporality in Christ gives humanity a matrix within which to understand the historical progression of God's coming as well as a direction in which to work in order to participate with God in the present coming of his future being. This eschatology answers questions of God's presence in history and humanity's existence in the presence of God.

Moltmann writes that eschatology in this context is simultaneously a doctrine of waiting and action:

> Eschatology is here *the doctrine of hope*, the doctrine of the future for which one can hope, and simultaneously the doctrine

---

31. Moltmann, "Theology as Eschatology," 9.

32. Ibid., 36.

33. Richard Bauckham notes that it is a difference between theologians who had judged eschatology unacceptable to the modern mind unless removed of all reference to "the real, temporal future of the world," and Moltmann's approach, which views in "future eschatology precisely the way to make Christian faith relevant in the modern world." Bauckham, "Jürgen Moltmann," 213. Moltmann discusses this at length in *Coming of God*, 6–22.

of the action of hope which brings the hoped-for future into the sufferings of the present age.... The universal horizon of eschatology reveals the reality of the *world as history*, manifests faith in Christ as *practical hope* for the coming God, and thus qualifies herein the past and the present as history of the future of God. This leads us to an understanding of the present as the *presence of the future*.[34]

The particularity of Christian theology is that it inherently "speaks of God historically and of history eschatologically." Christian faith speaks of God in specifically historical contexts, as in "the God of Abraham," or "the Father of Jesus Christ." These are historical situations in which God is involved and they unite "the proclamation of God with the memory of historical persons," and therefore Moltmann sees "the hermeneutical starting point of Christian theology is... the concrete history witnessed to in both the Old and the New Testaments."[35] Time is both the distance from and connection to the text. God's action in historical moments has definite effects for the present state and enactment of the drama.

God's action in past history intersected with the present is not the completion of the dynamic, however. This God in history is always set in the context of promise, that is, in the context of his coming in the future. All history is the history of the future, the history of God's coming. God's future is coming towards the present, and the present is always the realization of God's future. In this sense a future dimension is unified with past and present in the future promises of God. Therefore, "the end of history is not only its consummation, but also its key, the basis for understanding it."[36]

It is here that the theodicy and identity questions are taken up and answered. Since on the basis of the Christ event Christian theology asks for God in the context of the coming kingdom of God, "it recognizes in the resurrection of the crucified one the initiative of God for the overcoming of the predicament of man in the world."[37] In this light the theodicy question becomes the continued realization of the renewal of the world as God is made consummate over and against the present misery experienced by humanity. In terms of the identity question, that is, humanity's justification in the midst of the present misery of the world, humanity finds itself in a place of inescapable tension. We exist in time inbetween that which is presently evident in the world (misery and a continuing broken identity),

---

34. Moltmann, "Hope and History," 371. Emphasis original.
35. Ibid., 372.
36. Moltmann, "Theology as Eschatology," 7.
37. Ibid., 8.

and that which is proleptically present in and through the sufferings, resurrection and promises of Christ (healing, reconciliation, forgiveness, restoration). This unity of God's future with present and past makes realities such as redemption, ethical participation with Christ, and acclamation of the resurrected one, already present and possible.[38] In Christ the future of God's presence is proleptically present now. The past is the history of this presence. Past, present, and future of God are bound together.

This eschatological context of God's action provides a way past homiletical theologies that remove God's presence outside of time or ground it in human experience. Significantly, it does not represent a return to premodern or precritical theologies. Moltmann summarizes this thinking together of God and history as follows: "Theology as eschatology understands man and the world in view of the future which both shall find in the coming of God. It is a thinking between cross and parousia and holds up the hope for God's coming in the painful realities of this world. It can thus move beyond the modern dissent between cosmological and anthropological, objectifying and non-objectifying theology, in that it takes up the underlying questions, the theodicy question and the identity question, as questions of the future of God which changes present conditions in the world and in man."[39] In a focus on the present as the presence of God's future and on God's future as continually coming, Moltmann, moving away from an atomized view of time, brings together past, present, and future. This provides a way beyond modern theological and hermeneutical roadblocks in thinking through God in time. Consequently, this provides the preacher inroads in preaching together God's past, present, and future with God's people. Eschatology, formulated in this way, preserves God's action in the world as action, event-in-time as event-in-time.

This future has definite effect upon the present; indeed, "the future is in mastery of the present."[40] God arrives into each moment of the present from his promised future, and from God's promised future past and present come into focus. This future is preceded in the present by God's promise in the past, as well as in the here and now: "God now already sets present and past in the light of his eschatological arrival, an arrival which means the establishment of his eternal kingdom, and his indwelling in the creation renewed for that indwelling."[41] God's future casts light over past and present, and provides hope for humanity.

38. Ibid., 7.
39. Ibid., 8.
40. Ibid., 11.
41. Moltmann, *Coming of God*, 23.

Moltmann relates this observation about God as God of the coming kingdom to the dual questions of theodicy and identity: "God is not the ground of this world and not the ground of existence, but the God of the coming kingdom, which transforms this world and our existence radically";[42] and again: "God becomes the ground of the freedom from past and transiency and of the possibilities of the new, and, through both, the ground of the transformation of the world."[43] This eschatological theology affirms God's presence in past and present moments through asserting his future mode of being. Here we find a theology that unifies times in God's presence and action and which provides the foundation for a homiletic that does the same.

Anticipating God Now

In this unity of times a posture towards God's future shifts to *anticipation*, or, *prolepsis*. This differs from the current predominant view of the future as an *extrapolation* of the past. The biblical ground for the shift towards anticipating God's new future takes shape in Revelation 1:4 where the normal grammatical and temporal tense structure is broken. Jesus is not introduced as might be expected, as "him who was, who is, and who *will be*," but rather as "him who was, who is, and *who is coming*." God's advent already exists and is coming. Moltmann appeals to the category of *adventus* as having priority over the category of *futurum* in discussing modes of time. The difference may be slight, but profound. Extrapolation moves out of the past and seeks the future while anticipation participates now in God's announced coming from the future.[44]

The category *futurum* implies an extrapolation of the future out of past and present. Moltmann calls this a method of "futurology." This process relies on scientific and analytical functions applied to empirical data for the purpose of forecasting future actions or behaviors. As extrapolation moves beyond measurable and checkable data it becomes more questionable, better described as speculation, "the further it is removed from the realm of direct experience."[45] Futurology, trend-analysis, and computer-forecasting are examples of extrapolation. In these cases the practice means "the prolongation of lines of development from the past and present into the future,

---

42. Moltmann, "Theology as Eschatology," 10.
43. Ibid., 11.
44. Moltmann, *Coming of God*, 25.
45. Moltmann, *Future of Creation*, 42.

always presuming that everything goes on acting as it has done hitherto."[46] Reasonably, then, extrapolation is not "knowledge of the future at all; it is the calculated continuation of the present into the future; and this means that the present is thereby fixed and prescribed." This leads Moltmann to conclude that "extrapolation sees the future as an extrapolated and extended present and it hence kills the very future character of the future."[47] Modernity generally operates according to this principle, assuming that a calculated continuation of past and present processes is a reliable predictor of future processes or behavior.

The dubiousness of using extrapolation as a premise upon which to base one's eschatology, however, becomes apparent. If the future is extrapolated in this way it is merely a continuation of the present, which again breaks the unity of time altogether. Further, the only ones interested in prolonging the *status quo* are those "who possess and dominate the present." Those who are dispossessed and dominated in the present are asking "for change and liberation."[48] Therefore, there is a question of justice that arises in an extrapolated eschatology. In the concept of time operative in extrapolation "the future enjoys no primacy, there is no category *novum* [the new thing], and really no 'principle of hope' either."[49]

However, *adventus Dei* is an anticipation of God's coming, anticipated from its announcement in the past and continuation in the present, and it comes into reality from God's future.[50] Opposite extrapolation, anticipation (or prolepsis) is based on the promise in history of God's future. Moltmann refers to the Old Testament historical narratives as being a history of promise and fulfillment:

> To understand history as the history of promise means understanding promise as the verbal prolepsis of the promised good. Between promise and fulfillment the inchoative and partial fulfillments of history then come into being. They confirm the faithfulness of the promising God and at the same time point beyond into the wider future of the promised fulfillment. Anticipated fulfillment is then understood as the earnest and pledge of completed fulfillment. . . . On the basis of the promise that has been heard and the anticipation of God that has been experienced, man's faith, for its part, then becomes anticipation,

46. Ibid., 43.
47. Ibid.
48. Ibid.
49. Moltmann, *Coming of God*, 25.
50. Moltmann, *Future of Creation*. See especially 41–48.

that is, tense expectation, and the historical anticipation of fulfillment according to the forces and potentialities of history.[51]

Anticipation is a realization in the present of what is coming from the future—God's kingdom, the resurrection from the dead, the restoration of humanity's identity. Anticipation grants temporal priority to the future as one expects in hope Christ's parousia.[52] Removing theology and proclamation to some form of timelessness makes an anticipation of God's fulfillment of historical promises in and through time difficult to maintain.

This method of developing eschatology is evident in the New Testament where the reader is repeatedly encouraged to take action in the present on the basis of what is coming in the future. As such, present and future are bound together in present reality as a means for realization of the future. The implication for the follower of Christ is participation with God in the coming of God's kingdom, resulting in ethical implications based on the coming of God's promised future announced in advance. In short, the realization of God's promised future in every moment of the present makes particular demands on the follower of Christ. Moltmann notes that "anticipation is the hope of those, who, through the Spirit of Christ, have become poor, who with the poor hope for the new, liberating future of God."[53] As the believer in Christ has participated with God through the Spirit in the present moment of the drama because of promises made in Christ in the past, the effects of anticipatory eschatology move the future of those promises of God into the present moment in a theologically anachronistic manner. The proleptic event of Jesus Christ is the hinge upon which God's future swings into the present.

The Christological Unity of Time

What unifies all of time together in eschatology is the proleptic nature of God's promises in Christ and in God's Word. The theological center of Moltmann's eschatology, and indeed of a homiletic punctuated by eschatology in this way, is the death and resurrection of Jesus Christ:

> The hinge of history . . . or a Christian understanding of history lies in Jesus Christ himself. Jesus identified the eschatological kingdom of God with his Word, his activity, and his suffering, and thus with his person. The kingdom of God has identified

---

51. Ibid., 46–47.
52. Moltmann, *Coming of God*, 25–26.
53. Moltmann, *Future of Creation*, 47.

itself with Jesus in the resurrection of the crucified one. In his words and deeds Jesus has anticipated the kingdom of God and has opened the coming of the kingdom. In the resurrection from the dead God has anticipated in this *one* his kingdom of "life from the dead," and has herein, through this *one*, opened the future of the resurrection and the life.[54]

Any development of Christian eschatology must take Christ as its center and any development of Christology must be set against the horizon of eschatology. The person and work of Christ as eschatology's center further relates to the identity and theodicy questions discussed above. Humanity finds itself embroiled in the tension between that which has occurred in the person of Christ alone (resurrection and restoration of humanity and the world) and the promise of realized participation with Christ in death and resurrection for those who stand in solidarity with him. This is the tension of theodicy—that what God has promised has begun, but has not fully been accomplished for all. Moltmann's response is that Christ is the presence of the future reality of God occurring in the midst of history. Humanity finds identity in relation to the coming of God, already present in the person of Christ. In addition to Christ as the reality-prolepsis, the gospel, which "is the hidden epiphany, the verbal presence of the universal future of the risen Christ," provides humanity with hope for the eventual consummate revealing of Christ in glory.[55] This eschatological context for preaching reestablishes God's presence in the eventful history with his people, establishing the future of that history in promises. The life, death, and resurrection of Christ unifies all of time through event and promise, unifies the historical with the absolute, in an identifiable moment of time.

Promise and Prolepsis

The ideas of Christ as God's proleptic event, and gospel as God's proleptic word—that is, that these are the presence of God's future dramatically appearing in the present and past—link modes of time for the contemporary preacher. Moltmann distinguishes a promise from a prediction by noting that a promise "announces a reality which has not yet arrived."[56] In the announcement of this future reality, the reality becomes "word-present." A promise is the word-presence of a future reality in the present moment. As such, its significance is that as "the promise brings the future into the

54. Moltmann, "Theology as Eschatology," 23. Emphasis original.
55. Ibid., 20–21.
56. Moltmann, "Hope and History," 378.

present in the word, it compels the present to decisions."[57] The influence the promise brings derives from the hope that the promise provides.[58] The promise for humanity's future with God that has been made to those in the present is inherent and guaranteed in Jesus Christ and the events surrounding his life and death in the past. All of time is, therefore, unified in Christ and proclaimed in gospel. Christ is the reality-prolepsis, the incarnation of the future in the present moment. "What has happened to Christ is representative of what will happen to everybody: it is happening *pars pro toto*."[59] The gospel is the word-prolepsis, the manifestation of God's coming future in promised word. It is in this reality of prolepsis that the future is opened to the Christian, and he or she is able to reach into it and live presently according to God's promised and appearing future reality.

Christ: God's Proleptic Reality

Christ is the reality-prolepsis of God's promised future. Viewing the history and proclamation of Christ together as the Christ event, one finds two perspectives. The first is that in Christ there is a "real *anticipation* of the future of history in the midst of history."[60] It is a looking ahead to what is promised in the consummation of history. In addition to the anticipation Christ's death and resurrection manifests, in Christ there also is a genuine "incarnation of God's future" in the present moment.[61] Christian eschatology unites past, present, and future in Christ.

Moltmann proposes that God mediates his future reality through the crucified and resurrected one, and through this one humanity is afforded a glimpse of that future reality in the present moment:

> The historical mediation of salvation happens in the solidarity of the one who brings salvation with those who lack salvation and in his substitutionary suffering and death for them. The cross of Christ modifies the prolepsis of eternal life under the conditions of death in order to bring redemption from these conditions. . . . That is, it brings the future of God's kingdom into the presence of sin, death, and devil through substitutionary suffering. It brings God's coming freedom and peace into a hostile world through self-renouncing love. . . . In the prolepsis

---

57. Ibid.
58. Moltmann, *Theology of Hope*, 18.
59. Moltmann, *Way of Jesus Christ*, 155.
60. Moltmann, "Hope and History," 379. Emphasis original.
61. Ibid., 380.

> inherent in the Christ event, therefore, lies the making present of our future under the conditions of estrangement in which we live.[62]

Christ's future-bringing death and resurrection occur in the midst of the conditions of death and sin while simultaneously redeeming from these conditions. Christ brings the future to bear upon the present, prompting the present for action into the future.

Although humanity is caught between the "already" and the "not-yet" of God's promised future, the reality-prolepsis of Christ's resurrection serves as the anticipatory, proleptic event, and has meaning in the present moment through Word and faith: "The meaning that this reality-prolepsis has happened exclusively in him but not simultaneously in all can only be found in the understanding that it happened to him 'for' us all and to him ahead of us all. The reality-prolepsis pertains only initially to him. Its universal meaning is manifest primarily in the Word-prolepsis. In the Gospel the universal meaning inherent in the Christ event is made manifest."[63] Christ brings about the future of God in the midst of history, granting access to that future through his deeds and his Word, thereby uniting modes of time within the Christian drama.

Gospel: God's Proleptic Word

Christ, the resurrected one, experiences the presence of God's future as reality. For the rest of humanity the presence of God's future is experienced in word and in faith, in what Moltmann terms the word-prolepsis of God's future. The gospel, that is, the proclamation of Christ's crucifixion and resurrection, is God's future made present in word. This word-prolepsis binds together future and past in divine promise, recasting with what God's promise is to be associated:

> As Word-prolepsis of the future of God, however, it [the gospel] takes into itself the future of God in the past and is *epangelia*. It takes the promise away from its bond with the law and it makes it present with the reality-prolepsis in Christ. . . . The Word-prolepsis of the Gospel thus integrates in itself the pre-prolepsis of the traditions. The new covenant antiquates the law and preserves the promise into the future. Thus, the Gospel establishes on the basis of its own eschatological nature continuity with the

---

62. Moltmann, "Theology as Eschatology," 32–33.
63. Ibid., 20–21.

promises of history. It places one into the simultaneousness with "the future in the past."[64]

The promise of the gospel appropriates the past promise in a new way on the grounds of the new event, that is, the reality-prolepsis brought about in Christ. As the gospel reveals Christ, Moltmann refers to it as simultaneously "the forerunner of his universal appearance," and, quite literally as "the preliminary form of his revelation in glory."[65] The gospel places its reader in a new relationship to both past and future, catching him or her in a continuity of times. This essentially binds the reader between the future, which is becoming and being revealed in the present, and the past history of the future. The drama catches the participant between past and future, calling for an enactment of God's future in the present moment.

THE ESCHATOLOGICAL TRANSFORMATION OF TIME

This eschatology reveals an inherent emphasis on the future of the world and the coming of God that "requires the church to engage with the possibilities for change in the modern world, to promote them against all tendencies to stagnation, and to give them eschatological direction toward the coming kingdom of God."[66] The unity of time has the effect of transforming our times.

The response in faith to the future of God appearing in Christ and in the gospel, providing healing to the misery of history caused by the theological situation surrounding the theodicy and identity questions, works out in what Moltmann labels creative eschatology, or, deeds of eschatological hope. Creative eschatology relates directly to the dramatic and temporal aspects of the biblical text and our experiencing God in time. Eschatology, as the future coming into the present, prompts towards redemptive action in transforming the world now.

Moltmann asserts that the appearances of the resurrected one both illuminate the meaning of the cross in retrospect and "prospect the way in which the reality-anticipation of the future comes into the world."[67] That is, the appearances of the resurrected one point the way forward for the church as it awaits the eschatological consummation promised in the gospel and in Christ. Moltmann works from his identification of Christian theology as

64. Ibid., 21.
65. Ibid.
66. Bauckham, "Jürgen Moltmann," 213.
67. Moltmann, "Theology as Eschatology," 35.

inherently historical initiative that seeks to change reality through performative language. Another formulation of this thinking about the presence of God in time between past and parousia can be labeled drama, and it will be the subject of the following chapter.

As theology reflects on the promised future "realizable possibilities to overcome the misery of history" come within reach of the present.[68] In this context, Christian theology must be a theology moving towards its goal, a theology on the way, enacted and participated in rather than a theology stagnant or completed. Discipleship after Jesus as characteristic of this journey anticipates possibilities for the inbreaking and real transformative presence of God's future in the midst of the present. The call to follow Christ on the way is a call to become a coworker with God in the bringing about of his kingdom in the midst of history. It is a call to live already under the conditions promised in God's future. This is the inevitable and natural ethical extension of Moltmann's eschatological theology and it provides the participatory foundation for a homiletical theology that seeks to unite modes of time in God's action among God's people. In eschatological preaching that proclaims out of a unified temporality, what is largely appended application in the sermon will evolve into an organic call to participation in what the God of all time is doing right now as congregation is bound between God's past and promised future.

Transformation in Time: Conversion and Discipleship

For Moltmann, the imminence of God's judgment has made conversion necessary while Jesus's proclamation of God's pitying justice has made conversion possible. Conversion thus signals a "turning around, the turn from violence to justice, from isolation to community, from death to life."[69] Conversion is, then, an anticipation of the new life, a future promised and present in Christ under and within the circumstances of the present era. Or, as Moltmann states elsewhere, "conversion and rebirth to a new life change time and the experience of time, for they make present the ultimate in the penultimate, and the future of time in the midst of time."[70] Conversion acknowledges the lordship of Christ as mediator of God's future anticipated in the present moment. Hence, the Christ follower is compelled towards practical action in discipleship as he or she is confronted by the discrepancy

---

68. Moltmann, "Hope and History," 375.
69. Moltmann, *Way of Jesus Christ*, 102.
70. Moltmann, *Coming of God*, 22.

between the present and God's promised and coming future. Conversion makes future present now.

The discipleship brought about by conversion is indispensably linked with the path of the Messiah for his own life and death and inherently points to a program of making present God's future in present reality. The result is that "christology and christopraxis become one, so that a total, holistic knowledge of Christ puts its stamp not only on the mind and the heart, but on the whole of life in the community of Christ; and it also means that Christ is *perceived and known* not only with mind and heart, but through the experience and practice of the whole of life."[71] This eschatological view of history is focused centrally upon the disciple's participation in the transformation of the world rather than upon developing an objective history of existence. The Christian view of unified time sets the Christian's promised future in contradiction to the present state of the world, and therefore he or she is constantly seeking to bring about the reign of Christ in the present moment: "The eschatological concept of history in which the faith in the reality-prolepsis of God's future in the crucified Christ becomes conscious of itself is no theory of world history . . . but a 'battle doctrine' with the cross as victory emblem. This concept does not want to interpret the world religiously, but wants to transform it through the creation of the obedience of faith."[72] The disciple "on the way" finds him or herself in a position of contradiction to the misery of the world, believing in and working for the transformation of the world in the belief that Christ has appeared as the promise of God's future and is the guarantee of the new creation. In this way, the disciple seeks to reach into the promised future of God's drama through Christ and the Spirit in order to bring about the love, justice, peace, and forgiveness of God's coming kingdom, living these future realities in the present moment.

Conversion and discipleship always reach beyond the role of the individual. "None of us are given hope just for ourselves," Moltmann says. He continues: "The hope of Christians is always hope for Israel too; the hope of Jews and Christians is always hope for the peoples of the world as well; the hope of the peoples of the world is always also hope for this earth and everything that lives in it. And hope for the whole community of creation is ultimately hope that its Creator and Redeemer will arrive at his goal, and may find in creation his home."[73] Christian conversion and discipleship

---

71. Moltmann, *Way of Jesus Christ*, 118–19. Emphasis original.
72. Moltmann, "Theology as Eschatology," 39–40.
73. Moltmann, *Coming of God*, xiii.

extend the hope of God's future in the present through deeds of eschatological hope.

Transformation in Time: Deeds of Eschatological Hope

In the tension between the "already" and the "not-yet" of God's promised future Moltmann outlines practical implications for Christian mission. Ethics is defined as "the forward-moving, evolutionary and revolutionary initiative for the overcoming of man's bodily predicament and the plight of injustice."[74] For direction in this ethical endeavor the community of Christ looks to the New Testament with a hermeneutic that interprets it "apostolically as a manual of the Christian mission."[75] Moltmann bases this observation upon the claim that "the New Testament testimonies have one intention and one tendency: they originate in the movements of the apostolate and they point to the movement of the apostolate 'until he comes.'"[76] The New Testament text, as witness to the reality-prolepsis Christ and the word-prolepsis gospel, forms the community's basis of faith and practice as trajectory for anticipatory hope. Once again, the present Christian community is caught up between memory of the past and hope of the future—a future that has already broken into the present. The shape of this is drama.

The hope that is created "anticipates the future and brings it into the present." In this context the Christian is a coworker with God for the bringing about of God's kingdom:

> We are construction workers and not only interpreters of the future whose power in hope as well as in the fulfillment is God.... The Christians must understand themselves as "coworkers" of the promised kingdom of God and its universal peace and its righteousness. For they live not for a future which has not begun as yet, but which has already arrived in Christ and which—coming from him—will change the world. If the Christians hope for this future of God, they not only wait for it, but also look for it, love it, and strive for it. The eschatological will leads to decisions that are live options in the present.... Christian eschatology is, therefore, not only receptive but also productive, not only passive but also militant hope for the future.[77]

74. Moltmann, "Theology as Eschatology," 38.
75. Ibid. 44.
76. Ibid.
77. Ibid., 45–46.

Passivity is not something that finds a place in the eschatological unity of time and history. In a living correspondence to the promised future "the future already finds a real form" which the church/disciple can reach into in order to enact in word and deed in the present moment of the drama.[78]

In this context, the first deed of the eschatological hope Moltmann proposes is the present enactment of the proclamation of the gospel of the kingdom to the poor, and following on this, "the proclamation of the righteousness of God to Jews and Gentiles, insofar as all have sinned."[79] This facet of eschatological mission directly addresses the theodicy and identity questions which Moltmann views as intertwined barriers to modern theology, and indeed to modern preaching, and which are inherent in humanity's plight. The gospel reaches out to all of humanity without distinction. This challenges the dividing and distinctive positions humanity claims for itself—be it race, class, or other boundaries. The commonality that holds humanity together, however, is the deep-rooted misery brought about by "their common lack of true humanity, or their common plight of guilt, suffering, sorrow, and death," and it is this commonality in misery that the future hope appearing in Christ addresses in the present.[80] Christian eschatology announces to the poor, and indeed to all, hope for the restoration of humanity in the present enactment and anticipation of God's future. While humanity may stand in solidarity at the level of misery, "the Gospel anticipates the future of God at the front of man's real misery in that it offers the lost and the forsaken God's hope."[81] And it offers this in a tangible way in the present, as the future has already appeared in history in Christ. This gospel proclamation is actually identical with Christian mission: "Christian tradition is proclamation of the gospel in justification of the godless. It is made possible and necessary by the raising of the crucified Christ, inasmuch as the hope of the universal future of the world is therein guaranteed. It is thus identical with eschatological mission."[82] Proclamation, in preaching and in deed, announces and enacts the presence of God's future in the midst of history's present.

A second deed of eschatological hope is the founding of the Christian congregation. The congregation is the "new people of God" and is comprised of people from all reaches of society: "Jews and Gentiles, Greeks and

---

78. Ibid. 46.

79. Ibid., 37. Moltmann also discusses deeds of eschatological hope in *Way of Jesus Christ*, 94–116.

80. Moltmann, "Theology as Eschatology," 37.

81. Ibid.

82. Moltmann, *Theology of Hope*, 302.

barbarians, masters and servants, white and black, and so forth." In this way, the Christian congregation crosses artificial boundary lines and stands in agreement with the future of God in living unity and equality, becoming "the sign and sacrament of hope," an embodiment of God's future in the midst of the present.[83] The Christian congregation, reaching into God's coming future, can unite a humanity divided and therefore bring about a new reality in the church and world.

A third deed of eschatological hope is "the creative, battling, and loving obedience ready to suffer in the everyday situations of the present world."[84] It is pulling the conditions of God's future, already present in Christ, into the present and living them today as Christ's body. This can include a broad range of social and ecological reform initiatives that take place in the context of the proclamation of the gospel and in the congregation of God's people.[85] Moltmann expounds this: "It is transformation of life, transformation of society, transformation of the world in the possibilities that one is afforded or that one meets, favoring the new life, the new community, the new world. Obedience in the body is anticipation of the redemption of the body (1Cor. 6), and societal obedience is anticipation of the new humanity which is coming, and earthly obedience is anticipation of the renewal of the earth in the kingdom of God."[86] All of these active anticipations of God's future are "possible in the discipleship of Jesus who is the reality-prolepsis of God's future," the one who brings that future tangibly into the present.[87]

CONCLUSIONS

Moltmann's eschatology begins with the premise that the mode of God's being is future and that God's fullness is coming towards the present from the future. God's promise has reached into the past and present through the appearance of Christ who serves as the reality-prolepsis of God's promised future. In Christ the future of God is manifest in a real and reality-altering manner, with the events of Christ's life, death, resurrection, and glorification as representative and guarantee of the promise of God for the totality of those entering into solidarity with the risen one. Correspondingly, the gospel is the word-prolepsis of God's promised future, bringing that future into the present in word and faith and producing hope. Christ as reality-prolepsis

---

83. Moltmann, "Theology as Eschatology," 38.
84. Ibid.
85. Moltmann, *Way of Jesus Christ*, 121.
86. Moltmann, "Theology as Eschatology," 38.
87. Ibid.

and gospel as word-prolepsis of God's promised future prompt real change in the present realities of the human condition. Humanity responds to Christ and the gospel in conversion and discipleship, which affect the whole of human life and call for Christian mission. Christian mission identifies the Christian community as coworkers with God in the bringing about of his kingdom. This mission occurs within the tension of the already but not yet manifestation of God's kingdom. Creative eschatology moves towards living in active anticipation of the promised future within the real misery of humanity's shared condition. This is the presence of the future in the midst of the present. In Christ, all tenses of time, past, present, and future, are unified in a theology that presently anticipates the coming of God.

Christian theology, for Moltmann, must then be about the transformative power of God's future in the present overcoming the miseries of history.[88] Discipleship in this future-looking theology becomes a call to participate with God in the bringing about of the kingdom and its characteristics—justice, peace, forgiveness, mercy. In this sense Christian hope in the future, grounded in the person and work of Christ in the past, "anticipates the future and brings it into the present."[89] As a result, God's people have access to the ultimate act of God's drama while still enacting the penultimate. This allows God's people in the present to think, speak, and significantly to live God's future reality within history. God's people can, and indeed as a matter of eschatological identity they must, be active in reaching into that future that God has both incarnated in Christ and promised in the gospel, making it a living reality in the world. God's future has erupted in history's midst, bringing hope to humanity.

The call to preaching in the Christian community, then, is a call founded in a unity of time, past, present, and future, in Christ who has appeared and enacted God's future in the midst of history. The gospel that we preach must proclaim the presence of God in real time, in real event, rather than in timelessness. A hermeneutical move, process, or device that either moves outside of time or remains internal, practically does not proclaim the fullness of the God who was, and is, and is coming. However, a rediscovered and reframed eschatology gives us the unification of history that we lost in the Enlightenment while still respecting the distance between present and past, and anticipating the hope evident between present and promised and coming future. Indeed, time's unity has God's people creating the future now. With this temporal language which casts time unified in Christ as both the distance between the preacher and the text, and our ultimate connection

---

88. Moltmann, "Hope and History," 375.
89. Moltmann, "Theology as Eschatology," 45.

to it (the events recorded in the text, and indeed the eventfulness of the text itself, occur in the same historical temporality as we do), we are able to construct an eschatological hermeneutic. This hermeneutic takes time as its shape as we see the whole of God's story as perpetually enacted narrative. Another name for this is drama.

3

Now and Then
A Dramatic Organization of Time

ESCHATOLOGICAL THEOLOGY PROVIDES AN ORGANIC MEANS FOR UNIfying time. Within an eschatological unity of time a vision emerges of the present as bound between and affected by both past and future; times are held unified in temporal tension. If time is unified in the way that Moltmann and others propose, then how does one organize a framework for theological and homiletical thought for the here and now? In a context characterized by a temporal continuity between times, as opposed to the divisibility characteristic of Modernity, what is the fullest manner of organizing time for theological expression now? Further, how might one communicate the gospel in such a temporal continuum? These questions regarding the best mode for theological expression continue to address themselves to theology, biblical studies, and practical theology. In response to some traditional forms of theological expression that tend to cast Christian theology in terms of knowledge, personal experience, or communal language, there is a developing strain of theological expression that describes Christianity in accordance with its temporal and participatory natures—one that takes into consideration the boundedness of present between past and future, and seeks a proclamation between memory and hope. Eschatology unifies time. Drama organizes it.

The images of drama and anachronism present themselves as theological matrix and movement. The present chapter explores the development of this dramatic theological vision as a means of organizing time for a more temporally characterized hermeneutic, and finally homiletic. A dramatic theology is performative, or enacted, and utilizes metaphor to provide the basis for robust communication in the sermon. This paradigm may better account for the temporal and the participatory nature of Christian faith than do forms of theological expression based largely on modern presuppositions. The proposal here is for a hermeneutic rooted primarily in the temporal nature of living, rather than in the spatial metaphor of building bridges that has, at times uncritically, characterized much contemporary preaching.

The organization of time as participatory drama has been developed over the last century and a half, though only recently has it come into focus as a more viable theological option that accounts for the textual, contemporary, and future moments of God's story. In the mid-1800s one can see marks of an organization of time for theology and preaching in the theological, linguistic, and homiletical work of Congregational minister Horace Bushnell. Bushnell, whose theology of language and metaphor I will discuss in the next chapter, felt that doctrine must be more dynamic than both the predominant propositional and experiential theologies of his day. In response he sought a comprehensive theological method that attempted to reconcile opposite theological projects for a more dynamic way forward. At the core of Bushnell's theological convictions and homiletical practice was a reliance on metaphor, robust and dynamic speech designed to make the unknown known in language the hearer could enter into and in which he or she could participate in the creation of meaning through forms of living.

Nearly 150 years later distinctions of Bushnell's Romantic theology are identifiable in the work of contemporary theologians such as N. T. Wright, Richard Heyduck, and Kevin Vanhoozer. Vanhoozer and others (whose theology does not self-identify as Romantic or as connected to Bushnell), like Bushnell, respond to forms of theological expression that value propositions, experiences, or the communal agreement of meaning as the end product for theological enquiry. The matrix Vanhoozer and others propose works to organize the unity of time under the practice of drama—lived enactment of the story that God simultaneously tells and in which God calls his people to participate. Contemporary dramatic theologies take spatial systems to more fulsome and open ends, viewing time as both the real distance and inherent connection to the text's past and Christianity's future. While Vanhoozer, in his work *The Drama of Doctrine*,[1] has written most comprehensively on this subject, others such as N. T. Wright,[2] Richard Heyduck,[3] and Bernard An-

---

1. Vanhoozer, *The Drama of Doctrine*.
2. Wright, *The New Testament and the People of God*.
3. Heyduck, *The Recovery of Doctrine in the Contemporary Church*.

derson[4] contribute to this strain of theological thought, and I will reference them throughout the following.

For Vanhoozer in particular, Christianity is a life lived in participation with Christ in an ongoing drama, with metaphor the chief means of communicating the meaning of the old text within the horizon of the present. A "canonical-linguistic theology" is characterized as "giving scriptural direction for one's fitting participation in the drama of redemption today."[5] This theological reflection takes up themes such as the reevaluation of how language is used, a rejection of exclusively propositional or experiential categories as fully adequate for theology, a commitment to the biblical canon as authoritative script in reclaiming the Reformation principal of *sola scriptura*, the assertion of artistic and metaphoric language, and the emphasis on Christianity as life in participation with Christ.

Taking the insights provided by Vanhoozer and others a step further for preaching particularly, we will find the concept of anachronism as an essential device for theological thought and homiletical communication. A theological anachronism, as I have defined it, is a temporal metaphor in which two (or more) moments in time are brought together in a tensive relationship, each retaining its distinct temporal characteristics yet creating a new moment that demands participation from listeners. Theological anachronism brings together and holds in tension past, present, and future, providing a way to relate past and present, and to tangibly bring the present and future together as God's kingdom lived now. This chapter lays out a dramatic organization of time as the theological context for preaching. Out of this organization of time the following chapters will discuss anachronism with further development for preaching in particular.

ABSTRACT THEOLOGIES AND THE LOSS OF TIME

In setting the hermeneutical and homiletical context for a theologically dramatic organization of time it is important to see that Vanhoozer's work comes out of a dissatisfaction with contemporary formulations of doctrine. Propositional, experiential, or cultural-linguistic theological programs, in alignment with the hermeneutical commitments underlying homiletical practices explored in chapter 1, form the backdrop from which Vanhoozer's canonical-linguistic theology emerges. Another theological abstraction identified is the devaluation of time and history in modern theological thought.

4. Anderson, *The Unfolding Drama of the Bible*.
5. Vanhoozer, *Drama of Doctrine*, 22.

Theological Abstraction: Propositional and Experiential Theologies

The primary mode of theological expression from the Enlightenment to the present relies on scientific rationalism and emphasizes cognitive aspects of religion. George Lindbeck has identified that the propositional, or cognitive, approach to theology "stresses the ways in which church doctrines function as informative propositions or truth claims about objective realities. Religions are thus thought of as similar to philosophy or science as these were classically conceived. This was the approach of traditional orthodoxies (as well as of many heterodoxies), but it also has certain affinities to the outlook on religion adopted by much modern Anglo-American analytic philosophy with its preoccupation with the cognitive or informational meaningfulness of religious utterances."[6] According to this model truth claims about God are made as propositional statements and Christian faith is cast in terms of "right knowing."

Propositional theories of doctrine rely primarily on a referential theory of language and on the modern epistemology foundationalism. A referential theory of language holds that words correspond fully to that which they signify. As Heyduck observes, "When religion is seen as like a science (or, stronger yet, *as* a science), doctrines are understood as propositions that accurately and truthfully refer to objective reality, just like the propositions of science."[7] Foundationalism maintains that certain assertions of belief can be attained "by direct relation to indubitable first principles."[8] Doctrine becomes about mining the biblical data and transferring the right doctrinal knowledge. Further, preaching becomes the task of transferring this right knowledge from one person to another. The homiletical expression this produces is similar to that proposed by Cleland, above.

On another end of the theological spectrum one finds a strain of theological reflection that relies on spiritual experience for its truth claims. Termed "experiential-expressive" by Lindbeck, this approach "focuses on doctrines as noninformative and nondiscursive symbols of inner feelings, attitudes, or existential orientations."[9] What is important in this schema is the "experience of divine reality" expressed in a particular religious symbol:

> The general principle is that insofar as doctrines function as nondiscursive symbols, they are polyvalent in import and

---

6. Lindbeck, *Nature of Doctrine*, 16.
7. Heyduck, *Recovery of Doctrine*, 25. Emphasis original.
8. Ibid., 13.
9. Lindbeck, *Nature of Doctrine*, 16.

> therefore subject to changes of meaning or even to a total loss of meaningfulness.... They are not crucial for religious agreement or disagreement, because these are constituted by harmony or conflict in underlying feelings, attitudes, existential orientations, or practices rather than by what happens on the level of symbolic (including doctrinal) objectifications. There is thus at least the logical possibility that a Buddhist and a Christian might have basically the same faith, although expressed very differently.[10]

Experiential-expressive forms of religion simultaneously assert that religion cannot be understood as a science because a religion's claims are not provable scientifically, and that God is still real.[11] Therefore religion is reconceptualized. A religious symbol such as the resurrection is outward, malleable, or even discardable, while personal experience of the symbol is the locus of divine activity. In terms of language, "religious language has no external referent, being instead the expression of the inner depths of human consciousness."[12] For Vanhoozer, Heyduck, Wright, Lindbeck, and others, there are problems with both of these theories of doctrine, each being abstractive in its own way. Homiletically, this is the hermeneutic standing beneath much of the New Homiletic, explored in chapter 1.

While propositional statements of doctrine have benefited the church in the development of its theology—indeed, the transmission of an orthodox faith is an essential aspect of Christianity's persistence—problems potentially arise when doctrine is conceptualized as propositional and little else. To have an exclusively propositional view of doctrine flattens and abstracts the fullness of theological expression. Faced with this theological and linguistic abstraction Vanhoozer responds, "Hard questions will ... have to be asked of a method that appears to reduce the diverse modes of language in the Bible to the assertive and propositional."[13] Essentially, a reduction of the diverse genres, forms, and aesthetic language in the biblical text abstracts that text, removing its context and flattening it into something less pliable and dynamic, more static.

Further, a referential theory of language and foundationalism as an epistemology are inadequate models with which to work. As Bushnell argued more than a century ago, and numerous semiotic theorists since, a word can never fully represent that which it signifies, therefore precluding

---

10. Ibid. 17.
11. Heyduck, *Recovery of Doctrine*, 27.
12. Ibid.
13. Vanhoozer, *Drama of Doctrine*, 5.

the possibility of exact representation or the production of certainty in language.[14] Attempting to make language do things that it inherently cannot do (e.g., produce certain statements of truth, render exact correspondence between signifier and signified), leads to what Bushnell termed an "abstractive theology."[15] Contemporary authors like Vanhoozer are relying on more dynamic accounts of how language functions in human understanding.[16] Language is active, not merely saying something but doing things. I will discuss this more fully below.

The experiential-expressive injects static theology with something more dynamic: feeling and expression. No longer concerned with just knowledge, an experiential-expressive model acknowledges life and expression in the complex theological interaction that is faith. In the experiential-expressive model each religious symbol is experienced according to the subjective "I," which has the final say on matters of faith and practice. The Spirit becomes, then, one's own subjective experience of that symbol, defined in largely existential terms. Vanhoozer describes personal experience as the benchmark for this stream of religious doctrine, saying, "Human subjectivity becomes the locus of a revelation that is typically immediate and nonverbal."[17]

Experiential-expressive theological constructs have the potential to create a pastiche of theological beliefs in which all perceived experiences of the divine have equal standing and the ultimate arbiter of truth becomes each individual. One logical conclusion is, as Lindbeck points out, a potential universalism in which the uniqueness of Christ and Christianity is diminished in an increasing relativism: "The rationale suggested, though not necessitated, by an experiential-expressive approach is that the various religions are diverse symbolizations of one and the same core experience of the Ultimate, and that therefore they must respect each other, learn from each other, and reciprocally enrich each other."[18] The result is the decrease in distinctions among religions: an increasing universalism.

Further, historical aspects of faith are disposable as the events narrated become symbols as opposed to events in specific times, expendable historical containers for present experience of the divine. This, in itself, runs counter to the nature of Christian faith throughout this history of God's people

---

14. See Fiske, *Introduction to Communication Studies*; Scholes, *Semiotics and Interpretation*.
15. Bushnell, "Training for the Pulpit Manward," 226.
16. See Vanhoozer, *Biblical Narrative*.
17. Vanhoozer, *Drama of Doctrine*, 6.
18. Lindbeck, *Nature of Doctrine*, 23.

as a faith that declares God's activity precisely within the realm of history. Again, this is an abstraction of the necessary intersection within Christian faith of the concrete and the absolute, the sublime and the everyday. To translate history and event into simply experiential catalysts runs counter to God's movement in the incarnation which is essentially out of eternity and into time and place.

A dramatic and performative expression of Christian doctrine takes root in a theological context that abstracts an eventful faith in temporally flat forms, whether propositional or experiential.

Theological Abstraction: Removal of Time and History

An aspect of contemporary theologies that Vanhoozer pays special attention to is the decreasing attentiveness to history and temporality in contemporary formulations of theology. This characteristic is apparent in both propositional and experiential forms discussed above, but also in other contemporary theological projects such as the cultural-linguistic theological framework proposed by Lindbeck and the postliberal theologians. Directly related to this loss of time is a shifting locus of authority for theological reflection.

Heyduck makes the case that Modernity has contributed to the overall marginalization of doctrine in the church. Speaking mostly of propositional and experiential theologies, and the theological/philosophical movements underpinning them, he argues that modern conceptualizations of Christian theology, with their emphases on cognitive rationality and religious experience, lead to both individualism and dehistorization.[19] The problem with contemporary theologies founded upon modern epistemologies is that modern epistemologies seek access to foundational, secure, and certain knowledge. Temporality and historicity have difficulties finding a place in the modern models—time and history are too contingent and perspectival to provide certain knowledge. As such, these become dispensable:

> Foundationalist knowledge must be founded upon indubitable structures—not merely indubitable to you and me and our neighbors, but indubitable to any conceivable rational person, i.e., any person who thinks out the matter. In this drive toward the universal and the nonperspectival, history was found to be too messy, too varied, too undependable, and most of all, too contingent. . . . Therefore, if we assume foundationalism, history gets us nowhere in our quest to be rational. Once we take the

19. Heyduck, *Recovery of Doctrine*, 36.

fateful step of tying the essence of religion to reason, we have effectively severed any link between religion and history.[20]

The quest for certain expressions of knowledge in Modernity leads to the de-privileging of historical issues as serious sources for knowledge and attempts to move outside contingent time in order to find universal, timeless statements of truth.[21] A de-privileging of time in doctrinal formulations has served to undercut an understanding of Christianity's identity: "After history became marginal, it seemed only natural for the Christian to understand his or her 'religious' life as one compartment among many, decontextualized from the rest of the existence."[22] Christianity as an all-encompassing life that moves through time becomes difficult in this atomized view.

This diminishment of a temporal emphasis (or, the presence of a more static theology) is not difficult to identify in the two major forms of theological expression above. The form which propositional theology (and preaching) takes inherently moves away from historical or temporal action, favoring instead the distillation of so-called timeless truths. These are often presented as statements of certain or core theological knowledge, universal and non-perspectival (or, reclothed in contemporary dress after the shift through timelessness). The propositional theological statement abstracts the event it seeks to wring meaning out of so that the event itself tends to matter less than the timeless statement about it. Experiential theologies privilege the individual's experience of a religious symbol. The symbol itself (the resurrection, a miracle story) is pliable and even disposable. It is not an event's occurrence in time that makes it theologically important but rather the experience of that symbol in the present moment—and that experience can be ever changing. Both of these modes of theological expression tend towards the discounting of a text or symbol's context in time in favor of either viewing doctrine as right knowledge or religious experience.

One manner of theological expression finds itself primarily outside of time (timelessness), one primarily in the present experience of individuals. One quality lost is the temporality of the event described, and the flow of time in which it occurred and in relation to which it continues to yield meaning today. In essence, what is lost is the reality that the text is not primarily a repository of knowledge or a catalyst for experience, but a historical artifact recording events that exist in and through time. As Moltmann alluded to, a loss of this historical/temporal characteristic of Christianity has the potential to marginalize Christian identity. Again Heyduck articulates this:

20. Ibid., 19.
21. Ibid.
22. Ibid., 20.

> It takes no great powers of analysis to see that the primary form in Scripture is history-like narrative. A glance at the historic creeds of the church can discern their narrative structure. They purport not merely to state who Jesus is and how he is to be understood in relation to God, but also and centrally to assert that certain events transpired and that God was the chief agent in these events that were done for our salvation. Thus historical events certainly *appear* to be central to Christian identity. What would Christianity be without them?[23]

Christianity is centrally about walking with God in and through a life and the action of God with God's people in and through time. Propositional and experiential epistemologies and homiletics have the potential to miss this.

In response to the propositional and experiential doctrinal modes Lindbeck proposed another paradigm for theological expression that he termed "cultural-linguistic." According to this model, "emphasis is placed on those respects in which religions resemble languages together with their correlative forms of life and are thus similar to cultures."[24] Lindbeck utilizes a "rule theory," in which the most prominent function of church doctrines becomes "their use, not as expressive symbols or as truth claims, but as communally authoritative rules of discourse, attitude, and action."[25] He goes on to say that "stated more technically, a religion can be viewed as a kind of cultural and/or linguistic framework or medium that shapes the entirety of life and thought."[26] The cultural-linguistic mode of theological expression views doctrine as a language of the community of faith, a language that is internal to the community for which it functions to govern the community's divine language and experience. Further, as Vanhoozer explains, in this framework "the Bible is less a textbook of divinely revealed information than an identity narrative that both acquires and exerts meaning in the interpretative community for which it functions as Scripture."[27]

Lindbeck's proposal breaks the Modernist mold in that the cultural-linguistic takes up within it both propositional and experiential concerns—knowledge and experience are held in tension as a part of being religious, though not as the source of one's religiosity.[28] Religion is viewed in cultural terms as one is "encultured into the religious community," and hence it

---

23. Ibid., 21.
24. Lindbeck, *Nature of Doctrine*, 17–18.
25. Ibid., 18.
26. Ibid., 33.
27. Vanhoozer, *Drama of Doctrine*, 7.
28. Heyduck, *Recovery of Doctrine*, 28.

is understood and experienced as something more communal and more active than either propositional or experiential forms.[29] While propositional theology becomes about individual knowledge, and the experiential-expressive privileges personal experience, the cultural-linguistic places theology within the life of the church community. This moves toward a revival of the aspects of life and action to theological reflection, and is a welcome and valuable movement for theological thought.[30]

As for the charge of a loss of temporality leveled against both propositional and experiential-expressive systems, the cultural-linguistic model remains, at least partially, in a Modernist mire. The controlling image for the cultural-linguistic framework is that of a language, or grammar, for faith. It is notable that language, even while changing over time, does not have an inherent temporal quality. Languages are used to communicate narratives while not displaying a narrative of their own.[31] Further, in the cultural-linguistic model the biblical narrative can be viewed more centrally in terms of universal category than in terms of events occurring in time. Heyduck critiques Lindbeck, who states that the Bible "can therefore be taken seriously in the first respect as a delineator of the character of divine or human agents, even when its history or science is challenged. As parables such as that of the prodigal son remind us, the rendering of God's character is not in every instance logically dependent on the facticity of the story."[32] Heyduck responds, "Though 'the rendering of God's character is not in every instance logically dependent on the facticity of the story,' does it ever so depend?"[33] Is the historicity, or temporal quality, of any event recorded in the Bible to be maintained?

Additionally, a related issue asked of the cultural-linguistic framework has to do with a shifting locus of authority. Vanhoozer asks if the cultural-linguistic approach has more to do with sociology than with theology: "Does doctrine refer to God, or does it merely describe how members of the Christian community talk about God? If church practices serve as both source and norm for theology, how can we ever distinguish well-formed practices from those that are *deformed*? . . . It is important to recognize that there is something in the nature of theology's subject matter—God, the gospel—that resists being designated as mere 'local custom.'"[34] In es-

---

29. Ibid.
30. Ibid., 31.
31. Ibid., 35.
32. Lindbeck, *Nature of Doctrine*, 122.
33. Heyduck, *Recovery of Doctrine*, 34.
34. Vanhoozer, *Drama of Doctrine*, 7

sence, it is circular to see the church's life as both the source of and standard for theological expression. What role does the biblical text play in such a program? To what extent is it authoritative for the church community? As will be discussed below, for Vanhoozer the Bible serves to root the church community in and through time and history, while the cultural-linguistic model focuses on the practice of the church in the present as the authoritative arbiter of faith and practice.

The dominance of the historical-critical method, while making a contemporary study of the Bible both more academic and more credible, can tend towards a flattening of the biblical text in the diminishment of its historical/temporal elements. Vanhoozer, and others such as Heyduck and Wright, view the gloss over time as a theological abstraction lending to theology's loss of dynamism across time. A historical and eventful faith, ironically, has become rooted less in history and event. In light of this Vanhoozer seeks to preserve both the temporality of Christian faith and the historical nature of the biblical text. Doing so, he hopes to conceptualize theology as something active and participatory, occurring in time, and rooted in a historical narrative that moves toward a dramatic conclusion. While above we see concepts of doctrine as knowledge, or experience, or language, Vanhoozer proposes the concept of doctrine as dramatic performance. This preserves action, participation, temporality, and event.

DRAMA: LANGUAGE AND LIFE THROUGH TIME

In response to these forms of theological expression Vanhoozer has proposed a different lens through which to view, express, and converse about Christian theology that, when developed for homiletics proves beneficial for preaching faith rooted in time. Vanhoozer's paradigm relies on a participatory framework with an emphasis on drama, refers to Christianity as an ongoing dramatic narrative in which the present-day individual and church play distinct roles, and view's the Bible as the authoritative script from which present-day actors in the play take direction. In this view of doctrine, time is both the distance from and connection between the text and today. Vanhoozer's doctrinal paradigm is a participatory theology occurring through time, seeking a return to the eventful and temporal nature of the biblical text (though not uncritically). As a means of introducing this dramatic theological paradigm in full Vanhoozer engages in a reevaluation of the nature of language for theological expression. What emerges is the development of dynamic language in the form of metaphor for theological communication across time. This forms the foundation for anachronism as temporal metaphor in the following chapter.

Rehabilitating Language for Theological Expression

A primary aspect of Vanhoozer's reimaging of the theological project is a reevaluation of the nature of language. Propositional theologies utilize language in a primarily referential manner, and experiential-expressive theologies tend to view language as individually subjective.[35] Within Modernity, propositionalism and experiential-expressivism are the two most readily available conceptualizations of language and doctrine. However, Postmodernity has begun to challenge many of the foundational tenets of Modernity making different conceptualizations more accessible. For Vanhoozer performance is the alternative image for doctrinal reflection that is both dynamic and respects temporality. Performance includes the idea that doctrine is active rather than static and has as its basis a view of language as inherently dynamic and active because of its nature as speech-act.

Vanhoozer begins his reevaluation of language with the communicative action of God speaking into human history.[36] Relying on J. L. Austen among others, he argues that language is best understood as actively doing something rather than as merely saying something: "The great discovery of twentieth-century philosophy of language, however, is precisely the *speech-act*. After a century or so of detailed analysis of sense, predication, and reference, Anglo-American philosophers discovered the 'illocution,' namely, the notion that we *do* something in speaking. To speak is not simply to utter words but to ask questions, issue commands, make statements, express feelings, request help, and so forth."[37] This idea that language is intrinsically active recasts language in general, and the communication of God in Scripture in particular, as something performative rather than simply informative. He discusses this, in an echo of Moltmann's treatment of promise and prolepsis, with particular reference to the performative quality of promises:

> A promise, for example, has propositional content, but this is not what makes it a promise. An utterance becomes a promise only when an agent uses words to commit himself or herself to

---

35. Heyduck, *Recovery of Doctrine*, 27.
36. Vanhoozer, *Drama of Doctrine*, 62.
37. Ibid., 63. Emphasis original.

a course of future action. Promising is an act in its own right; to promise is to commit oneself to a future course of action that some hearer finds desirable. Promising is a form of *doing* something in *saying* something. To promise is to use words in such a way as to bring about a particular kind of interpersonal relationship.[38]

This active characteristic is not merely present in some speech or in certain types of speech but is integral to all language.

The principal significance of this recognition of language as inherently active is that it opens up at least one new way to conceptualize doctrine in the church. Whereas language models in Modernity largely restricted doctrine to being either a conveyance of right knowledge or a catalyst for personal experience, language as active, or performative, allows one to cast doctrine as a speech-act of the church, speech that calls for reception of and participation in the drama it constitutes. In addition to the propositional content of a statement are both what the speech does (the illocutionary), and what the speech effects (the perlocutionary). When all are taken into consideration one has a fuller vision of language's active quality. Scripture is then taken as the speech-act of God to the church, detailing God's speech to and action within humanity. God stands as the primary communicator, thereby identifying the speech in which the church participates (the drama of Scripture) as centrally God's. This speech-act necessarily calls for response. Vanhoozer explains it in this way: "The Bible is a divine communicative act that exists for the sake of covenantal relations."[39] Doctrine then, as reflection upon God's speech-act in Scripture, becomes a complex speech-act of the church—"the means for encountering God in communicative action."[40] This holds promise for preaching within time.

By viewing language as performative Vanhoozer opens the door for theological reflection to be conceptualized as dramatic, participatory and community focused, rather than merely informational or individually experiential. Organizationally, we may refer to the whole of the framework as drama. Drama organizes time with such dynamic qualities as plot, conflict, character, climax, and resolution. These observations and this framework help explain the action of language through time, both in speech and in a written text. This is also the case in relation to the understanding and communication of Scripture. The speech-act takes a further step towards describing the effect of language working in and through time, and in different

---

38. Ibid., 64. Emphasis original.
39. Ibid., 68.
40. Ibid.

moments of time—for instance, how something spoken or written in the past demands participation in the present. The tensive moment created in the speech-act is not only between disparate images, as with traditional formulations of metaphor, but it is between disparate moments in time—past and present moments, present and future moments. The dynamic inherent in the interaction of moments of time is metaphor set in motion through time, or anachronism.

Christianity as Participatory Drama

With a view of language as essentially performative and active Vanhoozer is able to construe theological expression as itself essentially performative. Casting theology as active performance in God's redemption narrative, Vanhoozer finds "drama" as the most fitting image in which to frame the theological project. There are at least four components of this theological program: gospel as living drama; Bible as authoritative script; theology as living performance; and metaphor as relational key.

Gospel as Living Drama

From the outset Vanhoozer gives a definition and purpose of doctrine that moves away from more modern formulations: "*Canonical-linguistic theology gives scriptural direction for one's fitting participation in the drama of redemption today.*"[41] It is unified eschatological time that binds the church in the present between its past history and future existence; between temporal memory of God and future promise of God. Vanhoozer borrows the image of biblical history as a drama from N. T. Wright,[42] who has proposed that the Bible's authoritative and participatory character derives from it having the form of an unfinished five-act play occurring in real time:

> Suppose there exists a Shakespeare play whose fifth act has been lost. The first four acts provide, let us suppose, such a wealth of characterization, such a crescendo of excitement within the plot, that it is generally agreed that the play ought to be staged. Nevertheless, it is felt inappropriate actually to write the fifth act once and for all: it would be to freeze the play into one form and commit Shakespeare as it were to being prospectively responsible for work not in fact his own. Better, it might be felt, to

41. Ibid. Emphasis original.
42. Ibid., 2 n. 4, 57.

give the key parts to highly trained, sensitive and experienced Shakespearian actors, who would immerse themselves in the first four acts, and in the language and culture of Shakespeare and his time, *and who would then be told to work out a fifth act for themselves.*[43]

Wright carries the analogy, contending that the first four acts would be the authoritative text upon which any decisions about or objections to the improvised living-out of the fifth act could be based. Connection with the biblical narrative is then made explicit, sketching a biblical outline of time that views "the five acts as follows: (1) Creation; (2) Fall; (3) Israel; (4) Jesus. The New Testament would then form the first scene in the fifth act, giving hints as well (Rom 8; 1 Cor 15; parts of the Apocalypse) of how the play is supposed to end. The church would then live under the 'authority' of the extant story, being required to offer something between an improvisation and an actual performance of the final act."[44] In this sense the Bible holds a primary and authoritative position in the life of the Christian community in that it is God's speech-act that gives the church the story from which its life proceeds, and through an eschatological lens, the goal toward which it is directed. Further, the biblical drama includes the life of the church in the present, thereby demanding participation in the unfolding drama right now. This participation is evaluated by what the script says is the narrative's past enactment and future arrival. Drama as theological matrix organizes time as well as provides the inroads for our participation in God's action in the world, in time.

Vanhoozer is keen to pick up on this dramatic imagery in casting theology as dynamic and inherently oriented towards practice and movement: "Christian theology seeks to *continue* the way of truth and life, not by admiring it from afar but by following and embodying it. Following this way involves more than adopting a certain ethic. . . . The Christian way is fundamentally *dramatic*, involving speech and action on behalf of Jesus' truth and life. It concerns the way of living truthfully, and its claim to truth

---

43. Wright, "How Can the Bible Be Authoritative?," 18. Emphasis original.

44. Ibid., 19. Samuel Wells proposes a revision of Wright's five acts: "Act One is creation, Act Two is Israel, Act Three is Jesus, Act Four is the church, and Act Five is the eschaton" (*Improvisation*, 53). The critique I bring to Wells's revision lies in the identification of the fourth and fifth acts. While Wells's outline may be appealing in that it gives the church its own "Act," Wright's scheme rightfully acknowledges, albeit implicitly, the biblical notion that the church exists already *in* the eschaton, rather than waits for it. However, it is possible that Wells's use of the term "eschaton" is meant to refer solely to Christ's Second Advent, but this is not clear.

cannot be isolated from the way of life with which it is associated."[45] What Vanhoozer has introduced into the theological endeavor, without saying it explicitly, is the notion of temporality—theology occurring in and through time. Indeed, the very imagery of Christianity as a lived drama, or of Christianity as a life, recognizes the inseparable temporal element in the process of theological reflection. Distinct from narrative, drama is *enacted* story in time. Doctrines are no longer static, locked as fixed entities. Instead they exist in a fluidity of movement that integrates life and thought in ways not possible in a static Modernity. This stands in contrast to the idea of doctrines as packets of information or experience waiting to be reinterpreted or redescribed in each generation, which works to shield doctrine from the integration of thought and life, theology and time. The dramatic theology involves a continual fluidity of movement enabling integration of life and thought. What Vanhoozer does is to bring this temporal, historical element into the conversation in a way that modern conceptualizations of theology have not.

Vanhoozer proposes that "the purpose of doctrine is to ensure that those who bear Christ's name walk in Christ's way. Far from being irrelevant to 'life,' then, doctrine gives shape to life 'in Christ.'"[46] This dramatic shape for theology is not something imposed upon it, but rather it is inherently biblical: "The gospel—God's self-giving in his Son through the Spirit—is intrinsically *dramatic*, a matter of signs and speeches, actions and sufferings." Vanhoozer goes on to say, "Doctrine is a response to something *beheld*—beheld not theoretically but, as it were, theatrically: a *lived* performance. For the 'word of life' is nothing less than the life of Jesus, the Word—a *historical drama*."[47]

Here, history and temporality are reintroduced into the theological equation.[48] Scripture is the eventful, historical revelation of God in time; the church's performance is the enacted narrative continued. One important implication of this is the reemergence of eschatology as an essential aspect of theology. Eschatology is the area of theology that most specifically addresses issues of time—past, present, and future.[49] Viewing Christianity in dramatic terms allows for a recovery of eschatology, which has been

---

45. Vanhoozer, *Drama of Doctrine*, 15. Emphasis original.
46. Ibid., 16.
47. Ibid., 17. Emphasis original.
48. Heyduck, *Recovery of Doctrine*, 139–47.
49. See the discussion of Moltmann in chapter 2. Further, see Sampley, *Walking*, and Hays, *The Moral Vision*, both of whom point to eschatology as the center of New Testament ethics and life.

devalued in the modern era.[50] Drama recovers eschatology and organizes time in continuity, seeking to discern meaning across the history (including present and future) of God's people, and in each moment of the drama. Christian theology and Christianity itself become participation in one's role in the faith through time. As Vanhoozer notes about participation in the life of faith with Jesus along the way, "*The proper end of the drama of doctrine is wisdom: lived knowledge, a performance of the truth.*"[51] One judges this performance according to the church's script: Scripture.

Bible as Authoritative Script

"Doctrine's role in the drama is to enable the church to build wisdom's house: a pattern of speech and action that fits in with creation and redemption alike to the glory of God."[52] It is here that Vanhoozer revitalizes the Reformation principle *sola scriptura*. The Bible serves as the church's script, outlining what Vanhoozer terms "canonical practices," which become guidelines for the church's action:

> The Bible is both the authoritative version of the drama of redemption and the authoritative script for the church's ongoing life. As a collection of authoritative stage directions for performing the Christian way of life in the truth, the script calls not only for responsive reading but for responsive action and embodiment. *The script demands to be played out*; the literary forms of Scripture call for forms of life. *Sola scriptura* is ultimately the name of a practice to be performed by the church in the power of the Spirit.[53]

The Bible functions as script, calling to action and directing the church in the performance of the Christian life.

There are at least two reasons Scripture and not something else serves as locus of authority in Christian theology. First, canon has been historically recognized as script for the ongoing drama and as such continues to be "the normative specification of what God was saying and doing in Christ." Second, "the canon, precisely as testimony to the theo-drama, is the charter document of the covenant that stands at the heart of the relationship of

---

50. Heyduck, *Recovery of Doctrine*, 141.
51. Vanhoozer, *Drama of Doctrine*, 21. Emphasis original.
52. Ibid., 59.
53. Ibid., 115. Emphasis original.

God and humankind."[54] Ultimately, God's use of Scripture rather than the church's makes it canon because Scripture is God's speech-act. The church is thereby authenticated by the canon, rather than the other way around, as the canon "needs no ecclesial approval to be what it is: the Word of God."[55] This distinction differentiates Vanhoozer's canonical-linguistic theology from Lindbeck's cultural-linguistic program.[56]

The canon in its entirety documents the covenant God has made with God's people. It "recounts the history of God's covenantal dealings with humanity and regulates God's ongoing covenantal relationship with his people."[57] Within this covenant narrative the church finds its identity as people of God in theo-dramatic continuity with God's people in the past:

> The church today is in continuity with the first Christian communities addressed by the authors of the New Testament because the theo-dramatic situation of the church after Pentecost is our situation today. The church today is part of the same worshipping assembly. The church today responds to the same divine communicative action of word and Spirit. There is no need to establish the relevance of the Bible by coordinating certain texts with felt needs of present-day readers. Scripture is already relevant because the church today is part of the same covenant community established at Pentecost: one body joined together by the Spirit.[58]

---

54. Ibid., 141.

55. Ibid., 150. Even so, the church is still tasked with faithful interpretation, exposition, and communication of Scripture. The Word of God comes to expression in the present through these tasks.

56. In Vanhoozer's model, the Bible as locus of community authority distinguishes his canonical-linguistic approach from the postliberal cultural-linguistic scheme: "The cultural-linguistic turn characteristic of postliberal and other types of postmodern theology is a salient reminder that theology exists to serve the life of the church. Yet the turn to church practice seems to have come at the expense of biblical authority. The *canonical*-linguistic approach . . . has much in common with its cultural-linguistic cousin. Both agree that meaning and truth are crucially related to language use; however, the canonical-linguistic approach maintains that the normative use is ultimately not that of ecclesial *culture* but of the biblical *canon*. . . . The supreme *norm* for church practice is Scripture itself: not Scripture as used by the church but Scripture as used by God, even, or perhaps especially, when such use is *over against* the church" (*Drama of Doctrine*, 16–17, emphasis original). While the cultural-linguistic approach sees the community's practice of the story as the authoritative source for doctrine, a dramatic model shifts the emphasis to the story and its performance.

57. Ibid., 137.

58. Ibid., 140.

Scripture as God's speech-act to the church brings together disparate moments in time in that the church today responds to "the same divine communicative action of word and Spirit" as the church just after Pentecost.

The canon calls the community to performance. The Bible as canonical script discloses God's interaction with humanity in history and calls the church to participation in the eschatological horizon of history opened up in the person and work of Jesus Christ. Vanhoozer, again echoing Moltmann's eschatological theology, declares that "Scripture thereby summons the reader to be part of a new thing that God is doing in the world."[59]

Theology as Living Performance

The Bible as canonical script provides the history of God's people by which the present community can judge the fittingness of its present actions in, or its performance of, the gospel drama. As Wright noted above, the first four acts of the play have been accomplished, and the church finds itself in the present in the midst of an eschatological Act 5. The present and future continue to intersect towards the eschatological horizon as God's people seek to participate in the ongoing drama through fitting spirited performance: "It is the unique privilege and responsibility of the people of God to perform the Scriptures and continue the way."[60] The goal of theological expression then becomes the fitting performance of one's role (or the community's role) in God's story in the present and into the future.

Being a member of the Christian community is a matter of "participatory drama," in which "to know Christ is to 'know the power of his resurrection' and to 'share in his sufferings' (Phil. 3:10)."[61] Doctrine in a canonical-linguistic context essentially penetrates community life: "*Theological interpretation is the process of keeping the canonical practices alive and well in the believing community.* The canon is not primarily the source of data for a theoretical science. On the contrary, the canon is a covenantal norm, a norm that regulates our life with God and with one another. We participate in the canonical practices by looking and living along the text in ways that recognize the lordship of Jesus Christ."[62] In the present-day performance of this drama the church must view itself as both audience to the historical drama as recorded and a principal player in the ongoing enacted

---

59. Ibid., 235.
60. Ibid., 22.
61. Ibid., 81.
62. Ibid., 219. Emphasis original.

narrative.⁶³ This observation has deep implications for practices and goals of preaching in the church.

Vanhoozer describes participating in Scripture's communicative practices as being "textualized" into the canon.⁶⁴ These communicative practices take genre-specific forms in Scripture with the purpose of forming the practice of the canonical community: "The Bible clearly embraces a variety of speech genres, language games, and literary forms. Included among the communicative practices in Scripture are the following: recounting history (narrative), praising God (psalms), foretelling (prophecy), cultivating the fear of the Lord (wisdom), anticipating the end of history (apocalyptic), and so forth, all for the sake of regulating the life, language, and faith of the believing community."⁶⁵ The illocutionary force within them thus characterizes literary genres of Scripture. Performing these communicative/canonical practices takes at least two forms. Interpretation of the biblical text is one form, in which "we begin to speak, see, judge, and act canonically [as] we learn to interpret the history recounted in the Bible, as well as our own ongoing history, as part and parcel of the drama of redemption in Christ." Prayer, a second form, is the "canonical practice whereby we do not merely envision the theo-drama but *indwell* it and assume a speaking part."⁶⁶ Interpretation and prayer provide a living and practical context in which to learn, appropriate, and integrate Scripture for one's life. In the practices of the canon it can be said that the canon is both closed and open—closed in the sense that the church recognizes God's definitive word in these particular books and in no others, yet open in the sense that the text itself invites, and indeed demands, the ongoing participation of the church in Christ, that is, the furthering of God's theo-dramatic narrative through time.⁶⁷ The church both accedes to God's word in matters of faith and practice, and lives God's word in its continued performance of God's drama. Doctrine finds its goal in practice of God's word eventfully, in and through time.

Vanhoozer notes that in its contemporary realization, "the drama may, and must, be the same, but the action now takes place with different actors, on a different stage, with new scenery," in essence, in a different temporal moment of the script.⁶⁸ Unless we make a commitment to recitation alone of the text (which, because of the different moment we occupy within the

---

63. Ibid., 111.
64. Ibid., 212.
65. Ibid., 216.
66. Ibid., 224. Emphasis original.
67. Ibid., 237.
68. Ibid., 240.

drama, does not replicate the text), one key question that must confront preachers in this paradigm is how the church in the present can be faithful to the past while retaining its present, distinct identity.[69] Or, how does doctrine relate the past history to the present moment and the church's future hope? This question, the hermeneutical question, is centrally related to homiletics in how one might preach within such a dramatic theological paradigm. In terms of communicating the drama, Vanhoozer, with others before him, relies on metaphor as the device that can relate moments across time. This blending of metaphor and time paves the way for theological anachronism.

Metaphor as Relational Key

Doctrine in the canonical-linguistic mode integrally employs imagination as a necessary component of theological expression. Scripture addresses the imagination, and in so doing addresses mind, will, and emotion.[70] It is imagination that allows something other than literal repetition of the drama thus far, a lived out continuity flowing from and connected to the past while retaining a unique identity. The relation of the church's present fitting performance to the past canonical script is achieved through use of metaphor:

> To achieve fidelity to Scripture and fittingness to the contemporary context—what we have termed a cross-modal similarity between yesterday and today—we need to think about our performance in terms other than literal repetition. The ability to discern fittingness between biblical and contemporary performances requires the creativity of metaphor as well as a good grasp of Scripture's literal sense. The etymology of *metaphor* is "to transfer": meaning that belongs to one mode is transferred (transposed) to another. . . . A good metaphor is one that enables us to perceive fittingness between things that we might not otherwise associate with one another.[71]

Moving away from literal repetition and imitation of the text one is confronted with the need for improvisation and innovation through faith. Direction for participation is attained through the practice of metaphor— purposefully bringing past into relationship with the present in order to perceive similarities in dissimilar moments in time. Metaphor is the manner

69. Ibid., 125.
70. Ibid., 12.
71. Ibid., 261.

of imaginatively discerning fittingness between the past or future of the text, and present performance of the drama.

Metaphor provides the foundation for discerning fitting performance in the present as the church's present action constitutes one dynamic moment of the overarching drama. Learning to translate biblical "patterns of action into contemporary patterns of action" is a process attended to in the canonical practices of biblical interpretation and prayer.[72] The player in the drama today must not only become familiar with the biblical script; he or she must also understand the contemporary cultural and sociological context. In bringing the two together, fittingness is discerned between two different yet similar moments in time. As Vanhoozer expresses it, "Patterns of speech, thought, and action will be fitting insofar as they discover and display a real similarity to the Christo-drama in spite of the culturally [or temporally] dissimilar."[73] Furthering Vanhoozer's observations about drama as theological matrix, and especially about metaphor within this matrix, will be the task of chapter 4.

CONCLUSIONS

God's drama is our theological, temporal matrix. Drama is an effective substitute for historical recital that treats the past as a time that is cut off from the present. Vanhoozer's paradigm for theological expression uses drama as the controlling image, yet more important than the image itself is the theological matrix for the practice of theology that drama enables. This performative theology reevaluates language, viewing it in terms of speech-acts in which language does not merely convey information but in which it acts; language does things. A dramatic theology seeks to respect continuity of time between interpretative communities, as well as retain the Bible as the community's constitutive text. According to this performative view of theology, the practice of doctrine provides direction for the proper performance of the church's ongoing dramatic narrative, authored by God, embodied and reaching its climax in Christ, and continued by the Spirit. Theology is recognized as an action, the living of one's life in participation with Christ. The canonical-linguistic mode of theological expression organizes time, and in doing so, elevates time for theological expression. This dramatic matrix for theological practice changes hermeneutical, temporal, and contextual lenses for homiletics, making demands upon the preacher. A reevaluation

72. Ibid., 262.
73. Ibid., 263.

of the traditional hermeneutical manner of moving through time comes into focus. The gap is temporal, and cannot be effectively bridged spatially.

The dramatic matrix proposed by Wright, Vanhoozer, Heyduck, and others situates the place of the church temporally within an overarching framework of God's interaction with God's people in this world, witnessed to in the biblical text but continuing today and beyond. In a dramatic theological matrix the present moment in time is understood in temporal terms as within the gap of the eschatological stretch of time opened between Christ's advents and includes the life and work of the church and individual believers from his ascension until his return. Literary critic Amos Wilder describes the eschatological and inherently participatory nature of the biblical drama's fifth act:

> We can make one general remark about the narrative-mode of the New Testament. These stories, long or short, in one way or another carry over into the future. The rounding off is usually in some sense still to come. The hearer or reader finds himself in the middle of the action. We are in the middle of the play, if not in Act V. Now this is certainly true of the Bible epic as a whole. God's last word is still to be spoken. Parts of the world-story are told in the future-tense.[74]

The reality of Christian living in this fifth act, as Wright describes it, seeks to participate in life among God's people in such a way as to be fitting with what has come before (memory) and with what is anticipated from the future (hope). The church and the disciple are caught between past and future, bound between memory and hope, offering an improvised enactment of the present course of the drama. The drama sees the intervening centuries between biblical events and our time as the "ongoing sacred history of God's people," as Krister Stendahl puts it.[75] Recognition of being bound in the

---

74. Wilder, *Early Christian Rhetoric*, 67–68.

75. Stendahl suggested a similar dramatic approach in answering the hermeneutical question in terms of a mode of hermeneutical translation consistent with a descriptive approach to biblical theology. He assessed that there were really only two available forms of translation that held consistency. The first Stendahl identified as Bultmann's program of demythologization, what Stendahl called a "radical ahistorical translation" of the text. After weighing the option of the "salvation-history" school, what he termed a "semihistorical translation," and judging it as containing "grave problems of inconsistency," Stendahl turned to a proposed "systematic theology where the bridge between the centuries of biblical events and our own time was found in the actual history of the church as still ongoing sacred history of God's people." Stendahl viewed this approach as promising for theology. This is, in large part, similar to what I am proposing here. Stendahl, "Biblical Theology, Contemporary," 428.

midst of this matrix recharacterizes Christianity from primarily cognitive or emotive to a more dynamic view of faith as a "life and living process."[76]

Drama provides the theological matrix in which the interpreter, the church, and the preacher live, interpret, worship, and preach. Every text is read against the backdrop of the overarching drama and not in isolation or as an encapsulation of the drama's entirety. This takes the temporal whole of the drama into consideration. The biblical text produced in the drama's past exists and emerges in the life of the church in the present while remaining anchored to the past. It further guides God's people in the performance of the drama towards its eschatological goal. Living in what Wright and Wilder identify as the drama's fifth act, the whole of the drama serves as a theological matrix in which life is lived. The sermon, then, becomes the proclamation of God's drama, and the forming of God's people for life in this moment of that drama—anchored in the story so far, acting out the action towards the story's goal. The distance between text and pulpit is reconfigured as time becomes both the distance from the past and the present's connection to that past history of God's people. A similar dynamic is apparent in the eschatological unity of present and future. In this reevaluation of hermeneutical distance, how might preaching be envisioned?

Metaphor, as traditionally envisioned, is rather two-dimensional in bringing together images and words. However, metaphor within the added dimension of a unified and dramatically organized temporality has the potential to be as dimensional as the drama it seeks to animate. Movement across time becomes the function of temporal metaphor, or, theological anachronism. Anachronism has the ability to unite moments of time across the drama, calling for participation in this moment of God's drama. Metaphor plus time gives us the theological and homiletical concept of anachronism—bringing two dissimilar moments of the drama into relationship in this moment, thereby creating a new moment of understanding which enables the preacher to navigate the time between text and today and to provide guidance for God's people living in this moment of the drama. Anachronism is the diachronic embodiment of synchronic metaphor, as it is the theological and communicative device able to connect the drama's present with its past and future, dynamically catching up the congregation in between. Developing anachronism as temporal metaphor will occupy chapter 4 before engaging in a fuller development of an anachronistic homiletic, in which the sermon unites moments of time across the drama, in chapter 5.

---

76. Coleridge, *Aids to Reflection*, 201.

4

Anachronism
Traveling through Time

Drama brings together the eschatological unity and temporal organization of time, so that one may approach the hermeneutical question based on time rather than space. It provides a theological, temporal, indeed ecclesiological context for the practice of preaching. Anachronism, that is, metaphor set free in time, applied practically in the sermon, binds modes of time together, brings the action of God to the center, and invites participation in the current enactment of the drama. As metaphor forms the core of the anachronistic device, what follows will first explore metaphor as a meaning-creating device. Set in the context of drama's unified and organized temporal quality, metaphor as a temporal device allows the preacher to travel through time, bringing disparate moments of the drama together in a new moment of dynamic understanding. This chapter first explores a definition of metaphor developed through the history of the church's practical theology and then sets metaphor in motion through time. This produces dynamic theological anachronism for temporally navigating the hermeneutical gap and effectively communicating the ancient text today. Examples of how this works practically in preaching are important aspects of this study. I will then explore anachronism as a theological practice historically in the church's premodern practices (Scripture, medieval practical theologies). While the concept of anachronism was eclipsed during the Enlightenment, Postmodernity displays anachronistic communication as a matter of art and communication. These cultural artifacts are beneficial to this study both in terms of examples of effective and artistic anachronistic communication and as guides for preaching moving forward.

ANACHRONISM: THEOLOGICAL MOVEMENT THROUGH TIME

In developing a working definition and practice for metaphor, and in turn anachronism, I turn to the Romantic theology of theologians Samuel Taylor Coleridge (1772–1834) and Horace Bushnell (1802–76). Coleridge, as a poet-theologian in the late eighteenth and early nineteenth centuries, gave definition to the concept of metaphor that would see the device as central for all theological thought. Bushnell, a New England Congregational pastor and theologian in the mid-1800s, took Coleridge's theology to practical ends in his preaching. Exploring metaphor from this starting point provides a base definition rooted in the church's practical speech and gives a jumping off point for setting metaphor in motion through time as theological anachronism. Bushnell especially, as one whose theological context, theological complaints, and proposed theological solutions so closely parallel contemporary dramatic theologians, is useful in seeing how preaching might manifest within the matrix of drama. This is something waiting to be developed in the dramatic theologies discussed in chapter 3. Here, we will look to Coleridge and Bushnell to develop metaphor for religious communication, and then take their work to even more dynamic conclusions through a developed dramatic theological matrix.

The religious and cultural landscapes of the middle years of the nineteenth century were dramatically shaped, according to historian James Duke, by "strong sociocultural forces—aftershocks of the Enlightenment, advances in scientific knowledge, shifting philosophical currents, changing patterns of social relations, and the processes of nation building, to name only a few."[1] The New England in which Bushnell ministered boasted theological battles raging among diametrically opposed schools. None of these schools of theology, because of language's limits, were able to claim a monopoly on theological truth. Rather than aligning with one side or the other, Bushnell's theological approach (in a characteristic Romantic fashion) sought to forge a path between them. The manner of developing a theology comprehensive enough to communicate God was a proposal for reevaluating language in general and theological language in particular. Relying on the imaginative thought and theology of Coleridge, Bushnell developed as central to his reformulated appraisal of language the idea of

1. Duke, *Horace Bushnell*, 2–3.

metaphor, or a reconciliation of opposites.[2] For Bushnell, a rehabilitation of biblical language would see metaphor as central for theological expression and would lead to a recognition of Christianity as a unity of life and spirit—something more dynamic and forward-moving than the typically propositional or experiential theologies of his day. All of this—parallels between context, complaint, and proposed theology—places Bushnell in alignment with dramatic theologians who would come a century and a half later. Taking Bushnell's emphasis on metaphor and setting it in motion through the canonical-linguistic theologies of today has the ability to produce a specific type of metaphor, one that is animated by time. Temporal metaphor, or anachronism, gives homiletical direction for the preacher speaking from within a canonical-linguistic matrix.

Theological Abstraction: Take Two

Bushnell's ecclesiological world found the pastor equally frustrated with theological abstractions both propositional and experiential. In this way, the pastor and Romantic theologian finds a good deal of affinity with Vanhoozer, Wright, and other more contemporary dramatic theologians. The theological climate was split between distinctively propositional and experiential theologies. On the one hand scientific rationality had gained a firm hold in academia in general and in theological studies in particular. Theological expression was, in this vein, a matter of forming propositional statements of truth about God; statements both timeless and exact. Opposite from the propositional theologies of which Bushnell was so critical were experiential theologies characteristic of preaching during the Second Great Awakening. The conversion experience was a staple of much nineteenth-century New England preaching and Bushnell was equally critical of what he viewed as an emotional appeal to religion. Characterizations of Christian faith as either the formulation of right knowledge or the creation of right experience tended towards lifelessness and vapidity for the Congregationalist. Revivalism and dogmatism both failed in terms of communicating and inspiring a faith that was life and Spirit.

For Bushnell the idea of revival was problematic. David Wells has observed that the view of society held in the middle years of nineteenth-century America, especially the view held by preachers, "fell under two headings: declension and revival."[3] Society was decaying in various aspects as there was a perceived loss of the values that had been held in previous

2. Coleridge, *Biographia Literaria*, chapter 13.
3. Wells, "Debate over the Atonement," 124.

generations. The prevailing theological response to this societal infidelity was the call for revival, with such prominent names of the nineteenth-century church as Charles Finney and Lyman Beecher fueling the flames of the Second Great Awakening.[4] Bushnell, however, saw revival as shallow, emotional, and producing a faith that was as impermanent as it was disintegrated from everyday life. Instead he sought to preach a Christianity that was characterized as a life lived. Acknowledging that there was the need for "some true renovation of the religious spirit,"[5] Bushnell was quite unconvinced that such a renovation was to come through the emotionalism and unstable spirituality produced by revivalists such as Finney.[6] In his lecture "Dogma and Spirit," Bushnell longed for a renewal of Christian faith that would "set us on a firmer ground of stability, produce a more acknowledged and visible Christian unity, and develop a more consistent, catholic, permanent, free and living exhibition of the renovation power of Christ and his truth."[7] Central to this rediscovery of Christianity's living quality was the idea that "Christianity fell into the world's bosom as a quickening power, as Life and Spirit from God."[8] Revivalism could not inspire or sustain this living, dramatic faith.

Bushnell also differed from the prevailing dogmatic theologies of the day, Unitarianism and Fundamentalism.[9] While he affirmed traditional positions such as the Trinity, Christ's divinity, and humanity's sinfulness and need for redemption,[10] what set Bushnell apart from his contemporaries, and in turn put him out of favor with them, was his attack on propositional theologies as inadequate for containing or absolutely communicating the life and Spirit that Christian faith demands. The propositional approach to faith, Bushnell asserts, is a replacement of historic Christian faith: "That historical and vital Christianity, which Christ presented in his life, is replaced, ere long, by what some call a doctrinal; that is, by a Christianity made up of propositions and articles. The teachers think they are shedding great light upon the new religion, but we, looking back, perceive a dark age just there gathering in upon Christendom."[11] For Bushnell a rehabilitation of Christianity would see the faith conceptualized as the unity of life and Spirit—a

---

4. Ibid., 140–41.
5. Bushnell, "Dogma and Spirit," 279.
6. Wells, "Debate over the Atonement," 141.
7. Bushnell, "Dogma and Spirit," 279–80.
8. Ibid., 280.
9. Edwards, *History of Preaching*, 632.
10. Ibid.
11. Bushnell, "Dogma and Spirit," 288.

reconciliation of opposites in the living out of faith. However, the Unitarians and Fundamentalists were both guilty of advocating an abstractive theology that raised propositional expressions of biblical truths to the level of certain and final statements of dogma.[12] This valuing of propositional theology was predicated on a flawed appropriation of scientific rationalism for theological expression. While his contemporaries were attempting to dogmatize theological truth, Bushnell would critique that the language they were working with was not, and inherently could not be, adequate for such a task.[13] His more typically organic perspective on language and Christian experience was "shocking to Bushnell's orthodox contemporaries, however, who thought that Christian preaching consisted of accurately arguing the doctrines of Calvin as they had received them," and was equally unacceptable to the New England Unitarians, who did not appreciate his comprehensive approach to theology.[14]

The chief medium of expression for Bushnell's theological ideas was the pulpit. Conrad Cherry observes that Bushnell "sought, above all else, to be an effective preacher rather than a scholar."[15] Bushnell judged that the dominant forms of preaching in his day did not achieve what should be the chief goal of preaching: cultivating the life of faith. Neither Fundamentalist, nor Unitarian, nor Revivalist homiletical paradigms "lifted before the minds of the auditors the imaginative wonder of the Christian tradition." Bushnell elevated preaching to "an art form which stirs the symbolic consciousness and invites one to undertake the pilgrimage of faith."[16] Out of these observations and resulting convictions Bushnell sought to move language, especially language for preaching, beyond proposition and experience and set it in motion through more dynamic communication: metaphor. It is here especially that Bushnell finds affinity with, and gives direction for, preaching within and for the enacted drama recognized by canonical-linguistic theologians.[17]

12. Bushnell, "Training for the Pulpit Manward," 491.
13. Bushnell, "Preliminary Dissertation on the Nature of Language."
14. Edwards, *History of Preaching*, 1:632–33.
15. Cherry, *Horace Bushnell*, 7.
16. Ibid., 12.
17. While Bushnell sought to rehabilitate language by holding in tension the elements of truth embedded in all forms of communication, his approach to theology, language, and preaching put him out of favor with his contemporaries. Theological arguments, such as those over the nature of theological expression or a proper understanding of the atonement, were to eventually lead to Bushnell's rejection, not by the members of his church but by other ministers and theologians. Edwards observes that so great was the break Bushnell was seen to advocate that "his North Church congregation was all but isolated, their minister unwelcome in neighboring pulpits, the

Truth in Contradiction: Spirit, Life, and Reconciling Opposites

Two central aspects of his theological reflections were developed as a result of Bushnell's reading of the Romantic poet and theologian Samuel Taylor Coleridge. The insistence that Christianity is a life rather than a set of dogmatic propositions find their roots in Coleridge's work. Second, the centrality of metaphor for communication in general and preaching in particular becomes prominent in Bushnell's theology. Both of these observations about faith in alignment with a dramatic organization of time offer a theological goal and the means that achieving that goal, for preaching.

Christianity Is a Life

The first significant insight gleaned from Coleridge has to do with the nature of Christian faith itself. This, in turn, opens into an evaluation of the ultimate goal of preaching. In his *Aids to Reflection* Coleridge writes that "Christianity is not a theory, or a speculation; but a life;—not a philosophy of life, but a life and a living process."[18] This meant that faith, rather than being a set of propositional doctrines or a conversion experience, was a continual life process in which one grew from the "religious nature" into the "religious life," the state of salvation.[19] Instead of a static, dogmatic or experiential belief system, Christianity is an active, dynamic, living process. Faith must be a life, and preaching must aim at this target. Cherry summarizes Bushnell's attitude toward Christianity as life: "The Christian religion was for Bushnell, as for Coleridge, a particular kind of life—a life of growth, of struggles of the free human spirit, of the counterforces of darkness and light. Such a dynamic phenomenon could never be captured by dogma nor preserved by a moral code; it could only be symbolized by imaginative metaphor and nurtured by vital persons and institutions."[20] Bushnell viewed

---

Association of Ministers to which he belonged split on his account, and the church's own ties with the North Consociation of Hartford County altogether broken" ("Portrait of a People," 158).

Bushnell's comprehensive theological method is a fascinating study in holding truth as vastly manifested in theological tension rather than finding a way through theological debate via liberalism or relativism. Bushnell, "Christian Comprehensiveness," 386–459.

18. Coleridge, *Aids to Reflection*, 201, quoted in Edwards, *History of Preaching*, 1:632; and Cherry, *Horace Bushnell*, 1.

19. See Edwards, *History of Preaching*, 1:633.

20. Cherry, *Horace Bushnell*, 2.

Christian faith as a life into which one grows. This is one aspect of his theology that set him apart from his contemporaries and from many forms of theological expression today. The language Bushnell used to characterize the very nature of Christian faith, and in turn the homiletic that would seek to produce it, is that Christianity is life and spirit.

In many ways prefiguring Moltmann, Bushnell speaks of Christianity as the unity of divine action and human experience. It is in uniting one's life with the Holy Spirit, in participating in the life of Christ, that one begins to understand God in living Christian faith. Knowledge of God is given through the Spirit of God, and to be joined with God's Spirit is to live the Christian life: "Therefore it is not in lectures or books, not in exegetic or dogmatic discipline, not in any and all other methods, so truly as in the elevations of prayer, and the inbreathings or inspirations of God, that a human soul may be truly initiated into the life and doctrine of Christ."[21] Bushnell advocates for the practice of the Christian life over and against the suggestion that Christianity is a matter of obtaining the right pieces of knowledge. It is this conviction that prompts Bushnell to suggest that the Christian minister's training should not consist merely of books and interpretation, but primarily it should consist of an almost mystical union with Christ: "He needs to be trained in a holy element, and be led along as a pupil of the Spirit, into that deep knowledge of the secrets of God, that pure and hallowed union of spirit with Jesus himself, which is the fountain of all Christian light."[22]

Bushnell's emphasis on Christianity as a life is clearly evidenced in his writings on Christian education. His most well-known work, *Christian Nurture,* proposed that in Christian education of children "the child is to grow up a Christian, and never know himself as being otherwise."[23] This was a departure from the prevailing attitude towards children, which generally stated that children were to grow up knowing themselves as sinners in need of redemption and then undergo a conversion experience at an age of maturity. The shift, which Bushnell states is the historical Christian position, points to a transition from an emphasis on teaching Christianity as merely doctrine and information and requiring a religious experience for conversion, to a stress on teaching Christianity as a manner of living, that is, being in relationship with God and with others in a loving, supportive community:

---

21. Bushnell, "Dogma and Spirit," 332.
22. Ibid., 333.
23. Bushnell, *Christian Nurture,* 4.

> Christ himself, by that renewing Spirit who can sanctify from the womb, should be practically infused into the childish mind; in other words, that the house, having a domestic Spirit of grace dwelling in it, should become the church of childhood, the table and hearth a holy rite, and life an element of saving power. Something is wanted that is better than teaching, something that transcends mere effort and will-work—the loveliness of a good life, the repose of faith, the confidence of righteous expectation, the sacred and cheerful liberty of the Spirit—all glowing about the young soul, as a warm and genial nurture, and forming in it, by methods that are silent and imperceptible, a spirit of duty and religious obedience to God.[24]

For Bushnell, both the method of Christian education and its outcome are centered upon the idea that Christianity is a life.

Bushnell summarizes his thoughts regarding what is central to the Christian faith in noting that until Christianity realizes its true nature as a unity of life and spirit it will remain stagnant: "By this cause Christianity has hitherto been dwarfed in all its results and manifestations. Nothing better can ever be realized, till, ascending into Christianity as spirit and life, in the fullest and freest sense, we submit our souls to God's universal movement. We are to receive the Spirit in his own measures, not any more in ours, and prepare ourselves, gradually, for an outspreading era of life, that shall be as the manifested Life of God."[25] Christianity, and just as importantly Christian preaching, must call for participation with God in a unity of Spirit and life. In this, and in his insistence upon metaphor, the commonality of goals in faith and sermon is seen with Vanhoozer's canonical-linguistic program: "The proper end of the drama of doctrine is wisdom: lived knowledge, a performance of the truth."[26]

Life through Reconciling Opposites

At the heart of Bushnell's calling to faith in life and Spirit is Coleridge's principle of reconciliation of opposites, or metaphor.[27] With reference to Coleridge, Paul Scott Wilson defines metaphor as the tension between two

---

24. Ibid., 12.
25. Bushnell, "Discourse on Dogma and Spirit," 354.
26. Vanhoozer, *Drama of Doctrine*, 21. Emphasis original.
27. Paul Scott Wilson uses the term "reconciliation of opposites" to describe the dynamic Coleridge refers to in his work. I will borrow this terminology throughout. Wilson, "Coherence," 451.

unlike ideas or images brought into relationship in order to create a new image or idea. Coleridge's *Biographia Literaria* describes imagination in these terms: "Now the transcendental philosophy demands; first, that two forces should be conceived which counteract each other by their essential nature; not only not in consequence of the accidental direction of each, but as prior to all direction, nay, as the primary forces from which the conditions of all possible directions are derivative and deducible; secondly, that these forces should be assumed to be both alike infinite, both alike indestructible."[28] This aspect of Coleridge's thought is the "balance or reconciliation of opposites."[29] Wilson explains that for Coleridge,

> Imagination functions in language by bringing two images or ideas into relationship. The tension or energy generated between the two poles produces a third identity (or spark). The result is not a compromise of the sort that may happen with thesis-antithesis-synthesis in logic. . . . the result Coleridge intended is metaphor, a language event or tensive relationship in which the reader must participate to gain understanding.[30]

According to Coleridge's principle it is in the existence of contradiction, rather than in its resolution, that meaning is created.[31] This understanding of metaphor as a reconciliation of opposites forms the basis for theological anachronism moving forward.

Bushnell himself exhibits this penchant for contradiction in one of his most quoted passages: "Accordingly, we never come so near to a truly well rounded view of any truth, as when it is offered paradoxically; that is, under contradictions; that is, under two or more dictions, which, taken as dictions, are contrary to one another."[32] As language in and of itself is inadequate to produce a full accounting of truth, especially theological truth, it must be approached from a multitude of angles. For Coleridge, and for Bushnell, this is metaphor. When two or more contradictory images or statements are brought together, this creates a new image that sparks new meaning or understanding without assimilating or absorbing the images or statements from which it is formed. It is a *language event*, as Wilson describes it, in which a fuller view of the truth is accomplished. Bushnell here trades a static view of language for a dynamic one—reconciliation of opposites, or metaphor, is

---

28. Coleridge, *Biographia Literaria*, 299; quoted in Wilson, "Coherence," 458.

29. See Wilson, "Coherence," 451.

30. Wilson, *Preaching and Homiletical Theory*, 92. See also, Wilson, *Concise History of Preaching*, 141–42.

31. Wilson, "Coherence," 459.

32. Bushnell, "Preliminary Dissertation," 55.

the mode of language in which language *does* something and in which the receiver must *participate*. This dynamic approach to language provides the means for communication across time between text and sermon.

These key ideas combined—that Christianity is a life process and that language is essentially at its best metaphorical and poetic—help provide a hermeneutic and homiletic today that is able to move through time, giving direction for the present enactment of the historical and future drama. Metaphor—the reconciliation of opposite ideas or images in language—set in motion through the unified time of the Christian drama in which one lives sets the stage for theological anachronism. The preacher, rather than pairing two objects, images, or ideas, sets in motion two moments in time (past and present, or present and future) by preaching the two near enough together, and so takes the theological reflection and creativity of Coleridge and Bushnell in developing metaphor to an even greater depth. By setting metaphor into motion through time we begin to create the homiletical outworking of the hermeneutical practice in the canonical-linguistic drama.

A STORY OF ANACHRONISM ACROSS TIME

The power of language for the contemporary sermon lies in bringing together Vanhoozer and Wright's insistence on drama as a theological matrix, with Coleridge and Bushnell's development of metaphor. Metaphor animated through dramatic time gives us the theological concept, and communicative device, anachronism. We have already defined drama as theological matrix for theology and preaching. While anachronism has played a role and received preliminary definition in previous chapters, here I will give it a more definite character as a theological concept, metaphor with the ability to move through time. Anachronism, quite simply, reconciles disparate moments in time by bringing them together and embracing their temporal contradictions. This is metaphor set free in time.

The *Oxford English Dictionary* defines *anachronism* as "anything done or existing out of date," and as "an error in computing time, or fixing dates; the erroneous reference of an event, circumstance, or custom to a wrong date." In Modernity, anachronism serves as a label attached to anything that appears out of line with a normative or logical temporal sequence. In this sense anachronisms tend to be violations of modern sensibilities that then dictate their removal. I am proposing a more theological and imaginative approach to anachronism, however. While anachronism may be a violation of modern understandings of time, it is precisely from these various aspects of modern temporal understanding that I am attempting to move. Another definition of anachronism is rooted in its characteristic of holding times together in the tradition of Coleridge's reconciliation of opposites.[33] Further, while the traditional view of anachronism generally deals with past and present time exclusively, which is in line with a more modern and less biblical view of time, within the unity of times assumed in the doctrine of eschatology, I regard anachronism as a temporal metaphor having a proleptic, eschatological quality of inbreaking the future in the present. Or, drawing on Moltmann's observations regarding time, conversion, and rebirth, anachronism makes present "the ultimate in the penultimate, and the future of time in the midst of time."[34] Anachronism as a theological concept holds modes of time together, and allows the preacher an organic manner of answering the hermeneutical question.

Adapting Coleridge's reconciliation of opposites as a definition of metaphor, and Bushnell's related maxim that truth is understood most fully in contradiction, anachronism can be recast and understood more poetically and imaginatively as a metaphor moving in and through time, or temporal metaphor. In a traditional metaphor one brings together opposing images, words, or ideas for the purpose of the constituent parts playing off of one another and creating a new image, word, or idea without damaging the original pieces. This is what Wilson describes as an imaginative spark.[35] Anachronism functions as a temporal metaphor in which temporal opposites within the drama are reconciled, past and present or present and future. When these two moments are brought near enough they create a new moment of both experience and understanding. Neither original moment is collapsed into the other, but both retain their distinct identities while creating something new.

In addressing the hermeneutical question, anachronism (and a homiletical theology built upon it) does much more than the bridge paradigm (or homiletical theologies built upon it). While the bridge approach seeks to traverse an imposed road between text then and knowledge or experience now, anachronism seeks to bring out inherent connections between moments in time in a dynamic and mimetic way. Continuity in the overarching

---

33. See Coleridge, *Biographia Literaria*, 299; Wilson, "Coherence in *Biographia Literaria*."

34. Moltmann, *Coming of God*, 22.

35. Wilson, *Imagination of the Heart*, 32–37.

drama is, in this way, preserved as past and future are brought into the horizon of the present. Anachronism sees the sermon live into application organically rather than in a more stilted manner. Taken together, drama and anachronism when brought into practice through preaching can produce an imaginative, artistic, and dynamic homiletic that navigates the hermeneutical gap temporally instead of spatially.

The traditional sense of metaphor usually functions as an idea or image frozen in time. Set in motion through drama, temporally static metaphor becomes temporally dynamic anachronism. Anachronism holds together two moments or events in time such that they come together to create something new, and thereby one or the other or both may be seen. In holding them together, anachronism makes a claim that they are similar, and the viewer or hearer must discern where the similarity lies. The drama of one time is connected to the drama of another, simply because they are the same drama in different times. The "poles" of metaphor are reimagined from ideas or images to events in time from the drama of God's presence with God's people.[36]

Anachronism brings a past moment from God's drama together with the present situation of the church, or, brings a promise of God's future into the present moment. Memory is wed to the present moment for guidance in present dramatic performance, and hope in God's future is enacted into the now. The preacher can bring together any particular moment from the ongoing drama with the present moment in the life of the church, either seeing the present as a descendent of the past moment or viewing the present and past as the set stage for the future. Contemporary images, ideas, or knowledge can be read into a past event from the script in order to provide relative familiarity to an unfamiliar time. Similarly, the past event from the script can be contemporized for greater understanding and participation in this present enactment. God's future promises can, through Jesus Christ, be called and enacted into the present.

Significantly, much Christian theology and practice presumes this continuity of time. For instance, the sacrament of communion makes present the real sacrifice of Christ in the midst of God's community today. The inbreaking of God's kingdom eschatologically makes future present now in a real, tangible way. Anachronism names this dynamic as a theological concept with theological application for practical theology. Further, anachronism is distinctly hermeneutical in highlighting the temporal relationships

---

36. This is similar to what Lash presents as necessary for interpretation—that one is working with patterns of human action, in time, rather than static bits of information that somehow contain quantifiable "meaning." Lash, "What Might Martyrdom Mean?"

between moments of time, in a sense bending time in on itself and providing a temporal means of moving from text to sermon.

Before developing this dynamic for the contemporary sermon in chapter 5 it will be beneficial to briefly work through the story of anachronism through time as it has appeared in the church's premodern practical theology and in Western culture's postmodern artistic communication. Anachronism as a theological and communicative dynamic is a hermeneutic that has existed but was only lost in the Enlightenment. However, in a postmodern milieu anachronism has now already been reimagined for communication outside the church in the arts.

Anachronism in Premodern Theologies

Anachronism, that is, the reconciliation of opposites set in motion through time, allows the preacher in the contemporary moment to move through time and bring moments in time together for the call to enacted meaning commensurate with the canonical drama. Anachronism calls for a faithful improvisation of the drama in the life of the disciple in the present moment and into the future. This reconciliation of temporal opposites sets a path toward answering the hermeneutical question in a temporal rather than a spatial manner. These dynamics of what I have named anachronism are on display in both biblical examples of anachronism as a theological device, and in medieval practical theologies as a means for making the biblical drama present and accessible to the contemporary church.

Biblical Anachronism: First Corinthians 10

First Corinthians 10:1–22 provides a fruitful discussion of anachronism as a theological and homiletical device in the early days of the Christian church.[37] Here, Paul addresses the concerns of the church in Corinth by intersecting the drama of Israel's past with the contemporary moment of Jesus Christ and the present theological issues faced by the church. In doing so he purposefully mixes up his interpretive communities, casting the Corinthians as participants in the ongoing drama which had its beginning long ago and the end of which they await. Paul's gospel intersects with and comes to expression within the present moment of the Corinthian church—the leading edge of the ongoing drama. The means by which Paul brings

---

37. Throughout this section translation of the First Corinthians text is my own.

these moments of the drama together is through a pervasive theological anachronism.

This text stands at the end of a longer section of the letter in which Paul is addressing the church's questions regarding meat sacrificed to idols. The practice of eating meat previously sacrificed to idols was a salient issue for the Corinthian Christians.[38] Craig Keener observes that much of the meat in Corinth, whether served in either a pagan temple or at people's homes or instead sold in the marketplace, had first been offered to idols in worship.[39] For Jews and Christians who might not always be certain of the origin of the meat served or sold to them, this posed a problem. Keener points out that this issue was probably even more pressing for converts from non-Jewish backgrounds: "Could they meet over lunch with business associates or fellow members of their trade guild, or attend a reception in a temple for a relative's wedding?"[40] Especially in light of the class and social struggles within Corinthian society, refusal to participate in such occasions could have been grounds for disassociation or worse.[41]

One of several angles Paul takes on the issue of idol meat and pagan meals presents excerpts from Israel's history, with Christ as the climax of that story, to decisively warn against participating in idol worship. Paul argues on the basis of God's actions with the community of faith in the past, enrolling the Corinthians in this ongoing drama in the present, by utilizing theological anachronism as the primary communicative/homiletical device within an overarching dramatic matrix.

In 1 Corinthians 10 Paul's gospel, that is, the story of Israel intersected with the story of Christ, comes to expression in an anachronism that brings together Israel's past failings with the Corinthians' present situation. The two moments of the story are not so much told alongside one another as they are told within each other. Paul begins this re-presentation of Israel's story by recalling the potential and blessing of their "fathers" (v. 1), Israel, and their subsequent failings in the desert. It is significant that as Paul begins to retell Israel's story he specifically identifies the Israelites in the story as the Corinthians' own "fathers" (οἱ πατέρες ἡμῶν; v. 1), especially given that the letter is written to a predominantly Gentile community. The force of

---

38. For fuller background, see Willis, *Idol Meat in Corinth*, and Blue, "Food Offered to Idols."

39. Keener, *IVP Bible Background Commentary*, 469.

40. Ibid., 469–70.

41. See Hays's discussion, *First Corinthians*, 137: "For those few Corinthian Christians who were among the wealthier class . . . their public and professional duties virtually required the networking that occurred through attending and sponsoring such events."

this is to identify from the outset of his argument that Corinthian believers are included in the theological history of the Jewish people—to indicate that they are a part, or continuation, of the theological story of Israel. Hays notes on this point that for Paul "the story of Israel is for the Gentile Corinthians not somebody else's story; it is the story of their own authentic spiritual ancestors."[42]

These first verses serve to highlight the blessings Israel received in the desert and to link the Israelites in the desert and the believers in Corinth in common faith in a common God. This specifically is the dramatic, or canonical-linguistic, framework of the Christian drama. Paul deliberately includes all of Israel in the blessings received, and he links the Corinthians to these blessings through theological anachronism in reading Christ into the past narrative:[43]

> For I do not want you to be ignorant brothers
> that our fathers
> *were all* [πάντες] under the cloud
> and
> *they all* [πάντες] passed through the sea.
> And
> *all* [πάντες] were baptized into Moses
> in the cloud and in the sea.
> And
> *all* [πάντες] ate the same spiritual food.
> And
> *all* [πάντες] drank the same spiritual drink.
> For, they were drinking from the spiritual rock following them,
> and the rock was Messiah.

Paul refers to the Exodus narrative, especially chapters 13 (pillars of cloud and fire, v. 21), 14 (the Red Sea crossing, v. 22), and 17 (water from the rock, v. 6). It is clear from Paul's repetition and parallelism that he understands the blessing of God to have been on all of Israel and that the Corinthian believers are included in this same blessing. There is a temporal/dramatic link here between Paul's identification of the Israelites' "baptism" into Moses and the Corinthians' implied baptism into Christ (v. 2). "Spiritual food" and "spiritual drink" (vv. 3, 4) parallel the Corinthians' own practice of the

---

42. Ibid., 160.

43. See also Thiselton, *First Epistle,* 724–25; Hays, *First Corinthians,* 160; Fee, *First Epistle to the Corinthians,* 443–44.

Lord's Supper. And, finally, Paul purposefully and anachronistically reads Christ into the Israel narrative, showing that "in every respect Israel enjoyed the grace and presence of God."[44]

Verse 5, with its adversative ἀλλά (nevertheless), introduces Israel's failing despite their relation to God.[45] Verses 6–11 outline specific examples from Israel's history in which their behavior provoked God's wrath. Paul presents this poetically through parallelism and in a grammatically chiastic pattern:

> A   Now these things happened as patterns for us
> > so that we would not desire evil
> > > just as they desired.
> > B   Do not become [imperative] idolaters
> > > just as some of them.
> > > > As it is written, "The people sat down to eat,
> > > > > and to drink,
> > > > > > and they stood up to play."
> > > C   Nor should we commit [subjunctive] sexual immorality
> > > > just as some of them committed [aorist] sexual immorality,
> > > > > and twenty three thousand fell in one day.
> > > C1 Nor should we test [subjunctive] Messiah
> > > > just as some of them tested [aorist],
> > > > > and by the serpents were destroyed.
> > B1 Do not complain [imperative]
> > > just as some of them complained [aorist],
> > > > and were destroyed by the Destroyer.
> A1 Now these things happened to them as a pattern,
> > and it was written down for our instruction,
> > > upon whom the ends of the ages have come.

Verses 6 and 11, both beginning with the phrase "Now these things happened as patterns/as a pattern," serve to frame the discussion as between communities interconnected through a unified temporality in the ongoing drama of God's presence with his people. The four examples of Israel's failings in spite of God's presence and blessings are set out as a pattern for the

---

44. Hays, *First Corinthians*, 160. See also Fee, *First Epistle to the Corinthians*, 445.
45. Fee, *First Epistle to the Corinthians*, 449.

Corinthians' moral direction. Hays phrases it this way: "The arrogant idolatry of the Israelites and the terrifying punishments imposed upon them by God actually foreshadow the perilous situation of the Corinthian church in the present time: anyone with eyes to see should learn the appropriate lessons."[46] Paul makes it clear that the incidents he describes were "written down for our instruction" (v. 11), that is, they are meant to serve as examples for Paul and the Corinthians in their present moment.

The four exhortations and their reinforcing examples are structured in parallel triplets with the form:

> Exhortation to the Corinthians : Israel's failure : Israel's consequences

The exhortation or command is given in either the imperative or subjunctive mood as Paul warns against potential actions. Israel's (poor) example is stated in the Greek aorist, indicating that it is something that has already happened: Do not do . . . as they *already did*. The consequences of Israel's actions allude to different incidents from Israel's history and serve to show how God has already acted in response to the behaviors Paul warns against and eventually links with the Corinthians' current situation. It is important to note that the incidents Paul cites here all occur in the context of idolatry. Through metonymy Paul alludes to one portion of Israel's drama in order to bring to memory the fuller narrative, both its context and its consequences.

The first historical warning occurs in verse 7 where Paul commands the Corinthians to not "become idolaters, just as some of them." Here Paul quotes from the Septuagint (LXX) of Exodus 32:6. On the surface, "the people sat down to eat and to drink and they stood up to play" does not come across as recording a consequence of Israel's behavior, but rather as the actual content of their action.[47] The context of Exodus 32, however, makes the force of Paul's usage more clear. Exodus 32 is occupied with Israel's betrayal of God in their creation and worship of an idol, the golden calf. Paul only quotes a portion of the incident, but as Hays notes, "the quotation works powerfully for any reader who recognizes its source."[48] The quotation of the text points to Israel's sin and alludes to the consequences of that sin.[49] Further, the one verse Paul chose from the story deals with the people eating

---

46. Hays, *First Corinthians*, 162.
47. Fee, *First Epistle to the Corinthians*, 454.
48. Hays, *First Corinthians*, 163.
49. Fee notes that the subtlety of this explanation may be too much for some modern interpreters, but that it may "indicate that these early Christians knew their Bibles better than most moderns do, so that the allusion itself was enough to give them recall of the biblical context" (*First Epistle to the Corinthians*, 454).

and drinking in the presence of an idol, behavior that strikes at the heart of the Corinthian practice of attending meals in the temples of idols.

The example Paul produces in verse 8 alludes to Numbers 25:1–9. Paul has already addressed the issue of sexual immorality in this Corinthian correspondence (5:1–13; 6:12–20; 7:2–5), and the allusion here to the passage in Numbers serves to highlight the connection between sexual immorality and idolatry.[50] Numbers 25:1–2 says, "While Israel lived at Shittim, the people began to whore with the daughters of Moab. These invited the people to the sacrifices of their gods [LXX=idols], and the people ate and bowed down to their gods [LXX=idols]." Again Paul alludes to an instance of Israel engaging in idolatry, this time through sexual immorality that included eating in the presence of foreign idols.[51] The consequence for Israel was a plague resulting in the death of twenty-three thousand in one day.[52]

The third and fourth incidents here follow the same pattern, utilizing a unified temporal hermeneutic. Verse 9 warns against testing Christ, or Messiah, "as some of them tested." This is the second instance in which Paul has read Christ into the historical Israel narrative in a purposefully anachronistic manner. Paul brings to mind an incident in Israel's wanderings recorded in Numbers 21:4–9 in which the Israelites "spoke against God and against Moses" (v. 5) and in which the Israelites' disobedience to God again has to do with food and drink. The consequence for Israel's testing of God was the death of many by serpents. Paul's specificity in commanding the Corinthians not to test "Messiah," though the Israelites were not, strictly speaking, testing Christ, links Israel and Corinth in temporal and theological unity.[53] Finally, verse 10 warns against complaint, and the incident is most likely that recounted in Numbers 14:26–38.[54] The comprehensiveness of God's judgment here, in which all of Israel is punished, serves as a fitting crescendo to Paul's walk through Israel's dramatic history.

The second bookend here comes in verse 11. Echoing verse 6, Paul reminds the Corinthians that "these things" (the events he has just referred to) happened to Israel "as a pattern." The implication is clear, as Hays sums up: "Paul's heaping up of examples from the Pentateuchal narratives has demonstrated emphatically that God is not to be trifled with. Those who defy God's authority by flirting with idolatry and 'craving' idol-tinged food

---

50. Hays, *First Corinthians*, 164.

51. Ibid.

52. Numbers 25:9 records the number as twenty-four thousand. Some Greek manuscripts have changed the number to reconcile it with the Numbers passage.

53. Hays, *First Corinthians*, 165; Fee, *First Epistle to the Corinthians*, 457.

54. Fee, *First Epistle to the Corinthians*, 457–58.

will suffer catastrophic consequences."⁵⁵ God has dealt with these instances in his past dealings with his people; God will address present, similar situations similarly. God is consistent throughout the drama.

Finally in verse 11, Paul notes his readers' position as ones "upon whom the ends of the ages have come" (εἰς οὓς τὰ τέλη τῶν αἰώνων κατήντηκεν). This specifically eschatological statement is loaded with a Jewish apocalyptic worldview, Paul's theological background, coming to collision with the narrative of Christ and thereby altering Paul's theology. The import of this statement for our current study is to show that for Paul, eschatology gives the dramatic framework a unified temporality in which all of these incidents from the past become relevant for the present.[56] Within this eschatological drama the Corinthians are enrolled as actors, participants in God's enacted narrative. The part of the story that has already unfolded, Paul says, has been recorded for the ethical direction of those in Christ in the present. It is precisely in this theological overlap of the ages that the stories of the Israelites and those of the Corinthians are told together. This shows the temporal, dramatic, and eschatological natures of Paul's worldview, and the anachronistic quality of his practical theology.

Paul's inclusion of the Corinthians as inheritors of the past yet ongoing narrative of their fathers Israel implies that he viewed the Corinthians (and one might include believers through time) as properly taking direction for the present performance of their faith from the previous enactment of the story. Paul engages in the activity of enrolling the Corinthian church in an ongoing drama of God's relationship with God's people. He draws on God's action in the past history of Israel and he refers to the more recent action of God in Christ with God's people, read anachronistically into the Israel narrative and as a very present reality in his invocation of the Lord's Supper (vv. 14–22). In this way, Paul paints a picture of God's action with God's people that encompasses all of human time, binding past, present, and future times, which catches the Corinthian Christians up in the middle.

In 1 Corinthians 10:1 Paul narrates the Corinthian, mostly Gentile, believers into God's drama by labeling the Israelites of the past "our fathers." Paul is not concerned that the Israelites are not literally the Corinthians' fathers, nor that a large number of the Corinthians are not of Israel at all. Instead, he brings together past and present by reading the Corinthians back into the Israel narrative anachronistically with imaginative, communicative, and theological purpose. Paul continues his broken-time description

---

55. Ibid.
56. For a larger discussion of Paul's eschatological framework as developed out of Jewish apocalyptic beliefs, see Dunn, *Theology of Paul*, 462–65.

of this pan-temporal drama in verse 4, saying, "For they [the Israelites] were drinking from the spiritual rock following them, and the rock was Messiah," and in verse 9, "Nor should we test Messiah, just as some of them tested." Identifying the Israelites as "fathers" and enacting Christ into the ancient narrative weaves present and past in an imaginative, participatory, and theological manner. The Israelites become characters in the Corinthians' story, and the Corinthians and Christ become explicit characters in Israel's. Anachronism here is a hermeneutical, homiletical, and relational device, bringing together past and present time and past and present characters in the drama.

Other Biblical Anachronisms

In addition to this text in Paul's letter to Corinth he uses theological anachronism elsewhere to explicitly bind present and future realities. This future-moving anachronism is present in the different tenses, for instance, in which Paul identifies his audience as "sons of God" in Romans 8. In verse 15 he says, "you have received the Spirit of adoption as sons." The verb λαμβάνω ("to receive") occurs in the aorist tense, indicating that this action has already been completed in the past. Further, verse 16 declares in the present tense (ἐσμὲν) "we are children of God," indicating a present reality. Nevertheless, Paul goes on to say in verses 19 and 23 that adoption is simultaneously a future reality still awaited: "We ourselves, who are the firstfruits of the Spirit, groan inwardly as we wait eagerly for adoption as sons" (v. 23). The already and not-yet nature of the believer's adoption as God's child catches him or her in a temporal tension between the completion of adoption in the past which affects the present reality that God's people are indeed God's children, while also awaiting the consummation of adoption as God's future promise. Here, Paul acknowledges the future promise but intentionally calls that promise into the present, an eschatological anachronism.

New Testament authors outside of Paul bend time in this way as well. While not using the term *anachronism*, homiletician Thomas Long describes Luke's temporal abnormalities in Acts' Pentecost narrative. Pointing to the list of ethnic groups present to witness the events of the day, Long notes the improbability of Luke's account:

> Customarily the presence of this lengthy list is thought simply to say, "Jews were in Jerusalem from all over the world—east and west, north and south." That's true, as far as it goes, but it doesn't go nearly far enough. This conglomeration of peoples is not only a diverse and pluralistic gathering of tourists, it is also

an historically impossible collection of folks, save in the sort of burlesque narrative Luke's eschatology evokes. Consider the Medes, for instance. They must have had a rather difficult journey to Jerusalem since they would not only have had to travel several hundred miles, but several hundred years as well, Medes having already disappeared from the canvas of history. The same is true evidently of Elamites, who seemed to have wandered over to this Pentecost story not from the Tigris River, where Elamites once lived, but rather from the annals of history and particularly the pages of the Old Testament (see especially Ezra 2:7).[57]

This is not a defect of Luke's narrative, however. Luke's list of nations both current and extinct is a function of his eschatology. Here one sees a reconstituted people of God created from every nation and tribe, both present and past, coming together in the last days when God's Spirit is poured out. Luke brings together "not only east and west, but the ancient and the contemporary, the living and the dead, the new and reconstituted Israel."[58] In this sense Luke's anachronism pulls both past and future together in the present, locating the present as the locus of eschatological promise.

These instances of anachronism, with others, within a dramatic theological matrix set the stage for contemporizing and eschatological anachronisms pervasive in medieval practical theologies.

Drama and Anachronism in Medieval Practical Theologies

In the medieval period of the church, especially throughout Europe, the communication of the gospel occurred in various and intertwined ways, largely rooted in a unified, dramatic understanding of time and driven into the present through purposeful anachronism. Two avenues of practical theology were the sermon and the religious drama.[59] G. R. Owst posits that the medieval sermon led the way and gave rise to dramatic interpretations of Scripture stories. He notes that "the sacred plays of the Middle Ages, which so obviously 'combined that moral and religious teaching of the homily with the exciting movement of the drama,' if independent in origin, at least must have had some subsequent points of contact with the sister art of the

---

57. Long, "Night at the Burlesque," 28.
58. Ibid.
59. The religious plays of the Middle Ages were dramatic enactments of the gospel or salvation history performed throughout society for the purpose of teaching a largely illiterate society with little access to Scripture.

pulpit."[60] While the answer to which came first is uncertain, it is unlikely that the two arts developed independently.[61] In both, a dramatic framework and theological anachronism are pervasive. Anachronism in medieval drama and pulpit both refines the anachronistic device as apparent in Paul and gives direction for the development of this device for the contemporary preacher.

While distinctly modern assessments of medieval theologies have argued otherwise, it is now evident that instances of anachronism in the medieval religious plays and sermons are purposeful and theological.[62] At least two distinct types of anachronism are evident in the church's practice: the contemporization of a narrative and use of an omnitemporal perspective. These can also be named contemporizing and eschatological anachronisms, respectively.

CONTEMPORIZATION OF A NARRATIVE

The first type of anachronism evident in the medieval church contemporizes the narrative and sees the biblical text recast into a decidedly medieval context. Action moves from its original location in the biblical text into the English countryside, for instance, it occurs in the vernacular and is enacted in the dress of the time. Kolve summarizes this dynamic of the anachronistic device in the religious dramas: "The Corpus Christi drama, then, establishes by costumes, settings and verbal reference a time and place that are roughly contemporary, and more or less English. This localizing of place must also be understood as part of the drama's interest in addressing its particular English audience in their particular moment in time, in holding up to them a mirror of their own society and its moral nature. This wish pervades the

---

60. Owst, *Literature and Pulpit*, 471. See also Owst, *Preaching in Medieval England*.

61. One compelling reason Owst presents for the sermon's precedence is that the sermon never ceased to be a part of the medieval drama, as most plays opened with a homily and included seemingly spontaneous sermonettes. Further, many of these sermonettes within the dramas were taken verbatim from medieval sermon manuscripts, exhibiting a dependence of the dramas on the pulpit—for instance, Lazarus's sermon in the Towneley/Wakefield play, which is recognized by Owst to be "practically word for word identical to the smallest detail with Bromyard's sermon upon the fate of the dead" (*Literature and Pulpit*, 486–87).

62. Auerbach has cautioned that one must "be very much on one's guard against taking such violations of chronology . . . as nothing more than a kind of medieval naïveté" (*Mimesis*, 158). For a distinctively modern assessment of medieval anachronism as naive or uncritical, see particularly Greene, *Vulnerable Text*, 220–22, and Bloch, *Feudal Society*, 90.

plays drawn from both the Old Testament and the New."[63] Contemporizing anachronism, which brings the past and the present moments together in temporal metaphor, keeps the central narrative intact but moves it into a new location or tells the story in different language, style, and scene. David Bevington refers to the styles brought together as "sacred" and "profane,"[64] while Auerbach labels them "sublime" and "everyday."[65]

Examples of contemporizing anachronisms abound in both medieval religious drama and preaching. The twelfth-century French play *Le Mystere d'Adam* (or *Ordo repraesentationis Adae*) uses anachronism in retelling the Genesis narrative in a manner immediately present and relatable to a medieval French audience. Auerbach notes that the drama shows elements of both sublime and humble styles in an effort to make the ancient story contemporary to the play's audience:

> The episode which is here presented to us in dramatic form is the starting point of the Christian drama of redemption, and hence is a subject of utmost sublimity from the point of view of the author and his audience. However, the presentation aims to be popular. The ancient and sublime occurrence is to become immediate and present; it is to be a current event which could happen any time, which every listener can imagine and is familiar with; it is to strike deep roots in the mind and the emotions of any random French contemporary. Adam talks and acts in a manner any member of his audience is accustomed to from his own neighbor's house; things would go exactly the same way in any townsman's home or on any farm where an upright but not very brilliant husband was tempted into a foolish and fateful act by his vain and ambitious wife who had been deceived by an unscrupulous swindler. The dialogue between Adam and Eve—this first man-woman dialogue of universal historical import—is turned into a scene of simplest everyday reality. Sublime as it is, it becomes a scene in simple, low style.[66]

The sublimity of the narrative is preserved in its subject, namely, that it is a biblical story about God, Adam, and Eve. The low style Auerbach notes is exercised in the drama's presentation of that essential narrative. The sublime event occurs within the audience's everyday life "so that it is spontaneously present to them." Simultaneously, the play does not lose its sublimity in that

63. Kolve, *Corpus Christi*, 113.
64. Bevington, *Medieval Drama*, 79.
65. Auerbach, *Mimesis*, 159.
66. Ibid., 151.

"it leads from the simplest reality directly to the highest, most secret, and divine truth."[67] The ancient narrative is made contemporary through this blending of styles and times. This practice holds modes of time and tension, drawing the story into the viewers' time and the viewers into participation in the narrative.

Kolve notes more specific examples of anachronism in the biblical plays and the device's purpose in teaching.[68] In the Towneley/Wakefield Judgment play a section of dialogue spoken by a demon criticizes the culture's preoccupation with fashion. Similarly, the sacrifice of Isaac is often presented in the plays to admonish children to obey their parents.[69] An exemplary model of this contemporizing is the Towneley/Wakefield play of Cain and Abel. Kolve describes the purposeful and unselfconscious anachronistic retelling of the story of Adam and Eve and their sons:

> The Towneley version allows Cain a boy servant, whom he insults and abuses and cannot entirely control; and after the murder, frightened of the bailiffs, Cain and his boy go through the streets of the town proclaiming a king's pardon for themselves. The first murder is shown as taking place in a highly organized medieval community. Its lesson is about murder, contemporary as well as historical; about unregenerate man, in any age, cut off from God; and, in a smaller, less important way, but also wholly contemporary, about men who cheat the Church in tithing. . . . The drama, in short, compensated for the formal unimportance of the audience moment by staging the past as though it were largely identical with present time, thereby honoring its specific audience while seeking (among other things) to amend their lives.[70]

In each of these examples the narrative is modernized, and in varying degrees it is also moralized.[71]

In the biblical plays localization is a significant aspect in the creation of meaning for the contemporary audience. Much of the action in the English plays, for instance, takes place in an English setting.[72] In the Towneley/

---

67. Ibid., 156.

68. Kolve and others have referred to these medieval plays collectively as Corpus Christi. The more recent trend is to name them simply biblical plays, as only the York cycle in England was consistently associated with the feast of Corpus Christi.

69. Kolve, *Corpus Christi*, 105.

70. Ibid.

71. Owst discusses the tendency towards moralization. Owst, *Literature and Pulpit*, 118–19.

72. Kolve notes that this "Anglicization" is most common in the Towneley and

Wakefield cycle, Noah's wife berates her husband for incompetence: "'thou were worthi be cled / In Stafford blew,' offering him a beating that will leave him the color of the famous blue cloth from Stafford."[73] In the Cain and Abel play above, after the murder and resultant judgment Cain requests that "he be buried at the head of Goodybower quarry, just outside the town" of Wakefield. Also in Towneley/Wakefield, a conversation between two demons makes it clear that the Judgment takes place up Watling Street in Wakefield:

> 1 DEMON. For to stand thus tome, thou gars me grete.
> 2 DEMON. Let us go to this dome, up Watlin Strete!
> 1 DEMON. I had lever go to Rome, yei, thrise, on my fete,
> Then for to grefe yonde grome, or with him for to mete![74]

Localization brings a narrative perceived as ancient and distant into an audience's immediate sphere of living. That the judgment occurs just down the street brings immediate import for the viewer, prompting contemporary recognition of and participation in the story.

Owst sees contemporizing anachronisms occurring frequently in the medieval sermon in addition to the plays. He notes that "the homilists are often wont to 'feudalize' scenes and characters of the sacred text": "With a deft touch here and there [preachers] bring [characters] 'up to date,' reclothing them like the ancients of the *Gesta Romanorum* or the sacred figures in early painting, in garments of the period, giving them contemporary titles and ranks, thus making them vivid and familiar to common English folks of the Middle Ages."[75] Drawing on various homiletical manuscripts from the Middle Ages, Owst gives numerous examples of sermons in which the narratives are brought into the present. Often this occurs through the use of contemporary titles for ancient characters. Moses is "a 'grett' and 'curious philosofre' of the schools, seeking to probe the mystery of the Burning Bush." Job "is clearly no other than a typical worthy 'frankelein' of Chaucer's England." Further, Jezebel is portrayed as a "tyrannic medieval queen" by Bromyard. John Myrc's sermons address Potiphar as "the maystyr of the kyngys knyghtys," and the High Priest as "the byschop of the Jewes lawe."[76]

Chester plays, a bit more rare in the Cornish cycle and the *Ludus Coventriae*, and almost absent from the York cycle. Kolve, *Corpus Christi*, 116.

73. Ibid., 112.

74. Bevington, *Medieval Drama*, 642. Quoted from "The Last Judgement (Wakefield)," lines 125–28. Also Kolve, *Corpus Christi*, 116.

75. Owst, *Literature and Pulpit*, 114.

76. Ibid., 115–16.

Owst points to a particular example "of the way in which a Scripture parable could be made not merely intelligible but vivid" for a medieval audience in a sermon on the Pharisee and the tax collector:

> But frendes, that thou spekest with thi mouthe thou must nedis thence itt with thin herte.... Ensampull hereof I rede in the gospell of seynte luke (Luc. xviii) that ther com a pharisew and a pupplicane into the tempull.... The phariseu, as sone as he com into the churche, he fell downe on ys knees amonge all the pepull oponly, and this was is preyor—"Now, lord god, thou knawiste my liff. I am no robbere, ne revere, ne no theff, as othur men are, ne no lechoure, ne proude man, ne noon extorcionere as this pupplicane is; and also I pey my tythes, and fastes ii daies in the weke for thi love." And when he had seid all this, he thanken god.[77]

In this scene the temple is transformed into a church, and the list of sins the Pharisee denies partaking in is tailored to the preacher's contemporary audience. The drama, with its added characteristic of performance, had even greater means of bringing the narrative into the moment. Costuming, setting, colloquial language, and contemporary titles were routinely used to bring the past event into present time.[78] This type of contemporizing anachronism reinforces the pan-temporal relationship between characters in the textual moment of God's overarching drama and those in the contemporary moment. In turn, the anachronism calls for participation in the ongoing and present moment of the drama.

An Omnitemporal Perspective

Omnitemporal perspective, an eschatologically based device, is another type of anachronism appearing in the medieval drama and sermon. Following Auerbach, omnitemporal perspective refers to characters within the play or sermon possessing knowledge that, temporally speaking, they should not possess.[79] Characters can see or know across time. This knowledge is imparted to characters on the basis of God's character as omniscient across time. Kolve notes that at times this device is used for the convenient purpose of providing "vivid, colloquial dialogue," as in the case of Noah

---

77. Quoted in ibid., 117.
78. Kolve, *Corpus Christi*, 113.
79. Auerbach, *Mimesis*, 160–61.

in the York cycle "speaking of the rainbow as a token sent 'tille all cristen men.'"[80] Noah, appearing in a medieval context, speaks as a historical character in a historical setting, while possessing later knowledge of Christ and fulfilled prophecy one would only have in the enactment's present moment. Alan Nelson observes, "Noah is a medieval man acting out the story of the Flood without discarding everything he knows from having lived after the Flood. He does not dissociate himself from his knowledge of Christ and His fulfillment of prophecies."[81]

The *Mystere d'Adam* (*Ordo repraesentationis Adae*) displays a sense of omnitemporality in its span of biblical history. The latter half of the play consists of a procession of Old Testament characters announcing the appearance of Christ. In this act of the play Abraham, Moses, David, Solomon, Daniel, Isaiah, and others give details about Christ that their historical characters, strictly speaking, should not know. Daniel predicts Christ's Passion as a direct result of his rejection by the Jewish authorities (lines 827–40).[82] Further, as the prophet Isaiah speaks about the coming of Christ someone rises to challenge, addressing him as "sire Ysaias" or "Sir Isaiah" (line 883), another example of contemporization of title. While the characters remain historical personages, their knowledge of biblical history after their own time is not impeded by the limited span of their lives. As this is predicated upon God's own omnitemporal knowledge, God's action is elevated in these works.

A homiletical example of omnitemporality can be found in St. Bernard of Clairvaux's eleventh-century "First Sermon for the Feast of Annunciation,"[83] and the related *Mary Play* from the N-Town Cycle.[84] Finding his generative idea in Psalm 85:10 ("Steadfast love and faithfulness meet; righteousness and peace kiss each other"), Bernard personifies the virtues as sisters, narrating a conflict between them over the salvation of humanity.[85] The omnitemporal perspective is evident in Bernard's sermon as he draws liberally on the New Testament to narrate this Old Testament text. The personified virtues in the *Mary Play*, as in Bernard's earlier sermon, come to conclusions about Christ and his work in removing enmity between God and humanity, between Mercy and Righteousness, that, strictly speak-

80. Kolve, *Corpus Christi*, 104.
81. Nelson, *Sacred and Secular*, 399, quoted in Kolve, *Corpus Christi*, 104.
82. Bevington, *Medieval Drama*, 117.
83. Bernard, *Sermons*, 134–52.
84. Language modernized by Johnston, ed., *The Mary Play*.
85. Bernard, *Sermons*, 145. Bernard records the text as Psalm 84:11 following the numbering of the Septuagint.

ing, would be a mystery in the historical moment of the psalm.[86] Both the sermon and the drama are constructed from eschatological anachronism, reading future revelation into the past/present.

Pulpit and stage in medieval England were undeniably connected, especially through the recurrence of artistic devices such as anachronism. Focusing on preachers' and dramatists' affinity for updating the biblical narratives and their related choice of themes for production, Owst concludes,

> The whole feudal array of tyrant-rulers and counselors, Bishops of the Jews' Law, knights and peasants, patriarchs and saints, sir Noe, sir Lazarus and the rest appear in their characteristic medieval dress. Furthermore, since both preacher and play-producer—like the artists of their period—are concerned pre-eminently with the same great mysteries of the Church as celebrated at Christmas, Epiphany, Lent and Eastertide, the one in his pulpit, the other upon his scaffold, we shall hardly be surprised to find a similar correspondence in their choice of Gospel themes.[87]

In these medieval arts of preaching and religious drama one repeatedly finds these anachronisms: the blending of narratives across style and time in the contemporization of narrative, and an omnitemporal stance towards time and history. The narratives are made familiar without losing their sublimity and approach past and future time as if it were present and local. Such a practical theology is made possible in a view of time as a unified whole and reveals an early dramatic organization of time.

Medieval Anachronism and Mimetic Communication

The medieval plays and sermons had a mimetic quality to them in calling for present enactment of the drama, rather than a more diegetic character that tends towards simple recitation. Kolve argues that one manner of looking at the biblical plays "is as a sequence of plays relating the history of the world in seven ages, offering to its audience, within that framework, an image of all human time."[88] Within this schema audiences occupy the sixth age, a time in history between that of Christ's advents (this is analogous to

---

86. Bernard's sermon is most likely earlier than *The Mary Play*, as Bernard lived between 1090 and 1153, while earliest manuscripts of *The Mary Play* date from the fifteenth century. See Kahrl and Johnston, *The N-Town Plays*. Lines 1247–50 of the play directly allude to the psalm.

87. Owst, *Literature and Pulpit*, 489–90.

88. Kolve, *Corpus Christi*, 101.

Wright's fifth act). While the sixth age is not especially important to the medieval mind in this context, witnessed to by the fact that events from the audience period are not dramatized in these plays, it is through a theological use of anachronism that the viewer's moment is incorporated into the drama and the viewer is confronted by his or her place within the drama of human time: "By means of a pervasive anachronism and anglicazation [the biblical plays] furnished a critical image of moral and social life in the latter Middle Ages. It is possible that these cycles felt no need to stage actions from present time because they staged all past actions as if they were present. The Corpus Christi drama managed to hold a mirror to the times while imitating the structure of human time."[89] The desired outcome of the dramas and the sermons was an amended life, an acting out of the drama in the present age by viewers and hearers. It was to be a present-enacted continuation of an ongoing and enveloping narrative—a mimetic performance.

Auerbach argues that "the figural 'omnitemporalness' of the events works most harmoniously and effectively toward the end of embedding them in the familiar setting of popular everyday life."[90] Kolve concludes about anachronism in the biblical plays as a mechanism for mimesis that "the wish to furnish moral lessons from history was important for both [drama and historiography], and the cycle-drama achieved this by a pervasive anachronism that made those lessons immediately and directly relevant for English medieval life. The technique may seem naïve, but its goal is conscious and sophisticated."[91] By presenting the past as occurring in present time, the sermons and dramas of the medieval liturgy elevated their present moment, seeking to have audiences see themselves through a biblical vision of reality and mimetically enact the continuation of that reality in the present.

One can also view anachronism in medieval drama and sermon within the context of a medieval theology of time. Auerbach suggests that instances of broken chronology should be understood as a simplified "expression of a unique, exalted, and hidden truth, the very truth of the figural structure of universal history."[92] Previous to the development of a historical consciousness in the Enlightenment and modern eras, and active in medieval religious drama and sermon, is a sense of time Auerbach characterizes as "mystical." He describes the conception of time informing medieval drama as itself dramatic:

89. Ibid., 104.
90. Auerbach, *Mimesis*, 161.
91. Kolve, *Corpus Christi*, 109.
92. Auerbach, *Mimesis*, 161.

> Everything in the dramatic play which grew out of the liturgy during the Middle Ages is part of one—and always the same—context: of one great drama whose beginning is God's creation of the world, whose climax is Christ's incarnation and passion, and whose expected conclusion will be Christ's second coming and the Last Judgment. . . . In principle, this great drama contains everything that occurs in world history. In it all the heights and depths of human conduct and all the heights and depths of stylistic expression find their morally or aesthetically established right to exist; and hence there is no basis . . . for concern with the unities of time, place, or, action, for there is but one place—the world; and but one action—man's fall and redemption.[93]

From this perspective the context for the plays and sermons is an omnitemporal reality that finds its basis in God's omnitemporality, holding modes of time in tension while placing an emphasis on God's work in the world across time.

Kolve comments on this temporal stance that in God there is no distinction between times. Drawing on Augustine's theology and its influence in the medieval period, Kolve states that if God stands above time then what is future to humanity must be present to God. Therefore, in God there is no distinction between past, present and future, and there is no foreknowledge with God in this sense, only knowledge of all time. In this way, past, present, and future are held in tension, and are viewed as essentially interrelated, or ultimately inseparable. This is a more holistic and dynamic view of time than the atomization displayed in more modern views of time.

Purposefully rooted in a theological view of time that saw God's omnitemporality as central, anachronism in the context of the medieval church's practical theology sought to communicate events of an ancient text within the life situation of the viewer/hearer, prompting towards an enactment of the present moment of the drama commensurate with what had come before and was still to come.[94] These past practices can serve as examples for contemporary preaching. I am not suggesting an uncritical emulation of all medieval practices. However, these are instructive for preaching in terms of the theology and function of drama and anachronism for homiletics today.

---

93. Ibid., 158.

94. In addition to being a function of the medieval view of time, Auerbach notes that the blending of sublime and low styles is a function of medieval Christology—the sublime and the lowly were merged ultimately in Christ's Incarnation. Ibid., 151.

Anachronism in Postmodern Communication

The rise of what we now refer to as the Enlightenment brought about significant shifts in thinking at the broadest levels. While shifts in scholarship provided considerable gains for theological thought, time's unity and organization suffered as time was increasingly atomized. In such a context the dynamic of temporal metaphor exhibited in medieval drama and sermon became not merely discardable, but largely logically impossible. Separating moments of time from the moments which gave rise to them and the moments that flow from them tends to objectify those events and diminish the eventfulness of God's drama. Alongside all of the gains in biblical scholarship and theology provided by a modern investigation into the text, the disintegration of time's unity and eventfulness is a lamentable loss.

Coming to the surface once again in a postmodern cultural milieu, currents within the arts have resisted the constraints of more modern conventions. It is not surprising that even in the medieval period it was the artistic endeavors of drama and sermon, and now in the postmodern context it is in the dramatic and artistic arenas, that artists feel unconfined by modern temporality in their creating. Time as conceived of in a modern hermeneutic does not inherently make a claim on the creation of meaning or experience in the dramatic arts. In the hands of the dramatist the unity and malleability of time work together to provide a powerful palette for creating new moments of participatory meaning and life affect. Postmodern drama has begun to recapture this feature of a temporal hermeneutic largely lost in Modernity. The sermon as dramatic art must recapture this as well. Contemporary cinema and graphic novel are two arenas of dramatic art that can inform preaching in a dramatic-anachronistic mode. With their ability to manipulate and create time and space through narrative presentation, these arts in particular have an ability to do more with drama, and specifically with time within the drama, than modern communicative paradigms.

Douglas Rushkoff: Testament

Media theorist and communication scholar Douglas Rushkoff has created a retelling of Pentateuchal narratives in the form of the graphic novel *Testament*.[95] The medium grants Rushkoff, and artist Liam Sharp, the ability to play and move inside and outside of time, telling an old story in two simultaneous moments: the ancient and the contemporary.

---

95. Rushkoff and Sharp, *Testament*.

Figure 1. Cover art from *Testament: Akedah*. Douglas Rushkoff and Liam Sharp, images used with permission.

In communicating ancient Jewish narratives Rushkoff (who comes at the text from a progressive Jewish perspective) wants to communicate that the Bible does not need to be stuck in time; it occurs in the real world today in a fluid temporality. He begins with the observation that we no longer maintain a sense of the fluidity of temporality, asserting that "we have lost access to the gaps in these stories. We're either afraid or forbidden to inhabit the places where temporality, interpretation, and sequence are up for grabs."[96] With a respect for the Bible ("I'm actually attempting to restore its integrity as perhaps the most transcendent narrative ever developed"), he insists that the comic book genre is the previously unavailable venue to present the ancient story, which "takes place in multiple universes at the same time—including our own."[97] Again, it is in the arts that temporality's unity and fluidity are restored: "For by insisting we 'believe' that the Bible happened at some point in distant history, the keepers of religion prevent us from realizing that the Bible is happening right now, in every moment."[98] Despite how one may react to Rushkoff's particular theology, his hermeneutic in communicating the biblical narrative is innovative.

Figure 2. Abraham prepares Isaac, and Alan prepares Jake, for the sacrifice. Douglas Rushkoff and Liam Sharp, *Testament: Akedah*.

96. Ibid.
97. Ibid.
98. Ibid.

The first story arc in the series tells the Akedah story of Abraham's willingness to sacrifice his son, and its aftermath. The ancient story is visually and narratively told alongside the same story playing out in contemporary time.[99] The characters are all present in both moments of time: an unseen yet not unheard God directing the story through divine surrogates Melchezidek and Elijah; Abraham and his son Isaac; Lot and his wife and daughters; a cadre of other gods set against God's people and God's story. In the retelling the story plays out as familiar in the ancient setting. In panels telling the story now the drama is re-presented as a father struggles with sacrificing his son to a militant and violent global capitalism. In both moments the father is faced with the question of whether he will sacrifice his son to society's gods. The ancient story is brought into the present as both stories are told simultaneously (the story panels for each time are presented together); neither ancient nor contemporary characters lose their own identities, and neither moment in the story loses its eventfulness as a moment in time. The stories are simultaneously unique and the same. The moment of reading creates a third moment in which the two narratives come together to create a new space for understanding and experience.

The story, and the visual and narrative imagery that compose it, continues through the events of and surrounding the sacrifice of Isaac. Abraham's negotiation over the fate of Sodom is retold in two times:

---

99. Ibid.

Figure 3. Abraham intercedes for Sodom. Douglas Rushkoff and Liam Sharp, *Testament: Akedah.*

Abraham's victory in battle over giants (literal then, military-technological now) occurs simultaneously in two separate moments as God directs the story for the formation of his people:

Figure 4. Defeat of the Anakim. Douglas Rushkoff and Liam Sharp, *Testament: Akedah*.

In some ways a thread of this dynamic of reality existing in temporal fluidity has pulled through in the practices of the church. The crucifixion and resurrection, for instance, were unique events in human history, yet we continue to experience these events in various ways moment by moment through time. This is especially true in the sacrament of communion, in which Christ's death and resurrection are experienced and proclaimed as often as the ritual occurs. Rushkoff takes a theology of time and temporality seriously in his interpretation and communication. Indeed, the temporal space between then and now becomes a feature rather than a bug of the hermeneutical question.

Baz Luhrmann: William Shakespeare's Romeo + Juliet

Anachronism as an artistic and communicative device within a dramatic matrix is evident outside of distinctly theological contexts. Homiletical theory can recognize and learn the hermeneutics of, as well as drama and anachronism from, popular media such as contemporary cinema. Cinema is an art form that regularly capitalizes on these artistic devices. The purposeful use of drama and anachronism in film has the potential to teach the preacher ways of taking advantage of these concepts for communicating from the pulpit. The films I explore below reveal the artistic nature of anachronism within a dramatic framework and can further show what these concepts look like in practice, both artistically and homiletically. The potential for this type of study, however, is not limited to these particular films. Preaching would benefit from paying greater attention to cultural arts such as cinema, television, music, and commercials.

I've chosen director and artist Baz Luhrmann's films for discussion. These films in particular highlight the use of purposeful anachronism within their dramatic matrix. Each of these provide vibrant examples of how the preacher as dramatic artist can use drama and anachronism in the pulpit. Specifically, these films arise out of a unique dramatic matrix that seeks to make ancient stories accessible through dramatic participation in the narrative in the present. This is similar to the preacher's task in a dramatic-anachronistic homiletic. Anachronism in these films is a primary vehicle for participation. These anachronisms are accomplished practically as the filmmaker purposefully shapes time within the drama (montage), and shapes scenes visually (mise-en-scène). Through a study of popular film beyond its use as sermon illustration the preacher wishing to engage a dramatic-anachronistic homiletic can gain insight on wrinkling time with anachronism, gaining participation in the drama in the present, how both backward- and forward-looking anachronisms are created through montage and mise-en-scène, and for the use of vibrant imagery to create the temporal metaphors desired. Here Luhrmann's films will serve as examples of the cinematic art. Chapter 5 will bring together a homiletic within a dramatic-anachronistic framework that pulls the threads discussed here together for preaching.

A Dramatic Matrix: Red Curtain Cinema

Dramatic narrative is the foundation of nearly all popular cinema.[100] Film serves as a prime example of enacted narrative. For the preacher, a dramatic framework and especially purposeful anachronism in contemporary cinema is beautifully displayed in Australian filmmaker Baz Luhrmann's distinct cinematic style. He showcases this style in at least three of his films, collectively titled the *Red Curtain Trilogy*. *Strictly Ballroom* (1992), *William Shakespeare's Romeo + Juliet* (1996, hereafter *Romeo + Juliet*) and *Moulin Rouge!* (2001) all display a distinct filmmaking style Luhrmann has named Red Curtain Cinema. Three specific artistic qualities in Red Curtain Cinema function as distinct characteristics of the dramatic narrative and can be substantial for the preacher seeking to preach from a dramatic framework.[101]

First, the writing process begins with a well-known foundational myth or story structure. This underlying story is recognizable to the audience. In *Strictly Ballroom* the "David and Goliath" and "Ugly Duckling" narratives are wed to tell a story about overcoming seemingly insurmountable odds. *Romeo + Juliet*, according to Luhrmann, is itself a primary myth with a core message of "youthful love in conflict with society." The "Orphean Journey" (or "Orpheus and Eurydice") forms the narrative basis of *Moulin Rouge!*[102] Luhrmann works with the core narrative in such a way as to have its meaning emerge within the present. This cinematic goal is similar to the preacher's commitment to the text: another moment in the overarching narrative emerges in the present for fitting enactment. Luhrmann's art makes that earlier narrative understandable and eventful for participation today. This is parallel to the preacher's homiletical art on many fronts.

In a second aspect of this dramatic style the foundational narrative is set in a "heightened creative world," that is, a setting that can be described as outside of the stories' original settings but that is recognizable to the audience. *Strictly Ballroom* is set in the world of competitive ballroom dancing,

---

100. See especially McKee, *Story*.
101. Luhrmann, *Behind the Red Curtain*.
102. Ibid.

a romanticized activity that many would recognize, even if not by firsthand experience. A fictional city named Verona Beach, modeled on Miami Beach and Los Angeles and with a South American feel, replaces Shakespeare's Verona in Luhrmann's *Romeo + Juliet*. The Orphean myth of *Moulin Rouge!* is set in 1899 Paris at the famous Moulin Rouge cabaret.[103] Luhrmann's move through time and setting is founded upon temporal metaphor within a dramatic matrix. At the core, Luhrmann brings the ancient story into contact with a contemporary moment, context, activity, or culture. This blending of styles through what is fundamentally anachronism is accomplished largely through first the drama itself, but also the film's montage and mise-en-scène. These will be discussed below. What Luhrmann does here with a story's entirety is what I have proposed in a dramatic-anachronistic homiletic. These films are anachronistic on the whole, which is one way in which the sermon can take advantage of anachronism—in creating the story in its entirety with an anachronistic quality. Luhrmann's films serve as a model for the preacher wishing to preach anachronistically.

The third element in Luhrmann's cinematic language is that in each film he develops a specific communicative and participatory device that runs through the narrative and serves a dual function. The dramatically embedded device serves to continually remind the audience that they are watching a film and not "reality through a keyhole."[104] The second function of this device is to invite the audience to participate in the experience of the film. This, too, corresponds to the practice of preaching. While the preacher affirms the reality of the biblical text, it is her or his goal to have the listener continue participating in the drama beyond the text itself and beyond the sermon. The moment of interaction between past and present or present and future is an important moment of participation, but it is not the moment most emphasized. The goal of preaching in a dramatic-anachronistic homiletic is the living out of the drama after the sermon ends. The sermon leads listeners to an ongoing life that is fitting with the script. The anachronistic moment leads to participation in all moments.

For Luhrmann, anachronism (a word he does not use but that is descriptive of his artistic style) can encompass the entirety of a narrative, as described above, or can be used as smaller image devices. There is insight here too for the preacher. Anachronism as image device is particularly suited to call for participation, both in film and sermon. Luhrmann comments, "They're [audiences] allowed to participate in [the movie] . . . It demands of the audience that they commune in the story that's playing out in front

103. Ibid.
104. Ibid.

of them."[105] An example of this is the preservation of the iambic pentameter and original dialogue of Shakespeare's script in *Romeo + Juliet*, even while moving the film into the present. This reinforces the age of the narrative while maintaining its classic status. As a musical, *Moulin Rouge!* relies on spontaneous musical numbers, presented almost as contemporary music videos, to involve the audience and drive the narrative forward. Though the ancient myth is set in 1899 the film continually makes use of twentieth-century popular music, employing songs ranging from Madonna's "Like a Virgin" to The Beatles' "All You Need Is Love." These songs are presented to make an antique narrative resonate with late twentieth-century viewers.

In the contemporary sermon, as moments are brought together and objects, dialogue, or scenery seem out of place, the hearer is reminded of the ancientness of the text and the simultaneous demands it makes on the contemporary moment. In terms of narrative-length anachronism, the text can be moved into the present, or the present moved into the past or future. These anachronisms are akin to contemporizing location or scene in the medieval plays, and in Luhrmann's cinema. In terms of anachronistic image devices, when the text talks about a "boat," the preacher may, through imaginative language and dynamic metaphor, talk about the presence of a Boston Whaler, an inflatable raft, or a ski boat, depending on the text's and congregation's contexts, as well as the story that the preacher is trying to tell. Medieval contemporization of dress or title is an example here, and Luhrmann's films provide vivid examples to the preacher for how one might do this.

Contemporary cinema begins with the dramatic framework that I am advocating for homiletics. It is within this temporal framework of action across time that anachronism becomes possible and effective. More guidance is found in the different ways of manipulating time and scene in cinema.

Shaping Time and Scene: Montage and Mise-en-scène

In cinema the drama is moved forward through two interrelated elements: montage and mise-en-scène. Montage refers to editing, the juxtaposition of images on the screen to create a desired effect, reaction, emotion, or narrative direction. It is a deliberate shaping of narrative time in a film. In montage, the filmmaker decides which images are placed before the viewer, in which order, and to what desired effect. Mise-en-scène refers to everything placed before the camera, everything in the scene. To shape the scene is to decide what images are placed in a scene, how they look, and to what

---

105. Ibid.

desired effect. Both of these elements play into the development of anachronism in film and sermon. Montage has the power to play with time in such a way that different moments are placed together to create *this* moment, bringing about a desired meaning/effect that is not contained in either individual shot alone.[106] Mise-en-scène determines how the viewer/listener will see these images visually. A practical study of how Luhrmann uses montage and mis-en-scène in one of his films, *Romeo + Juliet*, can reveal the creativeness and effectiveness of these devices, and point the preacher in this creative direction for the sermon. Luhrmann creates anachronism through manipulation of montage and mise-en-scène.[107]

In *Romeo + Juliet* the twentieth-century composite Verona Beach replaces sixteenth-century Verona.[108] The story's mis-en-scène is created out of images familiar to twentieth-century audiences and employs features foreign to Shakespeare's time period. With skyscrapers, muscle cars, bright Hawaiian-style shirts displaying religious iconography, and semiautomatic handguns, quickly it becomes evident that his is a different interpretation of the classic story. This marked difference between Luhrmann's interpretation of Shakespeare's Verona and traditional portrayals of the play becomes apparent when images are compared with those of other productions. Franco Zeffirelli's 1968 staging of the play for the screen remains one of the most critically acclaimed of all Romeo and Juliet films.[109] Comparing the two films' mise-en-scène one can see that the narratives are created in different moments for different purposes.

Figure 5. Mise-en-scène: Verona Beach, *William Shakespeare's Romeo + Juliet* (Bazmark and 20th Century Fox, 1996).

106. Bordwell and Thompson, *Film Art*, 504.

107. These examples of anachronism may also reveal a relative familiarity with such communicative devices in popular culture, making them already recognizable when used in the sermon.

108. Luhrmann, *Behind the Red Curtain*.

109. Ebert, review of *Romeo and Juliet*.

Figure 6. Mise-en-scène: Verona, *Romeo and Juliet* (Paramount Pictures, 1968).

Figure 7. Mise-en-scène in *William Shakespeare's Romeo + Juliet* (Bazmark and 20th Century Fox, 1996).

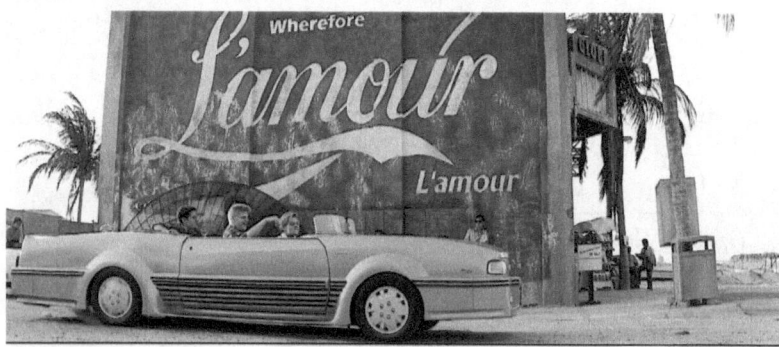

Figure 8. Mise-en-scène in *William Shakespeare's Romeo + Juliet* (Bazmark and 20th Century Fox, 1996).

Figure 9. Mise-en-scène in *Romeo and Juliet* (Paramount Pictures, 1968).

Costuming in each film provides another example of setting the ancient in the now:

Figure 10. Costuming in *William Shakespeare's Romeo + Juliet* (Bazmark and 20th Century Fox, 1996).

Figure 11. Costuming in *Romeo and Juliet* (Paramount Pictures, 1968).

The time and space shift of the drama is apparent in the mis-en-scène of the wedding ceremony:

Figure 12. Wedding scene in *William Shakespeare's Romeo + Juliet* (Bazmark and 20th Century Fox, 1996).

Figure 13. Wedding scene in *Romeo and Juliet* (Paramount Pictures, 1968).

Luhrmann has brought the narrative into a contemporary, more familiar setting through the appearance of present-day (as of 1996) clothing, mass-market billboards, and wedding fashion. He comments on his mise-en-scène that "Verona Beach is . . . the Elizabethan world created out of a collage of twentieth-century images to explain the circumstances of the world in which the play is set. And so you start to see images and references from the twentieth century brought together in a sort of potpourri that . . . was definitely twentieth century but absolutely Elizabethan."[110] Neither the original story (preserved through the narrative framework and in the original Shakespearean dialogue) nor the present moment (the viewer is aware of his or her own presence in the experience) is collapsed into the other in this temporal metaphor. Essentially, Luhrmann has brought the past text into the present, a comtemporizing anachronism of the story's dramatic matrix. He has done this through the creative manipulation of time and scene with montage and mise-en-scène.

Fusing Images in Anachronism

Participation is further called for in Luhrmann's films through the fusion of familiar narratives and mise-en-scène, a certain brand of anachronism. This involves mis-en-scène set in motion by montage. To help the audience make sense of an ancient story that is relatively unfamiliar, Luhrmann engages in a practice of fusing contradicting story styles and structures together to create a narrative experience that is new yet still familiar and faithful to the

110. Luhrmann, *Behind the Red Curtain*.

core of the central story/myth.[111] This is a facet of contemporary cinema that the preacher can create in the preaching art. Preaching deals with a text written in a time that is often unfamiliar to a sermon audience. In reaching for familiar images and fusing them with the unfamiliar, the preacher brings the ancient text into focus in a familiar context. This is akin to Bushnell's use of metaphor in explaining the unknown by means of the known, though for Luhrmann and for a dramatic-anachronistic homiletic the metaphor is dynamically set in time.

The opening scene of *Romeo + Juliet*, where all characters appear in a contemporary setting yet retain the dialogue of Shakespeare's text, is an example of this fusion. To help the audience make the narrative leap, Luhrmann uses recognizable imagery and narrative devices from a well-known genre of cinema, the Western. He brings them together through the devices of montage and mise-en-scène. In the establishing confrontation between the Montagues and Capulets, Elizabethan horses are traded for "pony cars" and handguns replace swords. The camera angles, close-ups of cowboy heels, cigarettes, and the sign swinging in the breeze, however, do not naturally conjure images of a Latin beach community or the Elizabethan world. Rather, they are elemental images that evoke an altogether different feeling: a Western gunfight. Luhrmann believed that despite not being a direct part of Shakespearean pastiche, or most contemporary lives, the Western shootout, a classic form of popular cinema, would be identifiable to his audience. These images and conventions anachronistically fused with the Shakespearean narrative help the audience understand this story retold.

Comparing mise-en-scène and montage from *Romeo + Juliet* and a Western from the same time period, *Tombstone* (1993), it is likely that Luhrmann has deliberately brought together many images from the Western in general, and possibly this film in particular, with his creation of the gas station scene:[112]

---

111. Wilson has written of fusion in terms of homiletics as "a process, first of the preacher finding the people's story in the biblical story and second of the congregation recognizing their faith story in it. Fusion has to do with finding or being found by God" (*Broken Words*, 80). What Luhrmann does here is similar, though not specifically theological. He is engaged in shaping an unfamiliar narrative according to familiar narrative, dramatic, and visual structures that will then make the ancient story as retold in the film accessible for present audiences.

112. This imagery is not limited to *Tombstone*, but as a part of the Western genre spans a large number of Western films. I have chosen *Tombstone* because of the relatively close release dates of the two films and the overt similarity between their mise-en-scène.

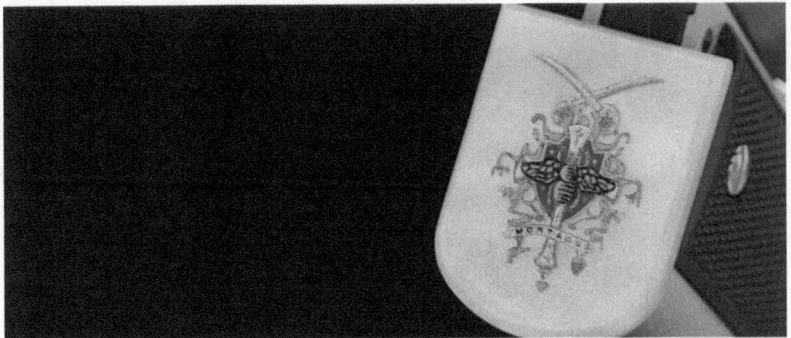

Figure 14. Engraved gun in *William Shakespeare's Romeo + Juliet* (Bazmark and 20th Century Fox, 1996).

Figure 15. Engraved gun in *Tombstone* (Hollywood Pictures and Cinergi Pictures, 1993).

Figure 16. Ornate boots in *William Shakespeare's Romeo + Juliet* (Bazmark and 20th Century Fox, 1996).

Figure 17. Ornate boots in *Tombstone* (Hollywood Pictures and Cinergi Pictures, 1993).

Figure 18. Gunfight in *William Shakespeare's Romeo + Juliet* (Bazmark and 20th Century Fox, 1996).

Figure 19. Gunfight in *Tombstone* (Hollywood Pictures and Cinergi Pictures, 1993).

Figure 20. Child with toy gun in *Romeo + Juliet* (Bazmark and 20th Century Fox, 1996).

Figure 21. Child with toy guns in *Tombstone* (Hollywood Pictures and Cinergi Pictures, 1993).

Figure 22. Scene on fire in *William Shakespeare's Romeo + Juliet* (Bazmark and 20th Century Fox, 1996).

Figure 23. Scene on fire in *Tombstone* (Hollywood Pictures and Cinergi Pictures, 1993).

Figure 24. Costuming in *William Shakespeare's Romeo + Juliet* (Bazmark and 20th Century Fox, 1996).

Figure 25. Costuming in *Tombstone* (Hollywood Pictures and Cinergi Pictures, 1993).

In re-creating the Shakespearean drama from a collage of twentieth-century images Luhrmann has purposefully contemporized the narrative by fusing images and narrative devices familiar to his audience with the language and dramatic core of *Romeo and Juliet* to have this story emerge within the viewer's temporal moment. Fusion begins to answer that question of where the preacher finds her or his images for anachronism. In short, the preacher uses the familiar to unmask the unfamiliar in a moment that is a strange blend of the two. This communicative strategy is anachronistic in its blending of times as it attempts to secure understanding of and participation in the presented drama.

The possibilities for this type of fusion of familiar and unfamiliar narratives, created through artistic manipulation of montage and mise-en-scène, are potent for preaching. Studying a film like *Romeo + Juliet* in terms of its anachronistic character created from a purposeful rendering of time and image helps the preacher shape the time and scenes of his or her sermon. That Luhrmann uses these strategies to create both story-length and image-specific anachronisms works to show the preacher how to use these devices within a dramatic matrix to push for participation in the drama and communicate the gospel. The preacher weds moments together artistically into a dynamic communication of God's word through shaping sermon time and scene.

In the anachronistic sermon moments in time collide, creating a new moment for the old and future story to be enacted in the present proclamation of the gospel. Contemporary cinema, as one of the most powerful storytelling media existing today, can give the preacher cues as to how to make drama an encompassing context (which may not be natural for the preacher steeped in more modern modes of homiletics) and metaphor set in motion through time an imaginative and compelling communicative and theological device. Cinema gives the preacher tools to use in the creation of a dramatic-anachronistic sermon, such as montage and mise-en-scène. Shaping time and the scene through juxtaposition of images and visual, vibrant language is central to anachronism in preaching. Films such as *Romeo + Juliet* provide visual examples of what I am calling for in the pulpit.

CONCLUSIONS

Anachronism, or metaphor set free through the temporal quality of the drama itself, is the means by which the preacher may travel, wrinkle, and navigate time in this moment of the drama. In anachronism the past is able to become immediately present while retaining its past quality. The present obtains the ability to make the future a reality right now, relying on the veracity of God's eschatological promises validated in Christ and in God's word. In the preacher's ongoing engagement with the hermeneutical question of how the ancient text can speak in the present moment, anachronism presents itself as the theological device that allows the preacher to travel time and navigate the drama's meaning.

Interestingly, anachronism is not necessarily a new theology for the preacher. Paul traveled the map of temporality anachronistically in revealing the drama for his readers. The church's practical theology adopted this type of temporal theology until the rules of the Enlightenment and then Modernity prevented it. And in postmodern works of art one can see the hermeneutic of time reemerge as a beautiful and viable mode of communication. A homiletic rooted in time and utilizing anachronism negotiates the drama out of a rich theological and artistic history. The need for bridges is diminished as anachronism participates in time as our distance from and connection to the text's history. Anachronism is the hermeneutic that brings together now and then.

A practical study of how drama and anachronism can be brought into relationship with preaching will be helpful. The remainder of this book will explore the practice of preaching within the dramatic tension described, focusing on the development of drama and anachronism for the contemporary sermon. The following practical anachronistic homiletic exhibits advantages for homiletics that offset the dangers of a disjointed temporality discussed previously.

5

The Anachronistic Sermon
Preaching Times Together

IN THIS FINAL CHAPTER I BRING TOGETHER PREVIOUS OBSERVATIONS IN an overview of a potential homiletical theology and process in the dramatic-anachronistic mode. Preaching from a dramatic-anachronistic homiletic creates the sermon through at least four broad moves that necessarily deviate in varying degrees from a traditional, space-conditioned hermeneutic and homiletic. To preach time together recasts the hermeneutical process as intrinsically narrative, dramatic and eventful. Shaping the story will engage exegetical tools to fashion the preacher's reading of the text, the sermon's goals, and the shape of the sermon. The preacher will then work towards shaping sermon space through mise-en-scène, and sermon time through montage. Finally, the preacher will create a timely language through the purposeful use of various anachronisms that serve to place the hearer within the drama of God's presence with God's people, in his or her unique moment. The following examples of sermons exhibit the dramatic-anachronistic dynamics I have presented. Through this discussion it will be possible to see both something of the homiletical practice I am promoting and the benefits of drama and anachronism for homiletics.

SHAPING STORY: SCRIPTING SERMON

At the center of a dramatic-anachronistic homiletical process is the dramatic theological framework discussed at length above. When the preacher comes to creating the sermon, he or she stands within this framework and creates from within its temporal currents. This framework changes our response to the hermeneutical question in terms of the sermon's shape and goals by imaging the reader as playing a role in an ongoing drama of God's interaction with God's people in the world. The biblical text constitutes the authoritative script by which enactments of the play's later acts must be played out and ultimately judged. Further, the drama has both past and future elements, with the present player bound between memory of the past and hope for God's future rooted in God's promise. In this reality we find a new vantage point from which to view and engage in the homiletical process. This matrix, with anchronism as the chief means of moving from text to sermon, guides the homiletical process from exegesis to sermon delivery. This is a theological beginning point, one that is at a distance from theological presuppositions in the bridge paradigm. A dramatic-anachronistic hermeneutic and homiletic shapes the way the preacher reads the text, sets her or his goals, and scripts the sermon.

Reading the Text: From Bridges to Drama

In a dramatic-anachronistic homiletic exegesis is revisioned against a dramatic backdrop which frames interpretation of the text in such a way as to open possibilities that may have been overshadowed in more modern approaches. In contrast to observations made concerning the bridge paradigm in chapter 1, a dramatic framework minimizes objectification of the text as something from which meaning, either knowledge or experience, may be extracted and then transported in some way into the present. Instead, events are viewed as events and meaning grows out of the organic and intrinsic relationship that exists between moments of time in the drama. Meaning, in this scheme, is characterized as the living process that occurs as the present moment of the drama is viewed as an outgrowth of the past moment, and the interpreter asks what forms of living are consistent with previous and future acts of the drama. A key question for biblical exegesis then becomes, Within the matrix of the overarching drama, how does this text affect the improvisation of the drama in the present? Answers to this question begin to emerge as the interpreter recognizes the pan-temporal relationship between him or herself and characters in the text, and between events in the time of the text (pronouncement of God, work of God, failing and forgiveness of God's people) and events in the present (especially contextual events in the life of the church). Once relationships across time are established, the question of fitting participation in the present moment of the drama begins to find answers.

This difference between a spatial and temporal hermeneutic can be represented in the following diagrams:

text
How does
this...
...relate
to this?
now

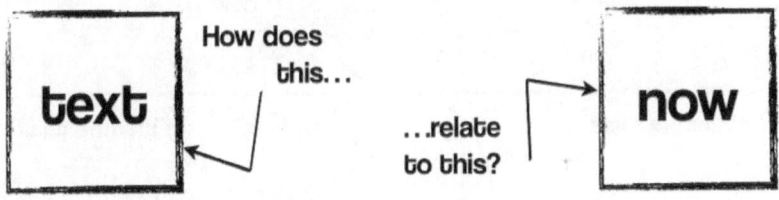

Figure 26. A more modern formulation of the hermeneutical question.

text
(bridge)
now

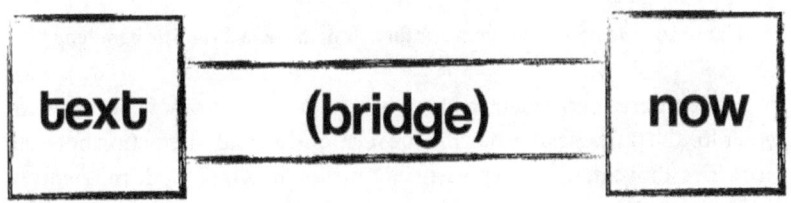

Figure 27. The creation of a bridge is a spatial solution to the modern hermeneutical question.

1: Creation
2 : Fall
3 : Israel
4 : Jesus
(Kingdom Inaugurated)
5 : Church
Christ's Return
(Promised Kingdom
Consummated)

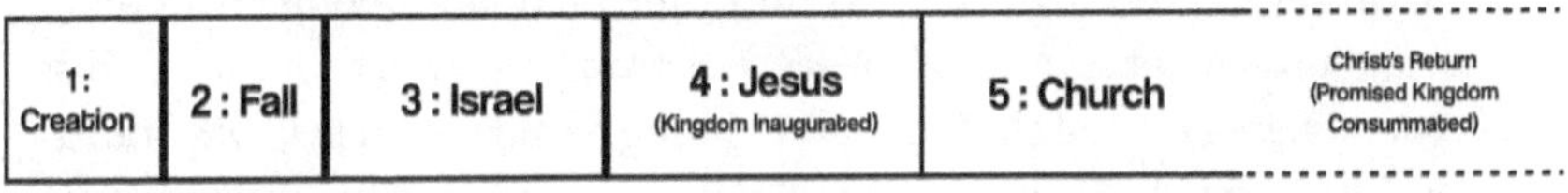

Figure 28. Scripture as drama in five acts, as proposed by N. T. Wright, sees all moments within the drama inherently connected through time. The hermeneutical question becomes temporal and participatory: "How can God's people fittingly play their part now, in relation to the whole?"

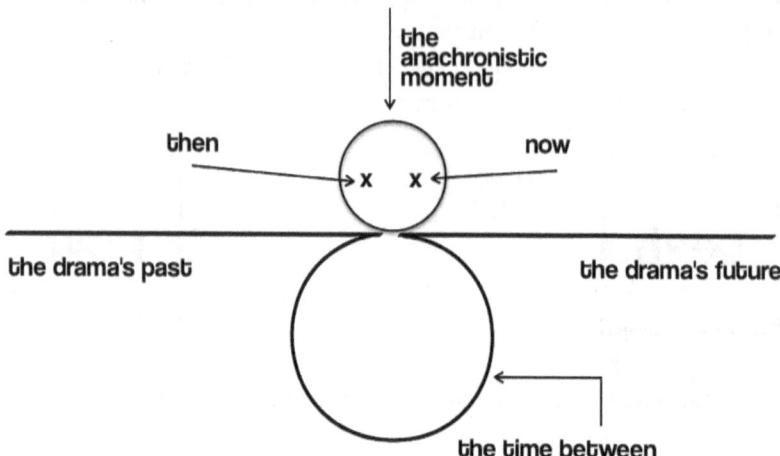

Figure 29. A temporal hermeneutic for a dramatic-anachronistic homiletic.

A temporal hermeneutic, then, is able to move moments of time together for the purpose of exploring the relationship and interaction between them. The above diagram represents a timeline in which both moments of the hermeneutical interaction are preserved as moments in time, and the temporal distance between the moments that the preacher is working with *wrinkle* between them (imagine the line as a string that has gone slack in the middle). The time between still exists and affects interpretation in necessary ways. However, meaning is created in the interaction of moments in time (past and present, or future and present) that are preserved as eventful. This calls the congregation of God's people to fitting participation in God's drama today. The hermeneutical question—"How can God's people fittingly play their part now, in relation to the whole?"—is proposed in the anachronistic moment, the temporal metaphor of disparate moments in time reconciled.

The exegetical process looks very much like the Apostle Paul's approach in 1 Corinthians 10. Paul, within the pan-temporal connection between God's people in the past and in the present, elucidated that connection in both reading the present into the past and the past into the present. The constant in the relationship for Paul was God and God's unchanging character and work across time. A temporal connection between Israel and the Corinthians served to lead the present-day church into more fitting participation in the drama than their historical fathers and mothers. Preaching from 1 Corinthians 10 today would follow a similar exegetical pattern, asking such questions as the following:

- What are the temporal and situational relationships between the Corinthians and the church today?
- What does idolatry look like in my culture, or church, today?
- What connection does the present moment of the drama have with the past moment?
- And then, when ready to move to anachronism, what moments of the drama can be brought together in a temporal relationship to create knowledge and experience in order to call for participation in the ongoing drama?

As time in a dramatic framework is held in tension across its modes, a future aspect of Christian eschatology opens interpretive possibilities that may be eclipsed in modern formulations. A dramatic-anachronistic homiletic, and the hermeneutic upon which it is based, eagerly hopes in the possibility of the future breaking into the midst of the present, and boldly proclaims this hope in the midst of history. With Moltmann, a dramatic-anachronistic homiletic looks for the possibility of the future breaking into the present. A practical example of this is what Moltmann referred to as eschatological deeds of hope. The preacher, looking into the future promises in the biblical text, calls that future into existence in the present, bringing present and future into relationship in eschatological anachronism. The future reign of God is characterized by peace, love, hope. The life called for in the sermon in the present calls for a full living of those future promises now.

As responsible exegetes we utilize exegetical tools such as translation, historical studies, social, contextual and literary criticism because these are valuable and necessary developments of Modernity for biblical interpretation. However, the context of these activities changes, and consequently the questions we ask of the text shift:

- What were God's people doing in the eventful moment of the text—either in alignment with or in deviation from God's covenant with God's people?
- What are God's people doing right now—either in alignment with or in deviation from God's covenant with God's people?
- What was God doing in the eventful moment of the text?
- What is God doing in this moment of the drama in the church?

While questions of God's action in the world, and of God's people's place in the world, are not particularly new to homiletical exegesis, in a dramatic-anachronistic homiletic they come to the center. The action of God in the eventful moment of the text and through history, including this present moment as it leads to God's promised future—and not a distillation of that action into proposition or experience or removal to another world outside of time—finds its powerful place in the quest for meaning.

In a dramatic-anachronistic homiletical process, then, exegesis is set apart from more modern counterparts largely in the hermeneutical and exegetical questions. It provides a vantage point for exegesis that is different from, and potentially not possible in, approaches based on modern formulations of time. Exegesis comes closer to the workings of life and Spirit that characterize a more organic and living Christianity, envisioned by Bushnell 150 years ago:

> The scriptures will be more studied than they have been, and in a different manner—not as a magazine of propositions and mere dialectic entities, but as inspirations and poetic forms of life; requiring also divine inbreathings and exaltations in us, that we may ascend into their meaning. Our opinions will be less catechetical and definite, using the word as our definers do, but they will be as much broader as they are more divine; as much truer, as they are more vital and closer to the plastic, undefinable mystery of spiritual life. We shall seem to understand less, and shall actually receive more.... It will not be our endeavor to pull the truth into analytic distinctions, as if theology were a kind of inorganic chemistry, and the last end of discovery, and atomic theory; but we shall delight in truth, more as a concrete, vital nature, incarnated in all fact and symbol round us—a vast, mysterious, incomprehensible power, which best we know, when most we love.[1]

The text is the church's script, authoritative for its life. Exegesis for the preaching of it will seek to proclaim God's action, and the response of God's people in a life and living process. This shift is evident in how a dramatic-anachronistic homiletic sets its goals.

Setting Our Goals: From Application to Participation

In previous chapters I have asserted that goals for the sermon flow from the emphases underlying each preacher's hermeneutical process.[2] Broadly,

---

1. Bushnell, "Preliminary Dissertation," 93.
2. I have simplified here, and it is notable that there are other ways to organize homiletical goals according to their hermeneutical commitments besides this one. Especially helpful here is Jacobsen, "Homiletical Exegesis," who appropriates Dulles's

the goals for preaching out of a bridge paradigm have been to transfer knowledge, create experience, or construct a world that overcomes that of the hearer. In a dramatic-anachronistic homiletic the goal of proclamation changes as the preacher narrates the hearer into the fabric of the drama. The sermon preaches either out of the drama's past or future, for participation in God's gospel drama in the world today.

Addressing the shift of a dramatic theology towards a more lived and practiced end, Vanhoozer observes that "Christian theology seeks to *continue* the way of truth and life, not by admiring it from afar but by following and embodying it. Following this way involves more than adopting a certain ethic. . . . The Christian way is fundamentally *dramatic*, involving speech and action on behalf of Jesus/truth and life. It concerns the way of living truthfully, and its claim to truth cannot be isolated from the way of life with which it is associated."[3] This embodied goal for theology carries over into proclamation of the drama. Preaching's goal is described in active verbs such as following and embodying, and the life aimed for inherently employs activities such as fitting speech and action. Drama encompasses goals of the homiletics operating within the bridge paradigm in calling for participation in the drama. It is a call to fittingly take one's place in the script of God's covenant relationship with God's people.

Significantly, this changes the development and application of the text for the sermon. Certain forms of homiletical thought have suggested that ideas can be developed in only particular ways for the creation of meaning. In a more traditional milieu, the preacher may explain, prove, or apply the idea of the text. However, as Vanhoozer and numerous others have shown, speech is more dynamic than this. Speech as an act does not merely say things cognitively; it does things dynamically, dramatically. This experiential quality of language stands at the core of the New Homiletic project, yet even here it seems to lack development beyond the experience created for the listener. Language has the power to do more than explain, prove, or apply an idea, or create an experience for a reader or hearer. Language retells the story, embodies the drama, creates the world (different from *a* world), and invites to an ascension to life and Spirit. Our preaching in a dramatic-anachronistic mode has the power and goal to call to participation in something larger than the preacher or the hearer specifically through a call to a life and living process.

Models of Revelation for homiletics. Jacobsen parses out distinctions in the New Homiletic to a greater degree than I have done here.

3. Vanhoozer, *Drama of Doctrine*, 15. Emphasis original.

This shift in homiletical goals happens as the view of the sermon extends beyond the moments spent at the pulpit. The preacher who calls for participation must embody his or her activity as more than the thirty minutes spent speaking, but rather as a part of the whole of the drama. Our atomization of time has permeated a view of the sermon as well as the text. The sermon has become merely a part of pastoral ministry, or one discipline (too often more disconnected from, less integrated with, both theology and Bible departments in the seminary curriculum) among the many that the theological student learns. However, the sermon along with the text is always in a tentative state of completion. The text is unfinished script, the sermon an unfinished rehearsing and call to participate in the drama once it is completed. As the sermon's priority shifts towards a fulsome call to participate, its conclusion is not left with an application appended to its end. Proclamation always finds its target in the ongoing participatory life of those who hear rather than at the moment the preacher sits down. This lifts the sermon to a more dynamic height, as it becomes ongoing dialogue between preacher, hearer, and God within the context of God's drama and the structure of God's people, the church. The sermon is an ongoing and cumulative activity—the proclamation of the gospel and call for a continuation of the action of the script. And so, the preacher moves away from simple application that seeks knowledge or experience towards calling God's people to create and participate in a living process. This move from application to participation will change the shape of the sermon from outline to script.

Forming the Sermon: From Outlines to Scripts

Working homiletically from a dramatic theological framework leads naturally to a more narrative or dramatic sermon structure. As a dramatic-anachronistic homiletic takes up within it both knowledge and experience, holding them in tension in an emphasis on life process, there are some sermon structures that may be less compatible with the theological framework underpinning the process. For instance, preaching forms that focus on organizing propositional statements of "timeless" truth are de-emphasized.[4] Truth is given to us specifically *in time* and the idea that we might be able to formulate truth outside of its constant is tenuous at best. The quest for a

---

4. I should note that I consider a propositional *central idea* in the sermon to be a communicatively important element in my preaching. But I consider this different from strictly *propositional* preaching. It is an example of how the dramatic-anachronistic homiletic takes up within it and utilizes proposition, without assigning the proposition a quality of timelessness or insisting that the sermon be constructed from propositional *points*.

timeless truth, experience, or reality/world is centrally atemporal and thus generally antithetical to a hermeneutic and homiletic, and life, immersed in time. Additionally, the rigid structure generally associated with point-form sermons is not very dramatic or mimetic at its core. This is not to say that propositions themselves must (or even *can*) be abandoned. Indeed, communication in general becomes difficult without propositional statements. It is, however, to remove propositional statements from the overweening position of priority they have in modern thinking and place them alongside more artistic communication such as narrative, drama, metaphor, anachronism, and the like. The same is true in terms of experience when it is sought as universal, or timeless. Experience apart from being put into practice in life strains to be completed. Structures that primarily aim for either knowledge or experience may not be comfortable in this program because sermon structure rooted in valuing timelessness is overshadowed by time in a dramatic-anachronistic hermeneutic and homiletic.[5]

At the core, a dramatic-anachronistic homiletic will demand a structure by which connections within the drama can be brought to the surface for the benefit of living the gospel in the present. The theological device that will make these connections in any homiletical structure is anachronism, and a structure that brings points of time within the drama into contact is effective. The structure will value the flow of time, both from text to sermon and within the structure of the sermon itself, as well as the pan-temporal connections between people and events that animate a dramatic-anachronistic homiletic to begin with.

One move to be made in preaching from the midst of the drama is that from outlining the sermon as an academic paper towards scripting the sermon itself as a drama.[6] This is the natural outcome of viewing the text as

---

5. Along these lines two more established sermon structures I find helpful when brought under the rubric of a dramatic-anachronistic framework are Lowry's "Homiletical Plot" and Wilson's "Four Pages." Lowry focuses on time in the sermon, ordering it according to temporal priorities rather than spatial ones. This structure is, however, focused more on the temporal nature of the sermon itself and not on the temporal aspect of the inherent theological framework in which the sermon is developed. Lowry's plot, when discussed in terms of the overarching drama or how individual moments in the drama can be plotted within the whole, can be helpful in a dramatic-anachronistic homiletic. Wilson's "Four Pages" focuses on the emergence of the gospel across times. This structure, with its then-now connective progression, has a built-in temporal relationship between the past event of the text and the present existence of the preacher/listener. Both Lowry and Wilson exhibit a focus on and respect for time. See Lowry, *Homiletical Plot*, and Wilson, *Four Pages*.

6. A commitment to academic outlines in modern homiletical thought is on display whenever academic form is imposed on sermons that do not intrinsically have that form. For instance, the sermon audio resource *Preaching Today*, in their publication of

unfinished script, especially in an eschatological context. As the preacher reads the script and engages in creating and calling for participation in the next moments of that drama, the sermon takes on qualities of script created for the stage or screen. A specifically dramatic sermon structure might script the sermon itself in five acts. The first four acts explore the text, scene by scene, in vivid language moved forward by a creative montage and mise-en-scène (discussed below). Act 5 is then reserved for the call of God's people in this moment to participate in the reality recorded by the text. Throughout, times are held together through a pervasive anachronism in which the overarching temporal metaphor holds together the event of the text (Acts 1–4) with the moment of the congregation (Act 5). A five-act sermon structure is itself anachronistic in its core form.

An Epiphany sermon rooted in the moments that Matthew records in 2:1–12, traditionally referred to as the Adoration of the Magi, may find its acts scripted as follows (the full sermon is presented in the Appendix):

> Act 1: Jesus is born and time moves on (v. 1).
> Act 2: The astrologers are compelled to follow (vv. 1–2).
> Act 3: The panic of the king (vv. 3–8).
> Act 4: The world sees the Son of God and gives him gifts (vv. 9–12).
> Act 5: Jesus is born, waiting to be found, waiting for you.

Here, the sermon imaginatively scripts events recorded in the text as events, bringing them into a dimensional relationship with God's people now. Acts 1–4 proclaim the drama scene by scene. Act 5 introduces the central calling of the sermon, which is purposefully a call to participate in what God has done and is doing. As the sermon is scripted, the shape will be filled out through the creation of sermon space, that is, mise-en-scène, and the creation of sermon time, or montage.

SHAPING SERMON: CREATING SPACE AND TIME ANACHRONISTICALLY

The development of the sermon in a dramatic-anachronistic homiletic will rely on theological anachronism to make connections between moments of the drama across time. In anachronism metaphor is set in motion through

---

Fred Craddock's "When the Roll Is Called Down Here," includes a print sermon outline with the audio file that imposes a deductive structure conditioned by an academic sense of what an outline should be, upon an inherently inductive sermon that is largely narrative. The outline is very likely the creation of an editor with an affinity for academic outlines and not of Craddock himself. Craddock, "Roll," 2.

time as two moments are brought together, past and present or present and future, and allowed to interact in such a way as to create a new moment for the gospel to emerge in the present. A then/now dynamic is still operative in the interaction, as temporal metaphor does not consume the moments of which it is comprised. The past and present (or present and future) moments of the drama remain intact even while coming together to create something new. Neither time loses its character; however, the moments together have an inherent power to bring the gospel to emergence in the now. This dynamic is illustrated in the graphic above.

As he or she discovers pan-temporal relationships across time, the preacher actively shapes time and scene in the creation of different types of anachronism for the sermon. Here, the concepts of montage and mise-en-scène become helpful in creating the anachronistic sermon. Montage and mise-en-scène, rather than being two separate tools or devices in the creation of the sermon, exist intertwined with one another. Mise-en-scène, all that shapes the scene, works to create the anachronism enabled by editing time through montage. Montage and mise-en-scène are two sides of the same coin, in this sense. However, I will consider them in turn before bringing them fully together in the homiletical examples below.

Anachronistically Shaping Sermon Time: Montage

Montage in the creation of a film (or in any dramatic performance) is the purposeful juxtaposition of images to create a desired experience, effect, reaction, emotion, or narrative direction. In creating a film, montage is the process of shaping dramatic time through editing images and scenes together. In writing a script for the sermon montage refers to how the preacher brings images together, in what order, and to what desired effect in the sermon for the hearer. Montage allows the preacher to shape the dramatic time of the sermon, bringing the moment of the text and the moment of the hearer into creative relationship, creating a new moment of meaning in the interaction. This practice, as I am defining it, is far from either illustrating textual points with stories or bouncing back and forth between images and descriptions of the "world" of the text and the "world" of the sermon. Montage creates metaphor in motion, scripting the present people of God into the overall and ongoing story that God is telling. To create anachronism with montage is to shape time by preaching time together.

We find direction for preaching here especially in the types of anachronisms created by the medieval theologians, and further illustrated in contemporary cinema. The contemporization of narratives and use of omnitemporal perspective, prolific in the medieval plays and pulpit, are adaptable for the contemporary sermon. This temporal editing gives the sermon a type of dramatic movement—contemporizing or eschatological. *Contemporizing anachronism* edits together the past moment of the drama with the present, calling the church into fitting participation in the story that has been enacted thus far. It does this with a mise-en-scène that purposefully moves forward the textual moment, retelling it in the present. A variation of contemporizing anachronism, and contained within the concept, is the biblicization of the present moment—that is, moving backwards in time by stitching the present congregation into the ancient setting. Contemporizing and biblicizing anachronisms are more fluid than distinct, as can be seen in the examples to follow. Baz Luhrmann's creation of Verona Beach out of a collage of images drawn from a Latin beach community and the cinematic Western is an example of the use of montage to contemporize a text.

Working with moments of present and future in the drama in a type of omnitemporal perspective (God has given his people a vision of the story's end, or new beginning) opens up *eschatological anachronism*, in which the preacher calls God's promised future reality into the present moment, inviting participation in God's future now. Eschatological anachronism is to call the church to, as Moltmann phrased it, eschatological deeds of hope. Each type of anachronism may be represented by the following diagrams:

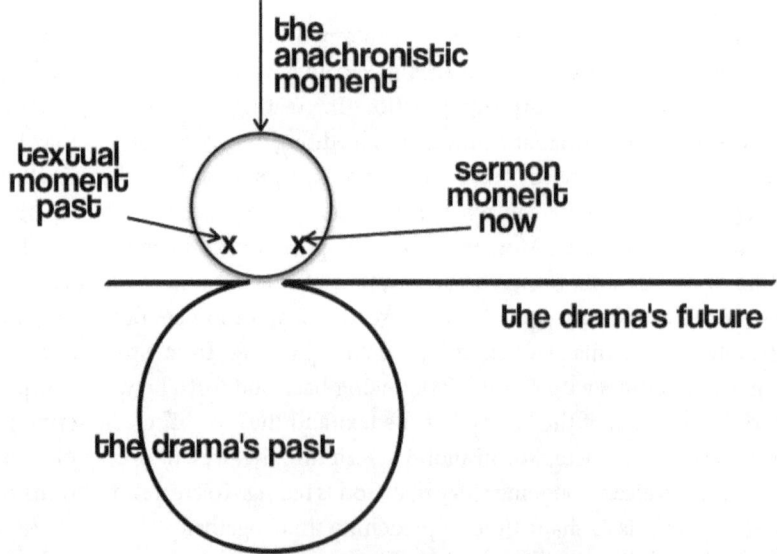

Figure 30. Contemporizing anachronism utilizes montage to bring together the past moment of the drama with the present moment, creating a new moment for the hearer and calling her or him to fitting participation now.

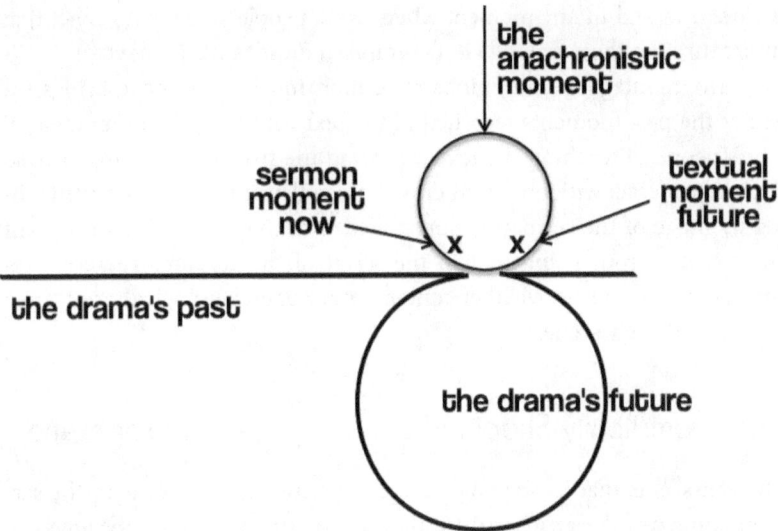

Figure 31. Eschatological anachronism utilizes montage to bring together the present moment of the hearer with the promised future of the drama. In doing so, the preacher is able to call the promise into the present by envisioning and proclaiming the future into the present.

Essentially, montage in an anachronistic context describes the dynamic of editing two moments of time together—past and present or present and future. When the preacher is working in the present with a biblical text that recounts the past of God's people together, contemporizing anachronism shapes the mise-en-scène and goals of the sermon as past and present time are played with. Contemporizing anachronism has as its goal the present exploration of the history of God's people, calling God's people present into fitting relationship with the God of the story. As the preacher proclaims moments of the story yet to come—consummation of God's kingdom in Christ's return; the state of the new creation described in future-proclaiming texts—anachronism takes on an eschatological quality. The dynamic of eschatological anachronism proclaims the revealed future into the present based on the veracity of God's promises, calling God's people to embody the consummation of love, peace, goodness, compassion, kindness, and the like, right now. The recovery of a future-looking eschatology, with an emphasis on Christ as the reality prolepsis and Scripture as the word prolepsis of the kingdom (described in chapter 2), makes this possible. This is true of preaching future-looking texts, and yet, eschatological anachronism also occurs in real time as the preacher calls God's people to enact the future in the present, and in any moment when God's people actually do enact that future through their making God's promised future a reality now.

The montage of the Epiphany sermon introduced above brings together the past moments recorded in the text with the present moment of God's people. Preaching the text will bring the two moments together so that they interact with one another without collapsing either. The overarching montage of the sermon is punctuated with the smaller images of past and present brought together in the script of the sermon. These image-specific anachronisms, whether contemporary or eschatological, are created through mise-en-scène.

Anachronistically Shaping Sermon Space: Mise-en-scène

Mise-en-scène, that is, shaping the space or creating the scene in the sermon, animates the anachronistic moment as times are brought together. While montage brought the two moments together, mise-en-scène creates those scenes in such a way that the sermon's hearer can see the event and so participate in the anachronistic moment of the drama. This is not a reliance on illustration. Instead, the preacher uses her words to populate moments of time with people, places, sights, smells, and any other creative image that serves to create the anachronistic moment and invite participation in the drama. The moment of the text (past or future) must be re-created in the imagination of the listener, while the present moment of the drama must be engaged with, described, investigated, and illuminated as a significant moment in the story of God's dramatic history. In mise-en-scène we encounter what might be the actual spatial aspect of the sermon—preaching time together creates a new moment comprised of its parts but standing on its own as well. Mise-en-scène is the action by which the preacher composes that moment out of dramatic imagery and imagination.

Paul Scott Wilson, while not using the language of mise-en-scène, calls the preacher to create the sermon out of vivid imagery worthy of our culture's best filmmakers. Encouraging the preacher to identify with directors, Wilson says, "As movie directors we place ourselves on the 'set' of the text, somewhere in the Middle East that the text identifies or suggests. Real geography surrounds us. Listeners should meet the main character (e.g., Paul, or the community members from or to whom he writes), observe his behavior, and overhear a few spoken words as a means of establishing realism."[7] In composing the scenes of the drama—both the textual and present scenes—

---

7. Wilson, *Four Pages*, 83.

the preacher is cast as filmmaker, creating the events through every image placed in the scene.

For Wilson, the sermon's mise-en-scène is sensory and invitational as the preacher creates scenery with color, offering the congregation something to "see, hear, touch, taste, or smell."[8] Similarly, as the camera points towards people and their actions the preacher must begin to make decisions about what these events looked like, and what they look like: What specifically does this person look like? How does she move into and out of the scene? What senses are engaged as I enter into the event of the text? What does that look like, and smell like, and sound like, right now? These are exegetical and imaginative questions that work towards creating the eventful moment of the sermon out of the moments of text and today. Wilson goes on to give this instruction: "Listeners can visualize someone if we give them visual clues, such as gray hair or the elegance of movement. In general, we should be as visual and sensory with the Bible as we are about current events, when we speak of someone today wearing jeans (name the color and the specific label) and a tee shirt from the Hard Rock Cafe, or of a hospital room with a single birthday card on the window ledge, for these small details paint bigger pictures of individual lives."[9] Preachers create these moments of time with what they place in the scene.

Within the new moment of time—the anachronistic moment—opened in editing times together, mise-en-scène imagines that moment and invites God's people to participate in it. In the Epiphany sermon from above, past and present are brought together in the overarching structure of the sermon, and in the sermon's smaller images. Images from past and present are preached together, largely without comment on the sometimes absurdly broken time discrepancies. These are the sermon's anachronistic moments that serve to create the new moment for the hearer. Setting the Matthew 2 scene might look something like this:

> Some time has passed since he's been laid in that manger. Months, a year maybe. Up from the manger Jesus has come, probably taking his first steps. Maybe clumsily mimicking sounds that sometimes can pass as words through the drool that drops from his gums sore with unseen teeth. He's a handful. Diapers changed multiple times a day and night—they went for reusables at the beginning. Now Mary is regretting it even though the disposables aren't as economical. All the new mothers complained about the price they paid for something you

8. Ibid.
9. Ibid., 87.

buy for the purpose of throwing away. She's young, Jesus is her first, they are still in Bethlehem and she doesn't even have her mother to coach her in the fine art of nursing. They couldn't even get a nurse from La Leche League to come all the way out here to help her out. The baby's toys are nice, but not the most fun. Joseph has carved him animals and an Ark out of leftover wood from his day job as a carpenter. Even as a baby you can only get excited about a playset that depicts the almost end of the earth for so long. And these are their days. Day in, day out. Day after day. Time moves by. Quickly, but not so much. They are mundane days. They are good days. A working-class family in a working-class town.

The following questions become important for the preacher: What images can I place before the hearer in order to create and communicate the scene? How can I arrange these images in the sermon in order to call for fitting participation in the drama? For instance, in scripting the Epiphany text, what aspects of the text are shared in common with, yet different from, life today? Or, how are the moments of time brought close enough together so that they retain their distinctive quality as unique events in the drama, yet interact in creating a new moment? The detail about diapers helps build affinity between those with this experience in the present as they relate to the characters in the text. The mundane detail about diapers, or nursing, and the overarching experience of worrying about your first child link the two times and elevate the story into the sublime in that it is a story about God's Son.

The similarities and differences between images and times all lend themselves to anachronism in the sermon. For instance, in scripting out the wedding at Cana (John 2:1–12), knowing that there are differences between the text and today, the preacher could merge mise-en-scène in terms of the reality of the past event stitched with contemporary images. The preacher calls into service the tradition of brides going dress shopping with mothers and bridesmaids, the groom and groomsmen in tuxedos, the minister in a collar. The wedding scene can be transported into the present, as the bride walks down the aisle of a large church with wooden pews, numerous candles, and a large cross affixed to the wall. All the guests might then travel to the community center for the reception, where the wine runs out. The winery and vintage of the first batch of wine is read from one of the empty bottles littering the floor, and an awkward moment ensues as the caterer, annoyed at being outdone, asks Jesus the year and region of his own wine.

Engaging in the purposeful shaping of time and scene through mise-en-scène and montage, a sermon exploring Luke's account of Christ's birth and its announcement to shepherds could, through imaginative and vibrant language, bring the past into relationship with the present:

> The farmers gather around a green-and-rust beat-up pickup truck out in the field. The key is turned "on" so that a slow, depressing country tune creeps through the speakers. Red embers of their cigarettes' ends are visible through the slight fog—a nasty habit, they know, but it keeps them warm through the cold night. To pass the time during lambing season they play cards on the tailgate, between delivering newborns and saving the orphaned ones from the cold. Poker. For cigarettes. Jimmy, in his oversized, dung-stained Carhartts, had already amassed a sizable pile of Camels.

Luke's mis-en-scène, "And in the same region there were shepherds out in the field, keeping watch over their flock by night" (2:8), is transformed through imaginative anachronism in its interaction with a contemporary setting in the dramatic matrix. This is achieved, as in Luhrmann's films, through bringing the ancient moment and the present together with adjustments to the scene (ancient fields to contemporary farm), the presence of modern items (pickup truck, cigarettes, poker, country music), and a change in costuming (from an imagined first-century shepherd to a present-day farmer in Carhartt coveralls). Visual language is included to add to the meshing of times: green-and-rust-colored truck, slow and depressing country music, dung-stained coveralls. All of these images are ordinary in that one would expect them on any present-day farm. They become sublime in that they are placed in the story of first-century shepherds visited by angels. Like *Romeo + Juliet*, the mis-en-scène is changed for the desired aesthetic, participatory, and theological effects.

In creating imagery that explores and calls for participation in Mark's recounting of Jesus calming the storm, one way to convey the potential fear the disciples might have felt as Jesus slept is to use an anachronistic image blurring temporal lines through use of contemporary imagery:

> All of them were out to sea when the storm hit. They tried to make it out of the storm's path but it became clear in their minds that they weren't going to make it home. As the waves ripped over the sides of the fishing vessel, and the motor choked, it seemed that these were their last moments. I wonder if in the middle of that storm, James and John didn't think back to their father and mother, standing on the dock watching after them as they left to follow Jesus, the boys' fishing poles left in the sand. Or if Peter didn't pull out his wallet, take out the picture of his

wife, and start to cry. "This is going to be really hard on my little boy."

The imagery here is inspired by the film *The Perfect Storm* (2000) and is created by stitching together mise-en-scène from the film with Mark's story of the disciples in the storm. Fusing sermon image with cinematic image has the potential to draw on a listener's relative familiarity with a film or cinematic conventions in general.

The rhetorical effect of mise-en-scène coupled with montage is to create the anachronistic moment of the sermon and the anachronistic moments within the sermon. This makes an unfamiliar scene familiar to a contemporary audience, but even more important, the dynamic calls the church to participate in the scene. Telling the story in the present can have the effect of placing the listener within the action so as to understand and experience it for the purpose of fitting participation in the drama today. This is the stated desire of Luhrmann in the creation of his mise-en-scène in the Red Curtain films, presented in chapter 4. *Romeo + Juliet* is created from a pastiche of familiar images so that the viewer enters the story (without losing her or himself) and participates in the action. *Moulin Rouge!* takes an ancient myth and sets it at the turn of the twentieth century and punctuates the story with the greatest pop love songs written *after* the action of the film takes place. This is mise-en-scène and montage with a mission—to create the anachronistic moment of the sermon and the anachronistic moments within the sermon, and thereby proclaim God's drama for participation in it today.

Anachronism Calls to Participation

Ultimately, the sermon itself becomes an anachronistic moment as the ancient/future text and present are preached in temporal relationship to one another. Simultaneously, the sermon utilizes imaginative anachronisms throughout by inserting out-of-time details for a timely proclamation.

An important consideration of preaching the anachronistic sermon is that anachronism—the whole of the sermon and the imagery that composes it—always serves the goal of calling God's people to participation. In this sense, anachronism as I have described it should be theological and meaningful rather than merely glib or decorative. It is easy to blend period styles out of a sense of simple novelty or entertainment. But I am not proposing decoration. I am proposing a temporal theology. The power of anachronism within a dramatic theological framework lies in its core identity as metaphor occurring through time. Using anachronism as decoration may render a powerful word event as mere illustration. We must ask the question, Does this anachronistic image in this context—does this blending of past/future and present in the whole of the sermon—serve preaching's goal of the growth of the gospel within the horizon of the listener's/church's present? Does it serve to take up both knowledge and experience and call for forms of living commensurate with the whole of the drama? Does the anachronistic sermon equip the church to continue writing the script as they act out the drama in the living process that is Christian faith?

Returning again to Epiphany, Act 5 of the sermon specifically calls the hearer to participate in the gospel today, asking him or her to find Jesus in the world right now:

> And that brings us to Act 5. Which happens to be the act when you and I are right now. The Child still appears. He still waits. He still looks to be found. Jesus is born, waiting to be found, waiting for you.
>
> So I ask you, where do you find him? And what do you bring him? You and I are called to him just as the kings before us. Where have you looked? Where have you found? What have you brought to him? What have you received in your finding? Jesus is born, waiting to be found, waiting for you.
>
> I can tell you where I've found him. It has been in what I would have considered unlikely places.... I only tell you so that you might make your own journey. Where do you find him? What do you give him? What have you received in your finding?
>
> Jesus is born, waiting to be found, waiting for you.

These qualities of the anachronistic sermon, shaping story and shaping sermon, are on display to a greater extent in the following sermons out of time.

SERMONS OUT OF TIME

Anachronism creates a new moment of understanding in bringing together two disparate moments of the drama and allowing them to interact. Participation is achieved dynamically and mimetically as the listener is called to a continuing enactment of the drama in each new moment. While the preachers of the sermons excerpted below have not used language of drama or anachronism to describe their preaching (except for myself), a dramatic-anachronistic quality is present in contemporizing and eschatological anachronisms in their work. These sample sermons will serve to present the sermon as anachronism, and anachronisms within the sermon, in action. First, Paul Scott Wilson works to update Mark's account of the rich young ruler, blending textual and contemporary styles through detailed contemporizing anachronism. Haddon Robinson brings forward in time the biblical text in his parabolic retelling of the text in a sermon titled "The Church of God in Christ Chicken Restaurant." Barbara Brown Taylor preaches the future into the present from Paul's letter to the Ephesians through eschatological anachronism. Finally, my own sermon attempts to display a range of anachronism, a blend of biblicizing and contemporizing, coupled with eschatological movement. In the following sermons, in varying degrees, time is held in tension, a temporal hermeneutic can be detected, sermon form largely follows that of a script, imaginative montage and mise-en-scène is called into service, and participation in Christianity as a life process (rather than sermon application) may be viewed as the sermon's goal.

Paul Scott Wilson: Contemporizing Anachronism

Paul Scott Wilson preaches a sermon rooted in Jesus's interaction with the one we commonly refer to as "the rich young ruler" (Mark 10:17-31). Wilson's juxtaposition of past and present in metaphorical relationship displays a deliberate move towards anachronism in its attempt to contemporize the text.[10] Discussing his homiletical process, he explains that in changing a few of the narrative's elements he has tried to update the ancient story for a contemporary audience: "Research tells us that Jesus and his disciples know the young man is rich because of his clothes and jewelry. In this sermon a more vivid symbol is needed. He is given a BMW, the sort of vehicle a rich young man might drive today. Further, the text is clear on the virtue of the young man. Here, to help the congregation imagine a devout person today, he is made to be a youth pastor whose faith is as devout as the biblical character."[11] The blending of styles is accomplished by preaching into the story a luxury automobile, vocation, and, as is later revealed in the sermon, a Heartbreak Hotel where one goes who's lost his or her dreams (and where "songs about broken hearts, failed jobs, lost loves, and disappointed hopes" play twenty-fours a day). The anachronism is not overwhelming or distracting, and it achieves a poignant effect.

Wilson begins the sermon by setting the scene and introducing the contemporized character:

> No matter what Synoptic Gospel we read, the story of the rich man who comes to Jesus is much the same. In Luke he is "a

---

10. Wilson, *Broken Words*, 66-70.
11. Ibid., 65.

certain ruler"; in Mark he is "a man"; and in Matthew he is "a young man." I follow Mark, yet in my mind I see him as a man in his early twenties, perhaps a rich young youth pastor 2000 years ago who has heard that Jesus is preaching at a small town, and he speeds over to try to catch Jesus before he leaves. The young man is ahead of his time in that he drives a black BMW with tinted windows, the kind you cannot see through; low profile tires so they look like they are about two inches deep; low-ride suspension to make it no distance from the road; and a racing exhaust system that sounds like the name of its manufacturer, Vibrant Muffler. In the trunk and where the backseat used to be are amplifiers and speakers that make the whole neighborhood throb with his Christian CDs. Tdddh, thddt, thddt-thddt.[12]

This contemporizing anachronism permeates the whole of the sermon and creates points of contact between the text and the listener in a way that is exegetically fitting. Wilson brings the two moments of the drama together with the dynamic of the past emerging within the present. A listener is brought into a new moment of understanding through participation in the creation of the scene out of two different times. Anachronism of this type has the potential for communicative resonance as it holds time in tension and calls for participation in the present moment of the drama.[13]

Haddon Robinson: Contemporizing Anachronism

Haddon Robinson creates a contemporary parable out of Paul's words from 1 Corinthians 9:19–23, especially verse 22, which reads in part, "I have become all things to all people." The whole of the sermon, titled "The Church of God in Christ Chicken Restaurant," transports the text into the setting of a present-day church that seems to have lost a meaningful relationship with the gospel.[14] Instead, through church growth strategies capitalizing on its main strength of facilitating community through fried chicken lunches,

12. Ibid., 67.

13. One point of departure I would have with Wilson's sermon is his manner of calling for audience participation in the ongoing drama. Wilson identifies the listener with the rich young man in an almost allegorical sense: "We are all that rich young man" (ibid., 69). While I think that preaching moments together into the same moment anachronistically holds homiletical potential, I am not convinced of the value in preaching together identities. One principle of temporal metaphor, and metaphor in general, is that neither part that comes together ultimately loses its identity in the process. Preserving identity becomes difficult when conflating two people/characters, especially in a universal manner.

14. Robinson, "Church of God in Christ Chicken Restaurant."

the church ends up as a restaurant. The whole of the sermon operates under the question, when has the church gone too far in becoming all things to all people? The elements of preaching the anachronistic sermon are evident: the sermon takes the shape of a script, contemporizing anachronism as the past and present moments of the drama are edited together in a pervasive montage, imaginative mise-en-scène creates the anachronistic moment of the sermon and anachronistic moments within the sermon, and the preacher calls the hearer to an organic participation in the drama beyond the sermon itself.

Robinson begins by creating the scene, using montage to set the ancient text in the present moment through vibrant and extensive mise-en-scène:

> As the road snakes up into the mountains it takes a strong turn to the left. Up on the right there's a very successful restaurant that has a very strange name. It's called the Church of God in Christ Chicken Restaurant. It's a successful restaurant. You get there on a Sunday or even a Wednesday evening and it's not unusual to have to wait for 45 minutes to an hour to be served. They give you one of those little beepers and you're able to walk around the grounds. And there's a great deal to see.
>
> For example back off the left of the eating area there's a church. It's called the Church in the Wildwood. Enter the church and by the use of electronic sound you can hear a congregation near the turn of the century singing some of the old hymns. Amazing Grace. Will the Circle Be Unbroken? And as you'd expect: Come to the church by the wildwood, come to the church in the dale. No place is so warm in my childhood as that little round church in the vale. And then following the music there's the voice of a country preacher exhorting the people to godliness and explaining to them the gospel.

The story then flashes back to the restaurant's humble beginnings as a church. It had been a small church in decline. At some time in the past the church elders shifted its ministry focus to play on the church's strengths. These strengths happened to be spending time together around the table. Fried chicken and fellowship were found hand in hand, and the church grew rapidly once they maximized their meals together and minimized their centeredness on the gospel. Robinson fuses the image of Paul becoming all things to all people with images of the church that many people in his audience would find imminently familiar:

> They had good fellowship and one of the ways that they inspired the fellowship was that every time there was a 5th Sunday in a

> month they would have dinner on the grounds. I gather that this wasn't an ordinary potluck. This was really something special. In fact, it was so special that on those Sundays that they had dinner on the grounds they would almost double their attendance. It was not unusual to have 125, 130 people come. Well, the elder in charge of evangelism and outreach knew a good thing when he saw it. He said if it worked once every quarter maybe it would work every month, and he suggested that every 4th Sunday in the month they would have dinner on the grounds. Folks agreed and he was right. I mean, the attendance shot up. On those Sundays they'd have 140 people and it went over to the other Sundays. The attendance just generally rose. . . .
>
> Folks responded well to that and there were women in the church who could cook. There was Carrie Campbell. Carrie made chicken from a recipe from her father who was a cook back in New York City, and he'd gotten it from a Great Aunt before him. I mean, it was good chicken. It made Colonel Sanders look like a buck private. Then there was Jenny Harrison. Jenny Harrison made biscuits. I mean, we're talking biscuits. I gather they were so light they would just float off the plate if it weren't for some of Jenny's raspberry preserves to hold them down, keep them stuck. Then there was Margaret Gibson. She made desserts. She didn't really make desserts. She created desserts. And one of here favorites was pecan pie. You folks who have been trapped in New England all your lives don't really know much about pecan pie. But down in the South it's a kind of fine art.

These are images of a church potluck that would resonate with many who have attended a small church like this one or who are familiar with the images from cultural cues.

As he reveals that the church at a certain point in its life became a full-service restaurant and largely abandoned its calling as the church, Robinson calls the hearer deeper into the story by asking him or her to participate in their moment of the drama:

> That story is true. It's absolutely true. I changed the names of the people and the place. And it wasn't really a restaurant. But the story is true. It's true in the same way that a parable is true. And that story presents to you certain questions you have to answer. One question that you might want to wonder about: Did the church step over a line? And what line did it step over? Was it wrong to give the name of the church to a chicken restaurant? I mean, churches give their names to hospitals, to insurance

companies, to bookstores. Even to used clothing outlets. Why not a chicken restaurant? Or was it wrong for them to really want to reach their community? Was it wrong for them to go down into Denver and ask a firm to help them with this operation? Would it have been more Christian if the chicken had been burned, or the biscuits hard, or the desserts flat?

Someplace along the line that church in its eagerness to reach its culture and its community seemed to cross the line. But the question is, what line did it cross? That's something you're going to have to wrestle with. It is really a theological question. I think one thing we'd agree on: that when a church becomes a chicken restaurant, it's probably gone too far.

The preacher calls the listener to participate in the drama through evaluating what it means in living practice to share the gospel as God's people, to "become all things to all people so that by all means I might save some." Robinson leaves the hearer with the question rather than fully answering, aiming at participation in the sermon and drama beyond the time occupied by the preacher's time in the pulpit.

Barbara Brown Taylor: Eschatological Anachronism

Barbara Brown Taylor's sermon on Paul's letter to the Ephesians brings into focus eschatological anachronism—bringing God's promised future moment into the present as an accomplished, and being accomplished, reality.[15] Taylor begins her sermon by creating a vivid scene of the ruined churches that dot the Kaçkar Mountains between modern Turkey and Russia. A church that has been battered, be it historically conquered or presently mired in scandal, controversy, or sin, stands at odds with Paul's vision of the church triumphant. Paul has a more glorious view of God's people gathered, says Taylor:

> The church shall be a colony of heaven on earth, Paul says, the divine gene pool from which the world shall be re-created in God's image.... That is what Paul can see, as clear as day—the perfection of creation through the agency of the church. I have been using the future tense out of sheer disbelief, but Paul does not. He uses the past and present tense: "And he has put all things under his feet and has made him the head over all things

---

15. Taylor, "He Who Fills All in All," in *Home by Another Way*, 136–42.

for the church, which is his body, the fullness of him who fills all in all."[16]

For Paul, Taylor says, God had already succeeded, and this in spite of what she sees in her own church and in others. And she asks her listeners to see it in their own churches also, churches that too often argue "about everything from what kind of music we will sing in church to who may marry whom." While we're divided on those things, "the next generation walks right past our doors without even looking in. . . . They are looking for a colony of God, and they are not finding it with us."[17] Here one might question whether Paul had it right to begin with.

However, Taylor brings Paul's hope back, emergent in the present through exploring the divine mystery of Paul's words, especially those of being already related to Christ. She does not admonish the church to just work harder in attaining Paul's lofty vision, as if such an ideal could be accomplished by human effort. Instead, focusing on the grace of the gospel in Christ, Taylor eschatologically and unapologetically asserts the actual present reality of Paul's vision. In contemplating that what Paul has said is already true of the church, and what is simultaneously obvious about the church's "spotted record," Taylor notes that "what Paul asks us to believe is that our twoness has already been healed in our oneness in Christ—not that it *will be* healed, but that it already *has been* healed—even if we cannot feel it yet, even if there is no startling evidence that it is so."[18] God's promised future is already a present reality in Christ. As such, Taylor offers that the church can see it constantly in its midst, even if this reality goes unrecognized. She ends with two realities imaging what she believes Paul is talking about, both eschatological anachronisms in that they bring the very promises of God, especially for relationship and healing, into the midst of the church's present moment:

> Based on my own experience this is not the kind of stuff that makes headlines, not the way declining membership numbers do. It's just your basic, raising-the-dead kind of stuff, stuff that happens in the church all the time.
>
> Like the brain-damaged young man who shows up one Sunday and asks to become a member of the church. As carefully as he tries to hide it, it is clear that he is out of everything—out of food, out of money, out of family to take him in. No one makes a big fuss. Very quietly, someone takes him grocery shopping

16. Ibid., 136–37.
17. Ibid., 137–38.
18. Ibid., 139.

while someone else finds him a room. Someone else finds out what happened to his disability check while someone else makes an appointment to get his teeth fixed. And do you know what? Years later he is still there, in the front pew on the right, surrounded by his family the church.

Or like the woman with recurrent cancer who is told she has six months to live. The church gathers around her and her husband, laying hands on them, bringing them casseroles, cleaning their house. Someone comes up with the idea of giving the woman a foot massage and painting her toenails red, which does more for her spirits than any visit from the pastor. She gives her jewelry away, she lets her driver's license expire, she starts writing poetry again. She prepares to die, but instead she gets better.

On Christmas Eve she is back in church for the first time in months, with her oxygen tank slung over her shoulder and a clear plastic tube running under her nose. After the first hymn she makes her way to the lectern to read the lesson from Isaiah. Her tank hisses every five seconds. Every candle in the place glitters in her eyes. "Strengthen the weak hands," she reads, bending her body toward the words, "and make firm the feeble knees. Say to those who are of a fearful heart, 'Be strong. Do not fear! Here is your God.'" And when she sits down, the congregation knows they have not just *heard* the word of the Lord. They have seen it in action.[19]

Taylor brings future promises of God, especially those dealing with the perfected reality and identity of God's people and the church as a whole, and declares her listeners to be what Paul has already identified them as: the colony of heaven on earth, joined to Christ, where the forgotten are adopted and cared for and where the sick and dying are loved, never left alone, and even healed.

Here one sees that as modes of time are held in tension, in this case future and present, God's future promises are brought into the present moment. Taylor accomplishes eschatology in the pulpit through vibrant mise-en-scène, which is more than mere illustration. This elevates the future aspect of Christian eschatology often lost in modern theology. Further, God's action in making the future present enrolls listeners into the present moment of the ongoing and future-moving drama. Taylor makes the hope of the future present for listeners as, in Moltmann's words, the present *is* the presence of the future.

---

19. Ibid., 139–40.

Casey Barton:
Comtemporizing and Eschatological Anachronism

John 12:1–8 records Jesus and the disciples' attendance at a meal in his honor, probably in celebration of Jesus raising Lazarus from the dead. The meal, occurring six days before Passover, before Christ's crucifixion, took place at the home of Lazarus, Mary, and Martha, and has as a climax Mary's anointing of Jesus for burial with expensive perfume using her hair. In retelling this story I have set the listener and myself at the dinner table, bringing together images from first- and twenty-first-century meal rituals; biblicizing and contemporizing anachronisms are blurred. Having set us at the table with Jesus and the disciples, the drama unfolds in such a way as to directly involve us, proceeding to a realization that in all of our meetings with Christ it is inevitable that our stories are retold from what they were to narratives of beauty in him. The drama is recounted in such a way that the perfection of these stories does not await a future fulfillment; rather, Christ has declared our stories healed and whole from our first encounter with him, even if within an eschatological tension. Contemporizing/biblicizing and eschatological anachronisms are evident as the audience and text are brought together, and the future perfection of our identities in Christ is declared a present reality.

The sermon begins by invoking images of a Thanksgiving-type meal. The scene is a family gathering where there is food, the kind of gathering that inevitably leads to remembering and storytelling. This is then wed to the scene from John's gospel:

> My favorite part of these meals is the mashed potatoes and gravy. But not just any mashed potatoes and gravy—Grandma's mashed potatoes and gravy.
>
> And probably even better than that is when we sit around after the meal and begin to tell stories. Some of the greatest, funniest, or most emotional words become: Remember when? Remember the time? Sometimes a photo album is produced, prompting even more remember whens and once upon a times. Childhood moments that embarrass you in front of your children. Last year's vacation on Maui. Pictures of Grandpa in his Navy blues, when he was young, long before he passed away. It's a time for remembering. A time for thanksgiving. A time for anticipating the future. It is, more than anything, a time for stories.
>
> That is pretty much exactly how I imagine the scene as Jesus visited Mary, Martha, and Lazarus. Sometimes we forget that the Son of God did some of the more mundane things like have

dinner with his friends ... with his family. But that mundane moment is where this story picks up: six days before the Passover, six days before Jesus had told his friends that he would die. And at a thanksgiving meal of sorts, Jesus has supper with his friends.

I imagine them all there, of course. The disciples. Mary, Martha, Lazarus who Jesus had raised from the dead, probably happier than any of them to be there. And of course Martha, channeling another notable Martha, prepared and served the meal. And what a meal it must have been—after all, Jesus had raised her brother from the dead. The house was filled with the smells of the meal: roast lamb, fresh bread, mashed potatoes and gravy. And as so often happens at a meal, friends laugh, family remembers, and stories are told. A photo album is produced. Memories emerge. This is a scene so familiar to me that I can see myself sitting there at the table too. Right there next to John. And I can see you sitting there too, all of us, all around the table, laughing, remembering, all of us in the presence of Jesus.

After establishing the scene in two distinct temporal moments I have brought them together, sitting characters who retain their unique identities across time at the same table, emphasizing the pan-temporal relationship between players in God's drama. In this sense the text is not fully contemporized into the present moment, nor is the present fully transported into the past. Instead, both moments are brought together in a new moment of participation and understanding. Inasmuch as the interpreter understands the text as the representation of a moment in time, a temporal event, rather than as a container from which he or she may extract meaning, the creation of the anachronistic moment is possible.

As the drama progresses the meal ends, and those reclining at the table are compelled to share their stories of Jesus:

> As the wine glasses empty and the coffee is poured, in the dim light of the fire everyone begins to tell their stories of Jesus: Remember when ...
>
> Now, the way I imagine it, Nathanael, one of the disciples, started things off: "Hey ... Hey ... Jesus ... Remember when we first met? Philip over there, he came and told me about this 'Jesus of Nazareth,' and I actually said, 'Can *anything* good come out of Nazareth?' But ... then you saw me, and you told me things about myself that only God could know. Right then and there I changed my mind: You are the Son of God! King of Israel! And you told me, 'Follow me and you will see greater things than these.'"

After a parade of disciples have shared stories of their encounters with Jesus, the style is purposefully blended once again as the sermon moves towards present testimony:

> And at that point, I just can't help myself—remember, I was there too—and looking down at my own reflection in my coffee, I timidly add my voice to the toast: "Remember, Jesus, when I didn't believe that there even was a God? I remember the emptiness I felt inside, felt it physically, like an aching ulcer. And I tried to fill it with whatever I could, anything to take away the pain. But nothing I did made my pain any less, it only made it worse. Until one day the pain was so much that I couldn't take it anymore. And that's where you found me, Jesus. You found me, picked me up, and have held me through all the pain and joy life has thrown ever since."
>
> And I looked up to see Jesus give me a wink, as if to say, "Yeah, I remember that."
>
> Then I heard you speak up about the time you met Jesus for the first time. How your parents had raised you from your beginning to have faith, and how Jesus had never left your side throughout your whole life.
>
> And then you told the story of how Jesus had given your mom strength when she was dying of cancer. Despite the prognosis she felt comforted in her faith, in her belief that she would soon be in the arms of Christ himself. And her faith comforted you, pulling you closer to Jesus yourself, a place you had resisted for a very long time. Jesus was there with you when she passed away.
>
> And you told about how you had really made a lousy mess of things in your life, and Jesus had come alongside and worked for you and with you, along with those here who have now become your family, to straighten things out.
>
> And around the table we go—stories of strength for pain, of orphans made children of God, of the loveless loved, of the homeless finding a place in God's family. All in and through Christ.

Not only has the contemporary audience been brought into the drama as characters who retain their own identities, but they now participate in and continue the story as themselves as they are compelled to recognize their own story in the scene played out. God's grace experienced is the theme of these incident reports, and the mildly specific though largely generic memories I have provided are meant to enthymemically draw listeners' minds to their own personal stories of interaction with Christ.[20]

The sermon comes to a close after Mary, both recognizing her own relationship to Jesus and the fact that his death would occur within days, displays a remarkable act of devotion in anointing him for burial with her hair. Judas rebukes her expression, and Jesus, speaking for the first time in the pericope, rebukes Judas. Our Thanksgiving meal with Christ comes to a close, tinged with eschatological anachronism in the tone of completion in what Christ has already done:

> The tension is thick. Slowly Martha gets up to tend to the dishes in the sink. Others of us nervously sip our coffees. One by one the guests, all of us, retire to bed.
>
> But something has changed. We've realized something. It wasn't so much that they sat around—that *we* sit around—and retell the stories of Jesus. Though we do that too. Even more, in the story of Jesus—his life, death, resurrection, his meeting with each one of us—in that meeting our stories get retold into something so much more beautiful, so much more exciting, so much more complete than they were before we knew him.
>
> God retells our stories in Christ. Nathanael's story, Philip's story, Peter's story, my story, your story, Mary, Martha, Lazarus—all of our stories are changed in our encounter with him. God has taken what we had—be it brokenness and pain, or failure and dishonesty, or earnest wandering, never knowing exactly what it is our hearts are longing for. He has taken what we had and retold it beautifully, amazingly in Jesus Christ. We cannot walk away from our meeting with him unchanged. Through Christ's love, forgiveness, and grace we are changed; he has taken our broken stories and retold them, whole and complete, in him.

Through bringing the two moments of text and present together, and bringing the reality of the listeners' completed retold stories into the present from the future, the sermon has attempted to foster understanding of the event and call for participation in the narrative. Through the sermon, the gospel comes to expression in the present moment of the congregation.

---

20. Enthymeme refers to the rhetorical device Aristotle identified in his *Rhetoric* as a logical syllogism in which one component is suppressed by the arguer and provided by the listener based on a collective body of shared information. In communication, the enthymeme causes the listener, or reader, to provide a portion of the argument or story him or herself, thereby participating in the meaning making of the conversation. Aristotle discusses the enthymeme in *Rhetoric*, sec. 8, ch. 2.22.

CONCLUSIONS

A dramatic theological framework and an anachronistic hermeneutic and homiletic allow the preacher to picture the sermon and the process of its development from a new vantage point. No longer navigating a spatial chasm between the world of the text and the world of the hearer, building bridges gives way to performing the drama. The goal of the sermon in a dramatic-anachronistic mode shifts from the appending of an application to the call for God's people to become full participants in the gospel drama today, disciples along the way. The dramatic-anachronistic matrix shifts our sermon shapes from academic outlines to spirited scripts. The preacher accomplishes all of this through an active creation of time and space by/in the practice of shaping montage and mise-en-scène, moving through time in contemporizing and eschatological anachronisms. These shifts, while a break from much homiletical practice over the past century, stand in continuity with the proclamation of God's drama throughout our history together. This anachronistic homiletic dynamically calls for participation in God's ongoing gospel drama in the world today. Further, these shifts towards a timely homiletic seek to address certain dangers previously observed in preaching out of a disjointed temporality (see chapter 1).

CONCLUSIONS _____

Restoring Time to Our Preaching

ANACHRONISM AND DRAMA LEND THEMSELVES TO A LARGER THEOlogical discussion any time the subject of time, and holding times in theological tension, is invoked. While drama and anachronism as theological context and concept are larger than any one practical, literary, or rhetorical quality they may possess, one particular aspect of their theological character is how drama and anachronism function in a practical manner in preaching. Preaching can be viewed as occurring within a dramatic context, with anachronism a key theological and hermeneutical concept for understanding and bringing together in tension past, present, and future modes of time. While drama and anachronism as theological concepts may be pursued along many theological, conceptual, or abstract avenues, I have attempted to lay a temporal theological and hermeneutical foundation for preaching specifically, and to bring theological insights gained from thinking through drama and anachronism as a theological matrix to bear on the sermon. The overarching goal has been the recovery of time in our hermeneutic, which produces a more timely homiletic, thereby calling for living participation in God's dramatic reality.

In pursuing drama and anachronism as the theological means of bringing moments of time together in the drama, I began in chapter 1 by attempting to sort through recent decades of homiletical theology with an eye towards uncovering hermeneutical commitments and their practical outworkings. The development of preaching in recent years has been tremendous, and tremendously helpful for me as a pastor who preaches at least weekly. What I've offered throughout this study is a homiletical theology that in some ways stands alongside those that have come before, in other ways grows out of them, and in still others, one that hopefully stands on its own in its recovery of time and the creation of a sermon caught between past and future, between memory and hope.

However, inasmuch as these homiletical theologies rely on the creation of a bridge that makes a hermeneutical move into a perceived timelessness they work from a disjointed temporality that abstracts the distance between then and now as space rather than time. The dangers associated with this disjointed temporality, again, are that it produces a sermon that fails to preserve the past event as an actual event; it breaks a temporal/absolute dialectic necessary to Christian faith; it flattens a pan-temporal conversation between God's people in their interpretive communities and contexts in their unique moments of time; it leads to an eclipse of the future tense of Christian eschatology; and it militates against a view of God at work in the actual world.

In the whole of this study I hope to have shown a theological temporality for preaching that exhibits certain benefits for homiletics that correspond to the dangers of atomizing time. By way of conclusion I present the following advantages to a dramatic-anachronistic homiletic. Drama and anachronism in preaching hold time in tension rather than working with a modern disjointed time. This temporal unity and organization preserves past events as events, animates the pan-temporal conversation between characters in the drama, and revives the future tense of Christian eschatology. There is a hermeneutical advantage in this program as drama and anachronism provide a means of navigating from text to sermon. In a temporally minded paradigm God's action is squarely in this world and through time, in contrast to more spatially oriented hermeneutics and homiletics. Further, drama and anachronism provide another homiletical option for the use of artistic and imaginative preaching forms. Underpinning these a dramatic and anachronistic homiletic asks for a shift in the way one approaches preparing and listening to sermons, and how the preacher conceives of the homiletical task and the foundational theology essential to it. Incorporating drama and anachronism into homiletics provides a dynamic view of the preaching task that calls for living participation in the overarching drama.

Holding Time in Tension: Eschatology and Continuity

In contrast to a separable and separated view of time characteristic of Modernity, a theology and homiletic predicated on the dramatic observations made throughout this work holds modes of time together in tension, putting forward a more holistic view of time as continuous and of time's modes as relatively equal. This is commensurate with a biblical approach to time. I noted previously that a divided view of time had the potential to fail in treating past events as events, for flattening a pan-temporal relationship between moments in the overarching drama, and eclipse the future aspect of Christian eschatology. Drama as matrix and anachronism as time travel begin to address some of these dangers. Recognizing a greater continuity between past, present, and future in a dramatic flow, and anachronism as a means of bringing together moments in that drama and moving between them, provides an animating dimension for preaching.

When we view the text as representing events in time, thereby respecting their authors' experience of them as events, then texts as events are addressed as real and vibrant parts of the drama. This does not necessitate a naïve literalism but recognizes that the events narrated in the text are, in many instances, presented as real events in the history of God's people. As such, those events have bearing as events on the present and future moments of the drama. The dramatic nature of the paradigm insists on a fulsome accounting of narrated events and their subsequent effect on the story. Further, the pan-temporal conversation between moments of and characters in the drama is animated to a greater extent than in a more atomized view of time. Time, bound together in continuous drama, provides an inherent connection between persons and events in the story.

Christian eschatology finds a renewed voice in a paradigm that holds future time in equal tension with both past and present. Recognizing this aspect of eschatology influences the interpretation of texts, the preparation of sermons, and the living of life. The future tense of the drama gives christological hope to the present living of the drama. If future eschatology is an essential aspect of New Testament theology and interpretation, as Stendahl, Moltmann, Dunn, Sampley, and others have noted, holding time in tension provides a more fulsome theology and homiletic. Drama brings the future into greater standing in terms of the past and present, and anachronism provides the means for living the future into the everyday of the present. The homiletical potential for preaching hope through use of a future-oriented, eschatological anachronism within the dramatic context is compelling.

Moving from Text to Sermon: A Temporally Relational Homiletic

A bridge hermeneutic predominantly relies on a spatial paradigm for moving from text to sermon in language that often centers upon moving between "worlds." These approaches refer to hermeneutical poles in a spatial manner. Biblical and contemporary worlds are the spatial images used to signify, and at times objectify, moments in time. This imagery is used to refer to the points of activity in the hermeneutical transition. On the one hand, narratives of various types of literature work to create narrative "worlds" into which one enters, finally to return to his or her own "world" with the insight and experience of that journey.[1] However, when with this spatial language temporal events are translated into fundamentally spatial realities, the particular nature of the biblical drama that claims to occur in and describe the only world, God's created world, becomes distorted. This is evident in the postliberal homiletic in which the work of God is removed into another world, another spatial reality. Further, propositional homiletics seek "timeless" truth, bits of truth removed from the conditionality of time, objectifying meaning and stripping a temporal quality from the text. Experiential schemes look for the experience of texts in the present, where the past event of the text is somewhat downplayed. While preaching in the bridge tradition may move temporally from past to present, it does so in a spatial manner, often objectifying texts and eclipsing their temporal and eventful nature.

One effect this has on preaching, and on faith generally, is that of relieving the reader or listener of responsibility for his or her place in the drama. If events occurred or characters exist in another spatial reality, in another world, or in a timeless reality, it is difficult to have a relationship with or to those events or characters, or to the drama itself. Spatial hermeneutics have negative repercussions on practical theology beyond homiletics, inserting distance between the individual's "world" and the "world" in which poverty, injustice, or unbelief exist. In the biblical drama neither spatial nor temporal distance alleviates responsibility for one's place within the drama, whereas compartmentalizing reality into different spaces removed by great or even insurmountable distances gives the impression that one is not affected by or responsible for realities in opposition to God's kingdom simply because they do not immediately affect the individual's immediate spatial realm. Principlizing the incarnation or racial injustice simply makes them less real as realities God's people are responsible for addressing in God's kingdom.

A practical example of this might be individuals who go on short-term mission trips to a third-world country and who return and say, "It was a whole other world." Or, in terms of social relationships, it becomes easier to dismiss an *other's* experience of the world (a man hearing the story of a woman's experience of sex discrimination, for example, or a

---

1. See Wolterstorff, *Works and Worlds*, and Tolkein, "On Fairy-Stories."

Caucasian hearing the story of systemic and institutional racism from an African American brother or sister) when we spatially distance ourselves from that story by removing it to an *other* world. Once it is in the realm of some other space, it can be compartmentalized, separated from one's own experience of reality, and disintegrated from personal responsibility. If poverty, injustice, or despair exists in the same world/space as I do, then as a disciple of Jesus I must respond. However, if these things exist in an *other* world/reality, the distance may become sufficient enough that felt responsibility wanes. We need one another's stories, each other's parts in the drama, to fill out the story of what God has done and is doing in the one world.

Shifting the focus to a temporal relationship between events and people within the same spatial reality (there is one world, and events happen and people exist in different times) brings the action of God in this world to center stage and elevates our responsibility to one another across time. If, as the drama claims, God has acted and continues to act in this world across time, then there is inherent relationship to God and God's acts and to characters throughout the temporal flow of the drama. Instead of removing God, characters, or events to another reality, drama and anachronism shift to a model of temporal relationship that connects them across time. This is a different way of conceiving of or analyzing the preaching experience, especially in relation to homiletics based on modern assumptions. A dramatic-anachronistic homiletic allows one to experience preaching differently. In a postmodern cultural and homiletical ethos, this hermeneutical facet may prove valuable for the preacher looking for a relational and dynamic move from text to sermon. A focus on a unified temporality that emphasizes a relative equality between modes of time and is interested in the future's effect on the present opens large areas of possibility for homiletics. Study of this subject in coming years will produce critical responses and a wider breadth of homiletical options.

Christianity as Life: Mimetic Communication

A further benefit of this program is that the goal of preaching becomes living participation in the drama. In a homiletic characterized by drama and anachronism preaching occurs within a dramatic theological context that sees Christianity and Christian doctrine as a life and a living process. The hearer lives the drama out of the past script in the present into the future. This practice of time is akin to what is affirmed in worship at the table when we are gathered with the communion of saints, past, present, and future.

Understanding and experience, then, are displaced as central goals of the sermon, important as they may be in calling for active and dynamic participation in the lived drama. Central is interpreting the biblical text and the present in light of the constitutive and ongoing drama of the gospel, and calling people to participate in this drama through a tensive relationship between modes of time. This takes up within it cognitive and experiential tasks in creating an intrinsically mimetic quality in the sermon.

A dramatic framework that uses anachronism to bring together moments of time deliberately holds time together in tension and creates a high level of dynamism. The benefit of this over against other homiletical options can be compared to the difference between diegetic and mimetic communication systems. Communication theorist Robert Scholes describes diegesis and mimesis as aspects of the representation of actions or events. Diegetic communication is characterized as what is told, summarized, or reported, and "in the strictest sense, a diegesis is a sequence of actions or events construed by an interpreter from a narrative text."[2] Mimesis, traditionally defined as representation or imitation, differs from diegesis in its emphasis on the enactment of the representation, rather than simply upon "imagination of the events based on a verbal text." Setting the contrast in terms of drama, Scholes explains, "The reader of a play engages in a diegetic activity; the actor of a play speaks the words and mimes the actions of the text."[3] Using the examples of Zeffirelli's and Luhrmann's respective productions of Romeo and Juliet, the 1968 film is more diegetic in seeking to reproduce the text through recitation. Luhrmann's film is more dynamic, mimetic, in re-creating the text for the present moment. There are different levels of enactment and dynamism at work in each activity. A dramatic-anachronistic homiletic exhibits a high level of dynamism in its mimetic quality. Refusing to be mere recitation of the past, the sermon and the life that comes from it is the creation of the future in the present.

In holding moments of time together anachronism, with its foundation of metaphor, creates a new moment of living as past and present or present and future are held together. Neither moment is destroyed in the relationship. Instead, the new moment created opens a space of understanding and experience, calling for a mimetic enactment of meaning in the present. This again addresses the process of moving from text to sermon, in addition to the subject of homiletical application. The call to participation, to mission, arises organically as times are brought into relationship and becomes a more natural outworking in life than an appended application of the text.

2. Scholes, *Semiotics and Interpretation*, 144.
3. Ibid., 145.

I am not suggesting that the hermeneutical or homiletical theologies discussed in chapter 1 are, or should be, characterized as strictly diegetic. Indeed, each of the approaches alongside which my own is set exhibit varying levels of both qualities in their treatment of the text and its proclamation in the pulpit. I am suggesting, however, that preaching from a dramatic matrix will be more mimetic intrinsically at its core, not seeking a reenactment or recitation of the text in the present but a fresh enactment of the drama for every fresh moment in which the story is lived. Indeed, the dramatic-anachronistic sermon is mimetic in seeking the performance of the drama both in the sermon and in calling God's people to continue to write the drama's script in each new moment of their enactment of it. This incorporates the goals of knowledge and experience into a more dynamic approach to homiletics and the theology that undergirds it. A dynamic, mimetic quality is inherent in a homiletic characterized by drama and anachronism as the sermon has as its goal a call to participation in the life of the drama. This quality of a dramatic-anachronistic homiletic may again provide a fresh vantage point from which to view the preaching task—its goals, sermon development, and theory.

An Artistic Homiletical Option

Fusing drama, anachronism, and preaching provides another option for preaching imaginatively and artistically. In recent years a host of works have been produced calling for greater imagination in preaching and offering creative suggestions for preaching more imaginatively.[4] The nature of the anachronistic pulpit—its being based in a theological view of drama and utilizing a creative form of metaphor—gives it a place alongside other creative, imaginative, and artistic homiletics. A dramatic-anachronistic homiletic gives the preacher another tool for thinking and preaching imaginatively, while calling the preacher to engage in deeper conversation with the artists of our time.

This dramatic-anachronistic homiletic provides artistic inroads for the preacher who finds engagement with contemporary popular arts valuable. Conversation with our time's most high-profile storytellers is not a necessity for the preacher engaged in preaching anachronistically. But, for those who find the conversation fruitful, engaging with filmmakers and other artists in the language and practice of artistic devices such as montage and

---

4. A sampling: Achtemeier, *Preaching as Theology and Art*; Elliott, *Creative Styles of Preaching*; Eslinger, *Narrative and Imagination*; Troeger, *Imagining a Sermon*; and Wilson, *Preaching as Poetry*.

mise-en-scène brings practical theologians into deeper conversation with some of our culture's most influential value-shapers. It is not the preacher's goal to copy what filmmakers and other artists do. It is, however, our calling to create art that points to what God has done, what God is doing, and where his kingdom is emerging. We improve our art as we engage in conversation with other artists at levels deeper than simply appropriating their art for the sermon. A dramatic-anachronistic homiletic encourages the preacher to seek out conversation partners outside of homiletical circles for artistic training in the work of proclamation. With drama and anachronism, the preacher is dramatic artist, engaged in creating dramatic art in the sermon. God, in his grace, takes that art and makes of it the dramatic art of his people's lives.

Appendix

Sermons Out of Time

Following are sermons that I have preached at Hilmar Covenant Church over the span of the last five years. The preparation for each of the sermons begins with the presupposition of a dramatic framework. Because this is something that my congregation may not naturally be used to I have prepared them over time, both in Christian Formation initiatives and on Sunday mornings, by teaching them how to listen to a sermon and how to view all of life and discipleship in a dramatic mode. Each of the sermons below displays various aspects of anachronism—contemporizing and eschatological, small images and whole sermons. They are drawn from different biblical genres, from psalms to gospel narrative to church letters. All of them utilize imagination in their creation, relying on the temporal movement of metaphor to answer the hermeneutical question presented in chapter 1.

These sermons are contextual, by which I mean that they have arisen specifically from the life and currents of one particular church. Preaching in each congregation sounds like the congregation that gave the sermon life. My congregation is a semirural, dairy farming community who are very educated and family minded. The people love their community, their work, God's Word, and our church. We struggle with our problems, with our sin, for sure. And in all of life we seek guidance from the past enactment of God's script to show us life today in fitting relationship with God's love for us.

The tone below is more sermonic, more scriptlike, than academic. These sentences were written really for hearing, in Hilmar, not primarily for reading.

THE SON HAS COME

A Christmas Sermon (Luke 2:1–14)

THIS MORNING'S SERMON WILL RECOUNT TWO SMALL MOMENTS—TWO small scenes—from a larger drama.

Both scenes are mundane, boring even. But don't mistake mundane for unimportant. Indeed, the drama, the whole of it, could not exist without these two little pieces of the drama. In both scenes we encounter a number of characters . . . but, in both scenes, only one is the major character. The others are important, but incidental. In both scenes we visit a number of locations . . . but, again in both scenes, the places we visit are really defined by the main character of the story itself. So that the places are only important insofar as he is present in them. He is present with the others in those places.

These scenes that we take time out for today have as their central importance what is the central importance of the whole of the drama, and of all scenes within it: The Son has come to show us God.

Scene 1: In those days . . .

The lights come up on a crazy amount of activity. The stage is crowded. The camera begins by showing us Nazareth as the whole of the region has been put on notice—Go and be counted.

At center stage, looking dazed and confused, is a young man leading his young fiancé, nine months pregnant, on the back of a donkey through the crowd. Through the busyness of this life he looks at her, she at him. They sigh and continue their journey, from Nazareth to Bethlehem.

The sun goes down. It comes up. Down again, then up. And down again. And as the sky changes from blue to orange and pink, and finally to black on the seventh day they reach their destination. Bethlehem. She's been in labor for a good twelve hours now. And there isn't a friendly face at even one door. Somehow the couple end up in a barn. A midwife helps her deliver as her husband paces, sweats. While he waits he cleans out a feed trough and lines it with straw. Too lowly a bed for any baby, really. But especially too lowly for this baby.

She wrapped him in cloth, and laid him in the manger. You could hear her whisper: Finally, God's Son has come to show us God.

In those days . . .

The stage quickly changes.

We're in a field thick with a fog that has set in. We hear laughing, voices, but can't make out the words. The farmers gather around a green-and-rust beat-up pickup truck out in the field. The key is turned "on" so that a slow, depressing country tune creeps through the speakers. Red embers of their cigarettes' ends are visible through the fog—a nasty habit, they know, but it keeps them warm through the cold night. To pass the time during lambing season they play cards on the tailgate between delivering newborns and saving the orphaned ones from the cold. Poker. For cigarettes. Jimmy, in his oversized, dung-stained Carhartts, had already amassed a sizable pile of Camels. The smoke from the small fire they've built to keep warm almost covers their smell, but . . . no . . . it doesn't. Shepherding is a dirty job, and these guys are dirty.

One of them is about to go all-in, ready to declare a cancer-promoting victory . . . when slowly the fog around them begins to illuminate with an eerie light and a man walks out of the fog right up to them and says, "Don't be afraid, I bring you good news!" And the men are afraid. Watching the scene, you could be forgiven for thinking that this was a man. He looks like a man. But the light that he emanates is not a man's. There is something different about him. And he delivers his message—after all, he is a messenger:

"For unto you is born this day in the city of David a Savior, who is Christ the Lord."

The stage lights up and singing begins. And you can hear one of the shepherds whisper: Finally, the Son has come to show us God.

As the lights come down on this scene there are a few things that you notice. Actually, one thing in particular. And that is the lowliness of it all, especially given who the central character turns out to be. It is Jesus, God's Son, who has come. And he has appeared lowly, to lowly parents. He has appeared lowly in a lowly place. He has appeared lowly, to a first audience of lowly shepherds. He has appeared lowly, to a lowly world. A baby, in a barn, the Son of God who has come to show us God. Lowly . . . but sacred.

In those days . . . Glory to God indeed. Glory to God in the lowest.

There is an intermission, and we return to our seats for Scene Two.

Scene 2: In these days . . .

The lights come up and the camera begins by showing us a cold morning. In the streets, and especially those between the fields, a fog has set in. There is a frost on windshields, and where sprinklers went off the night before the runoff on sidewalks has frozen. It is a quiet morning, but there is plenty happening. It is Christmas, and it is Sunday, and people are leaving their homes and coming to church.

They make their way from their cars through the parking lot and in through the doors. They check in their kids, come into the sanctuary and take their regular seats. Always their regular seats. There are more people here this Sunday than others. It is Christmas after all. At ten o'clock, the music begins. This morning the people sing several hymns and then the pastor stands up and gives the customary greeting. It varies little from week to week, but it is welcoming—at least he hopes it is. A few more songs. Someone stands up to pray, another stands to read the story. It is the same story we read each year at this time. The story of the baby born in a barn. The story of angels coming to announce his birth. While we've all heard the story before, there is excitement somehow. There is always excitement at the story.

The pastor stands to give the sermon and the people listen for God's Word. He thinks he's clever, but it's the story that does the work. It's always the story. At the end of it, the people stand and sing. We offer what we have in response to such a great reality—that God's Son has come to show us God. We offer our prayers, our songs, our possessions, all in response to the story of God's Son. And at the end of the service we stand and we receive yet again, now as then, God's blessing. We stand, and we receive God's Son.

It is a lowly scene, isn't it? I mean, Jesus, God's Son, has come. He has visited his people. He has come, and he comes again, and again, he comes to his people. In fact, since he came the first time, he's never really left us.

God's Son has come to show us God. But he's done it in such a lowly way. To a lowly people, who have nothing more to offer than what he gave us to begin with. To a lowly audience, whose unfinished lives too often don't reflect the glory that has come to them. To a lowly people, who, even though they are being renewed into the image of Christ himself, are not worthy vessels of that glory. To a lowly world, which, though it exists only by his effort and grace, too often receives him not. Glory to God. Glory to God in the lowest.

But, he comes. In those days, in these days, he comes. Every day, he comes to us. To his people. To love us, and to show us God, and to bring us home. God's Son has come to show us God.

In a few minutes the lights will go down on this scene. We'll ring the bells one last time for this year. We'll drink coffee and eat cookies. We'll celebrate Christ's coming together. But after that, this scene will fade into the next one, and into the next one, and into the one after that. And, regardless of how lowly each and every scene seems compared to the glory of the one who has entered the story, in every scene Christ has come to show us God. And Jesus, God with us, takes all of the lowliness and by his presence elevates us, revealing God in it all.

So, glory to God in the highest. And glory to God in the lowest. And glory to God all in between. Because God's Son has come to show us God.

WAITING TO BE FOUND

An Epiphany Sermon (Matt 2:1–12)

Today's text, and today's day, Epiphany, are so strange to me. But not strange at all. If you catch my drift. Today's is a story so familiar to us that we can recite it in our sleep. But it is because it is so familiar to us that somewhere right below the surface in all of our familiarity with it we can't get right to the heart of it all. Which, when it comes to Jesus, seems to me to be precisely where we want to be.

It is, of course, the story of the Wise Men, or the Magi, or the Three Kings, or Melchior and Balthazar and . . . I can't remember the third one's name. It is the story that we recite at Christmas. The story of the world coming to worship Jesus. The story we see in so many of our crèches. It is Epiphany. Jesus appears to the world. And the world sees him.

But let me be clear, right here at the beginning of the sermon. Right here at the beginning of this story. This story, the one just read for us, this story is about Jesus. It is not about wise men, kings, camels, kids in bathrobes, nativity scenes, gifts, gold, frankincense, myrrh, Herod being threatened, or a star. This is solely, only, absurdly, ridiculously about Jesus. Everything else here is incidental to him. All of this action happening around Jesus and Mary and Joseph (who isn't even present) is all for him and about him. And he, and his parents, have no idea that any of it is happening. It is all happening in the background noise of the world. All happening because of him, even if he's not done a thing in the world except get born. He's come, and that is enough. The whole world is abuzz. Even if he is not.

Act 1.

Some time has passed since he's been laid in that manger. Months, a year maybe. Up from the manger Jesus has come, probably taking his first steps. Maybe clumsily mimicking sounds that sometimes can pass as words through the drool that drops from his gums sore with unseen teeth. He's a handful. Diapers changed multiple times a day and night—they went for reusables at the beginning. Now Mary is regretting it even though the disposables aren't as economical. All the new mothers complained about the price they paid for something you buy for the purpose of throwing away. She's young, Jesus is her first, they are still in Bethlehem and she doesn't have her mother to coach her in the fine art of nursing. They couldn't even get a nurse from La Leche League to come all the way out here to help her out. The baby's toys are nice, but not the most fun. Joseph has carved him animals and an Ark out of leftover wood from his day job as a carpenter. Even as a baby you can only get excited about a playset that depicts the almost end of the earth for so long. And these are their days. Day in, day out. Day after day. Time moves by. Quickly, but not so much. They are mundane days. They are good days. A working-class family in a working-class town

And I wonder if Mary ever looked upon her child and tried to figure out what the angel had meant that he would be special. That he would save his people from their sins. She loved him. And wouldn't trade him for the world. But when would the world love him the way she did? When would the world know that God had come down? And another day. And another. And another.

Act 2.

The camera cuts to a far-off place. Different. Couldn't be more different than the place we've just left. It is a different kind of house in a different kind of land. No worries of diapers or wooden toys. Maps on a table, people looking quizzically at them, wondering what they were looking at when they'd been outside for the past few nights. It was a star, but not like any star they'd seen before. And, let's be honest, these guys knew a lot about stars. It was their job. It was the culture of their people, the talent of their fathers and their fathers' fathers. And some new light had stood up in the night and somehow had called out to them—called out to the world. They were compelled to follow. Even if they weren't completely sure of what they would find they knew that this star would not speak false. They would travel—weeks, months, through mountains and desert—to come to the king they would find on the other end. The journey, they knew, was not about them. The journey was about the one they would find. It was about the king.

Act 3.

The screen jumps now to an ornate palace in a beautiful city. It is evening and there is much rejoicing. It is rejoicing over the king. Nothing special, actually—this generally happened every night. The people who clung to the king, Herod was his name, had a pretty good idea that they needed to worship him if they liked remaining alive. Herod was king, and he liked to be king. And who wouldn't?

The sun set, and the oranges and pinks of evening ruined into the dark of night. There was that star that turned up in the East and now set over Jerusalem. On this night the guys from the East would arrive. They had known somehow the star would lead them to royalty; now that it brought them to Jerusalem they figured it was the Jewish king. But when they approached and were led to Herod, they pretty much knew that this guy hadn't just been born. It was someone else.

As you can imagine this threw Herod into a panic. A usurper! And a little one at that. If Herod could get his hands on the child he could kill this problem before he grew out of his diapers. Quick consultation of the prophets, directions given to Bethlehem, and the Easterners are back on their way. For Herod, for his fear, this story is about the baby. It is all about the baby. Only about the baby and how it will be the ruin of him. For the travelers, they are closer than ever to the center of the story. And they carry on.

Act 4.

Another day and Mary is home with baby. She tries to make playdates with other moms; sometimes she loads him into the hand-me-down stroller and takes him to the park. On occasion, on the way back she will stop at the 7-Eleven and get a Slurpee for herself. She's still a teen. She likes grape. She dreads the next time he's hungry because it hurts so badly. And she looks at her son and wonders when the world will see him the way that she does—a gift to the world from God.

That night as she fixes supper there's a knock. She goes to the door—they're no longer in that barn, mind you—and there is an entourage of strangers, speaking different languages, it seems from all over the world. Little did she know that in the background, in other lands and behind the scenes, the world was looking for him. And now they had found him. She welcomes them in. She puts on extra food. She offers them wine. Embarrassed, she hides the half-slurped Slurpee. She tries to hide the girl she is and put on the woman who is the mother of God's Son.

And here he is. Small and chubby. A heavy diaper. Showing these visitors his wooden tiger and elephant and monkey. And they give him gifts. Gifts befitting a king. They see him. They see who he is. And they respond. The Son of God revealed to the world. Here he is. And do you see? Do you see how they've responded? How the story is told? Jesus has done nothing. He can do nothing. And we're told his name six times in six different ways: Jesus, King of the Jews, the Christ, Ruler, Shepherd of Israel, the Child. Here he is. Do you see him? He has done nothing but get born, and these are the names he brings with him. These are the names he shows up with.

And do you see what he does? By doing nothing but get born he launches an exploring party from far off. He inspires a new star. Disrupts the rule of a king. Troubles a nation. Fulfills prophecy. Becomes the target of an assassination attempt, and simultaneously the object of worship. All because, and only because, he is revealed to the world. A baby who gives rise to seeking, finding, and giving.

Jesus is born, waiting to be found.

Act 5.

And that brings us to Act 5. Which happens to be the act when you and I are right now. The Child still appears. He still waits. He still looks to be found. Jesus is born, waiting to be found, waiting for you. So I ask you—where do you find him? And what do you bring him? You and I are called to him just as the kings and queens before us. Where have you looked? Where have you found? What have you brought to him? Jesus is Born, waiting to be found, waiting for you.

I can tell you where I've found him. It has been in what I would have considered unlikely places. One of those places is, over the past month or so, at the bus stop across the street, the one we made into a nativity scene—with Joseph standing next to the fire in the barrel, with Mary recovering on the bench, and finally with baby Jesus laid in the newspaper-lined recycling bin—I've found him there. And it seems like I'm not the only one. People have come to that bus stop, and instead of hailing a bus, they have left their gifts. Two dollars under Mary's hand. A PowerBar for her to keep up her strength. A note of love for the child. And as people have responded to the baby in this new nativity out of time, I have found Jesus.

As I've found him, wherever I've found him, I've realized that I don't have much to give. Certainly not gold. But like those who've come before me, I give him all that I have. I give him glory. I give him my prayers. And ultimately, I work through my life to give him myself. I don't have many gifts to give him. But I give him what I have. Simply because he has come.

I only tell you these things so that you might make your own journey. Where do you find him? What do you give him? Jesus is Born, waiting to be found, waiting for you.

THE BEGINNING OF HOPE (PS 137)

Note: This sermon was preached on the Sunday after the Paris terror attacks of November 13, 2015. The imagery of the sermon brings the congregation together with the psalmist at the river's edge. While imagery is less contemporized in this sermon than in some others here, it is in this sermon, I think, that I've come closest to Paul's hermeneutic in 1 Corinthians discussed in chapter 4. The whole of the sermon is enacted anachronism, setting God's people today into the continuous flow of tragedy and hope across time, from past and into the future.

There are times when it seems that hope is within our hands. Hope is there and we grasp it. It is in our fists and we hold it tight. You hear your kids in the other room laughing, safe. Anxiety disappears as you go to your prenatal appointment and they are able to find the heartbeat right away, and what's more they tell you it's a girl. Another year is marked as you exchange gifts on another anniversary. Food is on your table. Your heat is on. And we are grateful for these moments. Moments of peace. Moments of hope.

But then there are other times. Times when the hands with which we hold on to hope are violently ripped open and hope is stolen and peace is shattered as life is ripped in two. Suffering enters for us or for our world and hope moves from our hands to our fingertips and then finally it becomes an evanescent vapor just outside of our reach. In those moments we're in danger of losing hope, of losing sight of God in the midst of our pain. As we encounter the tragedy of the world, a world that is too often tragic, too often violent. Where do we find the beginning of hope once again?

I've felt that way since Friday, hearing the news coming out of Paris. You've seen the news, right? Coordinated terror attacks. In Paris, in France, half a world away, yet still closer to home. No longer violence in the Middle East, it is an attack in the West once again. In a matter of moments 129 people dead, more sure to be added to that number; 352 seriously wounded by guns and suicide bombers . . . and only 8 of them. A country thrown into a state of shock and panic. A world in mourning. Peace and hope evaporate.

Where do we find our hope? Where do we find our peace in the world? Especially when those things are in short supply. Where do we find hope in our broken world? Where does hope begin for us?

The one place, the first place for us to look, is to the story. The story of God with his people through all of time. Fortunately, and unfortunately, we aren't the first, or the last, of God's people upon whom the sky falls. Look back to the old story, which is written for us. And when we look there maybe we can find hope for hopeless time.

[Read Ps 137]

As we come to this psalm that is just steeped in pain we find our poet beginning his song on the edge of the river in Babylon. But the story begins much earlier than this. Israel had had years and years of goodness and blessing from God. Even in their sin, even in their love of idols, in placing everything in the world before God, God had given them grace upon grace. God had called them back over and over. But they didn't' turn back. For them at that point in their lives all of that God stuff was misty-eyed fairy tales and bedtime stories. And they were too old for that. And they had walked away from God.

But then one day the horses arrived. Horses with chariots and soldiers with spears and with fire. Line after line of mounted beasts on the horizon stamping dry earth into massive clouds of dust over the city. And when the armies hit they hit hard. They took everything that they wanted, and they killed everything that they didn't. And they did it with brutality. But not all, mind you. Warfare in that day had an ultimate victory that an army would strategize for. They didn't kill everyone. They kept aside for themselves some of the people of Israel—the best and brightest, artists and musicians, those younger Israelites—they would carry them off as prisoners into Babylon and they would enculturate them into Babylonian culture and lead them in the worship of Babylonian gods. In making good Babylonians out of the good Israelites, they would ultimately declare victory over the God of Israel. As they take our poet brother on the march from Jerusalem to Babylon, they are declaring victory over Israel's God himself.

And here we find our brother along the river in agony. He sings to us out of history and out of a broken hope. He says they demanded songs from us, but how can we sing the songs of God in a foreign land? If I forget you Jerusalem, if I forget you God, may I forget my skills. May my tongue stick to the roof of my mouth! May I never be able to sing again! May I never be able to worship you! If I forget who I am. If I forget from where I've come. Then he calls out to God: do to them, oh God, what they did to us.

I can see him there. Just there. Feet in a foreign river. Harp thrown high in a tree in protest against his captors. Feebly calling out to God for a scrap of hope. As the world around him has fallen apart, he's asking the question, where does hope begin?

It's easy to see him over there, isn't it? It's easy for us to identify with him even. We're not hauled off into a Babylonian exile . . . but, maybe, close enough. Terrorists marching into a theater and lining people up at the stage like some twisted tragic production, killing ninety people at once. Or a night out at a restaurant or the bar and thirty-nine people killed in less than fifteen minutes by bullets and bombs. Tragedy hits in all the scenes of the story.

But it doesn't have to be a terror attack in Paris. Peace is shattered with alarming regularity closer to home. How often do we see the cycle of bullying that leads to violence on a school campus with a gun? Or even closer to home than that, how often is hope in our world shattered by what might be described as humanity's inhumanity? Sometimes it seems like we invent ways to hurt one another with violence or with words, with our actions or with our inaction. And hope evaporates. And the world just hurts.

Now don't get me wrong. We look at the story of Israel and we see that very specifically in this part of the story in this context the judgment that comes upon Israel is because of their sin. And what I want to say to you is that ultimately all pain is the result of sin. But that doesn't mean that those who suffer pain specifically deserve it. Even if Israel suffered specifically because of their sin, it doesn't follow that the tragedy that we see in the world—in Paris or anywhere else—is specifically a judgment upon the people who suffer it. All tragedy and pain is the result of sin. It is the nature of living in a broken world. Tragedy is first and foremost tragedy, and we do well to first and foremost mourn tragedy and pain, rather than to judge. We sit next to our brother poet at the river, feet in the water next to his, and like our brother by the river we mourn. With him we cry for hope in tragedy's wake. Can you hear him there? Can you see him there in the river, searching, looking for something to hold on to?

As I see him there at the river in Babylon, I think it would have been the easy road for him to just write God off. To walk away: I've had enough, God. I can't believe that you'd let this happen. I'm going to take my ball and go home. It might be the easier path to walk away from God when we're at the river, unable to even sing his songs.

But for him, for our brother here at the river, there is no hope down the road of abandonment. To our ears it sounds like a call for revenge. In the last part of the song he says specifically, "O daughter of Babylon, doomed to be destroyed, blessed shall he be who repays you with what you have done to us! Blessed shall he be who takes your little ones and dashes them against the rock!" It is one of the saddest and most maligned texts in all of Scripture.

What sounds here like a call for vengeance is actually something so much deeper than that. It is a cry to God for hope. It is a cry for God to go back and remember his promises to his people. It is a cry that comes from a wound that it is so deep that it can only drive you back to God, and not farther from him, because there is no farther to go. It is the cry for God in the midst of tragedy to remember and fulfill his promises to his people. The cry of our brother as we sit by the river is rooted deep in the history and scripture of Israel. All the way back to Genesis chapter 12 our brother remembers that God made his promise to Abraham, which by default is God's promise to all of God's people throughout all of God's history: "Now the LORD said to Abram, 'Go from your country and your kindred and your father's house to the land that I will show you. And I will make of you a great nation, and I will bless you and make your name great, so that you will be a blessing. I will bless those who bless you, and him who dishonors you I will curse, and in you all the families of the earth shall be blessed.'"

God says to Abraham, and to all of God's people throughout all of history, "I will remember you—no matter what, I will remember you! Those who bless you I will bless. Those who dishonor you I will curse." And here our brother takes that promise in the most literal way possible. He says, "God, remember your promise! Do to them what they did to us. Repay them with the brutality that they showed toward us!" It is a desperate cry for God to remember his promises, for God to remember his people. Stuck very far from our Father, our brother cries out to God in the only voice he has. It is the voice of God's promise. "I will never forget you again, oh my God! Please, God, do not forget your children!"

And of course, God does not forget his children. God remembers his promise and fulfills his promise to the singer, to us, and to all of his people, even if it's not in the way that we imagine it with our feet in the river. But God fulfills his promise to bless and to judge, not in the carrying out of revenge, but in the grace offered and received in Jesus Christ. It is in Christ that his promises are fulfilled and the world is put to rights. As Jesus is the one who comes to take the judgment of the world upon himself—the pain of the world upon his own shoulders—we see God fulfilling his promises. As Christ comes and suffers the tragedy of us all, you see the hope that starts to shine through our brother's pain, and our own.

We cry out to God in our pain because God is the beginning of all things. Our God is the beginning of all hope. As our brother stands there in the river, in the current of all of God's hurting people, he cries with us!

He cries with Moses at the injustice of seeing an enslaved people in Egypt!

He cries with David, who cries out in repentance after his sin with Bathsheba and against Uriah.

He stands with Paul and Barnabas in a Philippian prison, singing the songs of God in a foreign land, waiting for the deliverance of God to be visited upon his servants!

And he stands and cries with us as we stand and plead for hope. As we plead for God to remember his promises in the midst of history's tragedies.

Our brother looked back to God's promise in Genesis, and he read it very literally. While his vision was clouded by the limitations of his moment in the story, not able to see God's full plan in the reality of history, the truth is that God would bring grace in Christ, fulfilling all of his promises. From his vantage point our brother looked back at the hope of the promise God made in Abraham.

For you and for me, though, our vantage point is different. We live after the life and death and life again of Jesus. With our feet in the river, in the reality of Christ, we look at the river ahead, not behind. We see the hope of God's promises as well as our brother did, but we look forward to the future promises and their fulfillment in our midst. We look for the consummation of all things in the goodness that God has promised. Our hope is in Christ, who is the beginning of all hope. Jesus is the beginning of all hope.

Jesus is the beginning of all hope for Paris. For Syria. For Iraq!

Jesus is the beginning of all hope for our nation. For Hilmar. For us!

Jesus is the beginning of all hope for you. The beginning of all hope for me.

Jesus is the beginning of all hope.

Jesus died, and he died in tragedy, with the tragedy of the whole world upon him. And when he did, he inaugurated the promise of hope when he rose from the dead. And the promise is this: Even as you are caught in between the pain of history and the looked-for consummation of his promises, Jesus is the one who was, and who is, and who is coming again. He is coming to put the world to rights. To bring God's kingdom in its fullness.

John writes about the fulfillment of the promise: "Then the angel showed me the river of the water of life, bright as crystal, flowing from the throne of God and of the Lamb through the middle of the street of the city; also, on either side of the river, the tree of life with its twelve kinds of fruit, yielding its fruit each month. The leaves of the tree were for the healing of the nations. No longer will there be anything accursed, but the throne of God and of the Lamb will be in it, and his servants will worship him. They will see his face, and his name will be on their foreheads. And night will be no more. They will need no light of lamp or sun, for the Lord God will be their light, and they will reign forever and ever. And he said to me, 'These words are trustworthy and true. And the Lord, the God of the spirits of the prophets, has sent his angel to show his servants what must soon take place. And behold, I am coming soon. Blessed is the one who keeps the words of the prophecy of this book.'"

Tragedy comes, but hope overcomes because God's promise is sure. In our hurting in the water of a foreign river, when songs are hard to sing and when pain abounds, we cry to God to remember his promises to us, for the fulfillment of his promise to come soon. Jesus is the beginning of all hope.

In the meantime, we who have his promise cling to it and share it with the world. Those who have received the hope of Christ share the hope of Christ with a world shadowed with suffering. So today, as we go from this place and we watch the news and hear what happens next . . . as we go from this place, we go as those who have received in Christ the hope of resurrection, of restoration, of justice, of love, of forgiveness, of peace. As we go out today we are those who cry out to God to soon fulfill his promises. Go in hope and share with the world the hope that is in Christ. Because Jesus is the beginning of your hope. Jesus is the beginning of all hope.

THE WORLD UPSIDE DOWN

An Easter Sermon (Mark 16:1–8)

Note: The form of this sermon utilizes Lowry's loop. As an Easter sermon, it is a bit longer than I typically preach in my church.

[1: upsetting the equilibrium]

It had been a long night. Not just long, but dark. And not just night, but an entire night, the next day, and night again. There had been little eating or sleeping. Even less talking about what had happened. Friday Jesus had been taken, nailed to a cross. They had all been there. They had all watched. They saw the nails put through his hands and his feet. They forced themselves to look even when the spear pierced his side. And they followed at a distance when Joseph and Nicodemus laid Jesus in the tomb and rolled the stone in front. That was Friday. And now it was Sunday. And it seemed to them as if the light of the sun had not shown its face since their Lord had died. Darkness and disbelief punctuated the slow minutes as time marched ahead. Now it was Sunday morning, and it was time to attend to his body. Tradition and despair kept them from visiting the tomb before that morning, but three women steeled themselves for what lay ahead. Mary and Mary and Salome journeyed to the graveyard, to his tomb, to give him a proper burial. It was a quiet walk. While the reality of his death had by this time set in, acceptance is at times no comfort when your greatest love and your greatest hope has been murdered. They inched along in silence, tears more difficult to hold back the closer they came to seeing their Lord once again, this time with his life drained from him.

The sun had risen and they went to the tomb. The large stone that had sat in front had already been rolled back, indicating that they weren't the first ones here. Panic-fueled adrenaline rushed as they set themselves to walk through the opening into the grave, not knowing who had beaten them to the body or what they would find. To say that they were "alarmed," as Mark says here, might have been the greatest understatement in all of God's whole story. I mean, would alarmed be an adequate descriptor if you were to walk into a mausoleum expecting to lay flowers and what you saw was a young man dressed in white and waiting for you? I mean, how creepy is that? How frightening? How . . . horrible, in fact. This is the shot in the movie punctuated by the background music suddenly shifting into silence as the plot is set in motion.

The women turn the corner and they see an angel, who speaks to them, telling them that Jesus has left the building, promising that they will see the one they watched die and be buried, alive and well, in Galilee. This is, in a word, unsettling. But it is, in fact, everything that Jesus said would happen. And it is, in fact, everything that the disciples and these women had ever hoped for. That Jesus would, in his death, come back to life just as he said he would. And Mark records for us the joy of their discovery.

Just kidding. What Mark records is actually their abject flight-inducing fear: "And they went out and fled from the tomb, for trembling and astonishment had seized them, and they said nothing to anyone, for they were afraid."

This . . . is not the Easter story that we are generally used to. Is it? It strikes me that it shows quite a different side of the morning than we are used to celebrating: entering the garden at sunrise, the voice tenderly speaking to Mary, Mary mistaking Jesus for the gardener, running to tell the disciples the news of the resurrected savior. Matthew and Luke—they give us the Easter story of a sunrise and a garden. Not Mark, no. Mark just gives us a picture of terror that can come only from seeing an empty tomb and an angel where you fully expected a dead body to be.

On the one hand, I find their fear a completely rational response to something that is generally so far outside of human experience. But at the same time I find it strange, in that this is exactly what Jesus had told them would happen. Jesus told those closest to him that he would die but that he would live again. It isn't as if he hadn't tried to prepare them for this. He told them how this would go down. The angel here even explains it all to them. And what's more, this is everything that they had ever hoped for—that Jesus would rise like a phoenix from the ashes and triumph over sin and death! And yet, they tremble and shake and flee and shut their mouths out of fear. Fear is generally not the emotion we associate with Easter morning. But here, the writer of the gospel emphasizes that it was the only emotion that seized those who first came upon the emptiness of the tomb.

And it makes me wonder: why? Why are these women afraid of what they've seen here? What is there on Easter to inspire such a deadening fear as we look upon the tomb that does not hold the dead? It may be that before we get to the joy of Easter's resurrection, we must face the fear inspired by the empty tomb.

[2: analyzing the discrepancy]

You might approach the question by asking why anyone fears anything at all.

Maybe the most common reason that we fear anything at all has to do with our own well-being. We experience fear in relation to imminent danger, risk, harm. This is intimately related to our fear of the unknown. Watch any scary movie—the most intense moment of the film comes when you aren't quite sure what is going to happen but you are pretty positive that it is going to involve that dumb guy over there getting killed. You ride a ski lift to the absolute top of the mountain and you stand at the precipice of a sheer drop-off that is sure to leave you in a cast once you tip your board past the point of no return. Most of us have an aversion to pain and are good enough at prediction to let fear get the best of us in that situation. Those who do not have that fear either end up in a cast or on the medal stand at the Olympics. And it is fear that prevents either you or me from being the one in the cast or the guy with the gold.

But while all of those most basic fundamentals of self-preservation are totally legit reasons for fear, it strikes me that the women at the tomb didn't face any of them. Read the story—there is no danger, no fear of personal harm. There is a young man in a white robe. Moms of teenagers face that every morning as the family wakes up to get ready for school. He calms their fears, gives them the good news that Jesus has risen from the dead, and tells them where they can find him. There is no secret, no suspense, no scary-movie tension. He tells them the end of the story, what is going to come next. There is only Jesus doing exactly what he said he would do—rise after three days. And so, it seems to me, this can't be the reason for their fears.

Another reason that we fear is having to face a reality that we really do not want to face. We wake up to something disappointing, or witness the fabric of our lives altered in ways that we find deeply unpleasant. Looking out onto the landscape of this new reality we fear the unknown that we haven't yet experienced. It might be the loss of a loved one in our life who has always been there—a parent, a friend, a child. It could be the brokenness of a relationship that we love, with someone that we love. We experience this fear when someone turns up missing in our lives. We fail the people around us, or they fail us, and we wake up to new realities that we never wanted to live in. And we experience fear at the loss of stability in the life we thought we had and yet have lost, and now stare into the unknowable future.

But that isn't what they encountered at the tomb. It wasn't a moment of unthinkable loss, of waking up to a reality that they had never envisioned. That had already happened when they woke up Saturday morning to a world in which Jesus had died. Now, this first morning of the week they actually wake to the reality that Jesus had promised. A reality that, if they'd heard any word that he'd said, they would have hoped for with all of their hearts. This was, in fact, the best-case scenario for them. Jesus is alive! If they were to do a cost-benefit analysis on this particular reality, they would find themselves coming out quite ahead.

Consistently, when American teens are asked what they fear most in the world, the top responses are (in this order) terror attacks, spiders, death, failure, war, harm, being alone, the future, and nuclear war. Two things there are striking to me: fear of spiders more than death? And where are clowns on that list?

But no. No indication of any of those things at the tomb. In fact, when I examine the scene—as the sun rises and light creeps over the valley, as they arrive to find their loved one, their Lord, now living, having conquered death, as they meet the herald of this news in the freshness of an empty tomb, no longer smelling of death but only of the spices and flowers that they've brought with them—I can really only see cause for joy, and singing, and dancing, and laughing, and kicking death while he's down! But still, there's something that inspired their shudders and silence and fleeing and fear.

So, it has to be something else then. Maybe it is another thing altogether, more fundamental, more simple, more simply overlooked by us who were not there, us who sit back and analyze years later.

[3: sudden shift]

There are times in life when the truth hurts. And there are other times altogether when the truth comforts. And there are other moments, admittedly more rare than the others, when the truth does absolutely everything all at once. And when it does the world turns upside down; everything changes.

The very nature of your life changes. That, I think, is what terrified these first visitors to the empty tomb.

[4: experiencing the gospel]

Think of it. They show up at the tomb expecting to find a body. I think that they probably had hopes of a resurrection—Jesus himself had told them of it—but I wonder if they ever really had the expectation that those hopes would be realized with a body actually coming back to life. Look at them: they stand in an empty tomb. If they had been able to believe Jesus's words, they would not have looked for him there. Their presence at the tomb indicates they never expected their greatest hopes to be realized. Yet it is empty, not because no one's ever been there—it is empty because its former occupant has stood up and walked out. It is everything that they've ever hoped for. Everything that Jesus had told them. Yet they had never really expected any of it would actually come to pass. And now, here it is, all of it, played out right before them. Can you imagine everything that this moment in time validates for them? For us?

If Jesus has risen from the dead:

His words—all of his words—are God's words. And if he told the truth in walking away from death, then he told the truth about everything else too. This empty tomb validates all of Jesus's words as God's words, full of truth and power. His promises are promises that will come to pass. You know that because his promises have come to pass, in the emptiness of the tomb.

His love—all of his love—is God's love. And nothing now, nothing, not even our sin or death, can separate us from that love. God's love in Jesus led Jesus to the cross and death. And God's love in Jesus led Jesus out of death and into life. And Jesus invites us into that same life beyond death. The barrier between us and God is removed in Jesus's life and death and life again.

Life—all of life in the life that he gives—has conquered death. There is now no fear in death. There is now no anxiety in life. And now, death no longer reigns in tyranny over our lives' ends. Life has conquered death.

Do you see it? In this one moment in the tomb, this moment when the women, and us, stand before the young man, this one moment has changed the nature of everything. It has turned the world on its head. All of life is upside down. In the face of it the women are disoriented. They walked into the tomb in the comfort of knowing that Jesus was dead and that the world went on—life ends in death. The status quo makes no demands on its adherents.

But they walk out in complete and total discomfort in the reality that everything has changed—in Christ, death ends in life. They walked into the tomb out of a world that they knew, knowing that Jesus had died and was lying there dead. They walked out into a world where none of the rules applied anymore. Where everything was up for grabs. Where nothing could be taken for granted, since the most certain thing in the entire world—death—no longer existed because Jesus walked out of death and into life ahead of them. In the tomb we meet a reality that we have always hoped for but have never really expected to exist: in Christ, in the transaction at the tomb, death has met its end and all of reality has changed.

Is it any wonder that they trembled? Is it any wonder that they were overtaken by the shudders, that they fled? The sun had dawned on a world in which God was near, sin was beaten, and death no longer had the final word. How disorienting is that? It is like, well, it is like being born again into a world you did not know and could not hope for and whose realities are yet to be learned. It is like being born once again as a child born into the vastness of an unknown world, with God as our Father, and Jesus as the one who leads us home.

We enter the tomb from a world where life ends in death. We exit the tomb onto a world where death merely opens up into life—life eternal with God.

The reality is big. It is new. It is scary. It is the fear that comes with realizing that everything you have ever hoped for in the depth of your being is true, and it has actually come to pass. And the world has changed, and you must change with it. It is the fear at the realization that the world has turned upside down. And yet, it is glorious. That in Christ all our hurts and fears are repaired! That in Christ, our death is merely a rest stop on the journey to the eternal life we were created for—life together with God.

[5: anticipating the consequences]

Please note well: their fear must not have lasted long. As is the case when you crest the first big hill on a roller coaster, screams of terror soon give way to incredible excitement. From this moment Jesus appears. First to the women. Then, as Paul recounts in 1 Corinthians 15, to the disciples, and then to more than five hundred, to James, to all the apostles, and finally to Paul. And, Paul argues, the risen Christ has appeared to you as well. He says in that place that this is the message that you first received, it is the reality of the world in which you currently stand, and it is the new world in which you are ever and always being saved.

When those women walked out onto a new world stretched before them as born again into a new place, you walked out of the tomb with them, and with Jesus. It is in the disorienting newness of this world that we walk into the world of Easter. And fear gives way to faith. And faith, as it matures and we grow into our forgiveness and into a world where death and sin hold no fear, faith gives way to joy, and discipleship; and we, as newborns in a new world, first crawl and then walk and then, if we are lucky, run after the one who has entered life ahead of us.

Peter says it this way:

> Blessed be the God and Father of our Lord Jesus Christ! According to his great mercy, he has caused us to be born again to a living hope through the resurrection of Jesus Christ from the dead, to an inheritance that is imperishable, undefiled, and unfading, kept in heaven for you, who by God's power are being guarded through faith for a salvation ready to be revealed in the last time. In this you rejoice, though now for a little while, if necessary, you have been grieved by various trials, so that the tested genuineness of your faith—more precious than gold that perishes though it is tested by fire—may be found to result in praise and glory and honor at the revelation of Jesus Christ. Though you have not seen him, you love him. Though you do not now see him, you believe in him and rejoice with joy that is inexpressible and filled with glory, obtaining the outcome of your faith, the salvation of your souls. (1 Pet 1:3–9)

We are born again into a new world with new rules. Disorienting, but it is the world as it was created to be. Where death has lost its sting, sin has lost its power, and the God who loves us has really, really, actually, in truth and in reality, gone into and through death in order to bring us into life—real, actual, true life. It is a new world where Jesus has overturned our separation from God by eliminating the specter of death. Jesus raised turns the world upside down.

THE MIDDLE (2 COR 5:11–21)

Note: This sermon was followed immediately by the sacraments of baptism and communion.

"And so, we were at church camp, and I framed the kid for selling cocaine. I had the head counselor threaten him with calling the police and, worse, his dad . . ."

You ever walked in on the middle of a conversation? No context. No beginning. And you can't imagine that any ending that might be coming would make sense of the piece that you just heard? The middle of the story I just told you could have heard from me, in a group of youth pastors, at a denominational conference, at dinner, when the question on the table was, what's the worst thing you've ever done in youth ministry? The story has a beginning . . . toilet paper and the lust for revenge. It has a complication—the kid so hurt and scared over being framed that he locked himself in the bathroom until four in the morning. It has a twist towards resolution of the plot—a moment when the kid, in the grace of Christ, offered me forgiveness. And a larger ending, with a bunch of youth pastors eating dinner together in Denver, Colorado, everyone stopping what they are doing, looking at me, and saying, "I would never do that," and "Did you keep your job?"

Someone once said—I can't tell who it was anymore—that every story has a beginning, a middle, and an end. And that is true. The beginning gives the context, introduces characters, and provides the plot points for the rest of the story. The middle explores some kind of trouble, something that by cause-and-effect relationship through time gets undone. And in the end, something new is done up again. We like to call it resolution. If the story is a comedy, there is a happily ever after. If it is a tragedy, there is just an ever after as characters live with the consequences of life. In any case, that's how stories work.

Each and every one of us has entered into the story in the middle. In fact, every day that we wake up and put our feet on the floor and brush our teeth and wash our hair, we enter again into the Middle of the Story. The Story, God's Story, started long before us. "In the beginning . . ." the book says. In the beginning God created the heavens and the earth. And all along we get to know this God, who is simultaneously the storyteller and the story's main character. In recent months, we've tried to get a fix on just who this God is: Father, Son, Holy Spirit.

God our Father is the one who is all over the place. The one who authors the story. The one who brings resolution out of trouble. He is the one who has created the story and everything in it. He is the one who directs the plot. God the Son is the one who comes in the midst of it all. He is God with us, the one who has died to bring us back to God. He is the one who comes in the middle of the story to point the way to the end. To point the way, really, to new beginning: an eternity with the one who loves us best. God the Holy Spirit is the one who has been here all along, and yet in this part of the story comes to dwell within God's people. To call them, to set apart and send into the world, in order to call and give the ability to God's people to love God and love neighbor.

To the mix of these main characters comes the supporting cast for the story. We've been there from the beginning, really, with Adam and Eve on the scene early on. But all through the story God's people have been present, providing the tragedies and comedies all through the story's middle. And into the midst of the story enters the church. That's you, that's me, together, waking up each day, throughout our days, to occupy the story's middle, telling it through on to the end . . . or, really, through on to its new beginning.

This is the story. The story of God, creating the world, in the world, in his people. The story of God bringing the world close to him, in each and every minute the story is told, his kingdom more and more into the reality of the world, even if we're so close to the story we don't see the bigger plot. That's the story. And me and you, we walk into the middle of it. Every day, we walk into the middle of it. And we do our best to get our bearings and keep it going. God tells the story, and we live its middle every day.

In this letter to the church, Paul writes about the middle. He writes to us, "For the love of Christ controls us, because we have concluded this: that one has died for all, therefore all have died; and he died for all, that those who live might no longer live for themselves but for him who for their sake died and was raised." There it is, the core plot line of the middle: Christ died for us, we died with Christ, Christ controls us, that those who live might not live for themselves, but would live for Christ.

That is it. That is the middle. That is God, here and now. That is our lives as we live in the middle. The great exchange: Christ died for us, and so we live for Christ and for others. From every day we wake up until the day he returns. We tell the middle of this story with our lives until he comes.

And, if you didn't get it the first go-round, Paul repeats himself in different words: "Therefore, if anyone is in Christ, he is a new creation. The old has passed away; behold, the new has come. All this is from God, who through Christ reconciled us to himself and gave us the ministry of reconciliation; that is, in Christ God was reconciling the world to himself, not counting their trespasses against them, and entrusting to us the message of reconciliation. Therefore, we are ambassadors for Christ, God making his appeal through us. We implore you on behalf of Christ, be reconciled to God."

In this story's middle, which we wake up into every day, God has made you a new creature. No longer yourself, no longer considering others or the world according to yourself, but only seeing others and the world through the person and work of Christ. In fact, Paul says that we, you and me, are ambassadors for Christ, and in this middle of the story, God makes his appeal to the world directly through us. You, me, us—we represent Jesus as we live the story with our lives, from the middle until the end.

On Sundays we come together and talk a lot about the story's beginnings: creation, Israel, Jesus.... Sometimes we talk about the story's end (or new beginning), when we talk about the hope of Jesus's return. The beginning and the end of the story are important, giving us bearings for living right now. The beginning gives us the history from which we've come. The end gives us the trajectory along which we're headed. And now, each and every day, we've walked in on this thing in the middle.

Let me tell you what this means. Paul writes to you, to our church, that in every moment of every day God is telling his story though you, through your life. God is making his appeal to the world, through you. God is reconciling the world to himself, through Christ, in you. In this middle of the story, it is your calling to enter in and tell it for yourself and to others. That is, you live in reconciliation to God. You live the hope of God in the midst of what might be hopelessness. You treat others with the love that Christ has given you. You tell the story of the kingdom already come, because in you, the kingdom already has. You forgive in an unforgiving world, you love when love is scarce and when you are confronted with the unlovable, you live in peace when all around there is unrest, you live into goodness even when confronted with the bad.

We do these things because this is what Christ did for us. We do these things because Christ calls us. We do these things because God's Spirit empowers us. We do these things because God tells the story, and we live its middle every day. And following Christ through the story, from one minute of it to another, is what living the middle is all about. God tells the story, and we live its middle every day.

We're lucky in this. You don't always get the whole of the story. Sometimes you just walk in on a part of it. You catch the beginning of the movie on USA Network on a Saturday afternoon after doing the dishes or mowing the lawn, but you can't stay for the end because your wife says you have to help with Trunk or Treat. Or you just catch the tail end of the joke your friend is telling to the group, and while everyone is laughing you halfheartedly laugh along, pretending you know the punch line. Or you walk in on the middle of the story of a youth pastor executing an ill-conceived prank, and the context and conclusion are lost somewhere along the way.

But we, God's people, his church, we have the whole story. In the beginning, God created. We have the hope of the end from the beginning: someday Christ returns, and God will create again, whole and new and beautiful, just like in the beginning, out of dirt this time enriched by the blood of his Son. And all along the way, all along the middle, you and me live as those who Christ has made his own, and live as ambassadors of the story we live along the way. The church is the middle of God's story. And we live and love every day that God places before us. God tells the story, and we live its middle every day.

We come this morning to both baptism and communion together. Both are activities in the church when we look back on the story's beginning, when we anticipate its new beginning, and join ourselves to the whole, together, in participation with God in the drama of our covenant together. So, let us join together, with one another and with Christ, as those who tell the story from its middle, out of its beginning, to the very end.

Bibliography

Achtemeier, Elizabeth. "The Artful Dialogue: Some Thoughts on the Relation of Biblical Studies and Homiletics." *Interpretation* 35 (1981) 18–31.
———. *Preaching as Theology and Art*. Nashville: Abingdon, 1984.
Allmen, John-Jacques von. *Preaching and Congregation*. Translated by B. L. Nicholas. London: Lutterworth, 1962.
Anderson, Bernard W. *The Unfolding Drama of the Bible*. 4th ed. Minneapolis: Fortress, 2006.
Aristotle. *The Art of Rhetoric*. Translated by H. C. Lawson-Tancred. London: Penguin, 1991.
Auerbach, Erich. *Mimesis: The Representation of Reality in Western Literature*. Princeton: Princeton University Press, 2003.
Austin, J. L. *How to Do Things with Words*. Oxford: Clarendon, 1962.
Balthasar, Hans Urs von. *Theo-drama: Theological Dramatic Theory*. Translated by Graham Harrison. 5 vols. San Francisco: Ignatius, 1988–98.
Barth, Karl. *The Word of God and the Word of Man*. New York: Harper & Row, 1957.
Barthes, Roland. *S/Z*. Translated by Richard Miller. New York: Farrar, Straus and Giroux, 1974.
Bartlett, David L. "Allegory, Allegoresis." In *The New Interpreter's Handbook of Preaching*, edited by Paul Scott Wilson, 5–9. Nashville: Abingdon, 2008.
———. *Between the Bible and the Church: New Methods for Biblical Preaching*. Nashville: Abingdon, 1999.
Bauckham, Richard. "Jürgen Moltmann." In *The Modern Theologians: An Introduction to Christian Theology in the Twentieth Century*, edited by David F. Ford, 209–24. Oxford: Blackwell, 1997.
Bernard of Clairvaux. *St. Bernard's Sermons for the Seasons and Principal Festivals of the Year*. Vol. 3. Dublin: Browne and Nolan, 1925.
Bevington, David, ed. *Medieval Drama*. Boston: Houghton Mifflin, 1975.
Blackwood, Andrew W. *Preaching from the Bible*. New York: Abingdon, 1941.
———. *The Preparation of Sermons*. New York: Abingdon-Cokesbury, 1948.
Bloch, Mark. *Feudal Society*. Translated by L. A. Manyon. Chicago: University of Chicago Press, 1964.

Blue, B. B. "Food Offered to Idols and Jewish Food Laws." In *Dictionary of Paul and His Letters*, edited by Gerald F. Hawthorne et al., 306–10. Downers Grove, IL: InterVarsity, 1993.

Bordwell, David, and Kristen Thompson. *Film Art: An Introduction*. 7th ed. Boston: Mcgraw Hill, 2004.

Brøndsted, Gustav. "Two World Concepts—Two Languages." In vol. 2 of *Kerygma and Myth: A Theological Debate*, edited by Hans-Werner Bartsch, 216–305. London: SPCK, 1962.

Bultmann, Rudolf. *Jesus Christ and Mythology*. New York: Scribner, 1958.

Burke, Peter. "The Sense of Anachronism from Petrarch to Poussin." In *Time in the Medieval World*, edited by Chris Humphrey and W. M. Ormrod, 157–73. Rochester, NY: York Medieval Press, 2001.

Bushnell, Horace. "Christian Comprehensiveness." In *Building Eras in Religion*, 386–459. New York: Scribner's, 1881.

———. *Christian Nurture*. New Haven: Yale University Press, 1953.

———. "A Discourse on Dogma and Spirit; or the True Reviving of Religion: Delivered before the Porter Rhetorical Society, at Andover, September 1848." In *God in Christ: Three Discourses Delivered at New Haven, Cambridge, and Andover, with a Preliminary Dissertation on Language*, 277–356. New York: Scribner's, 1876.

———. *Nature and the Supernatural as Together Constituting the One System of God*. New York: Scribner, Armstrong, 1877.

———. "Preliminary Dissertation on the Nature of Language as Related to Thought and Spirit." In *God in Christ: Three Discourses, Delivered at New Haven, Cambridge, and Andover, with a Preliminary Dissertation on Language*, 9–117. New York: Scribner's, 1876.

———. "The Reason of Faith." In *Sermons for the New Life*, 87–105. New York: Scribner, 1858.

———. "Training for the Pulpit Manward." In *Building Eras in Religion*, 221–48. New York: Scribner's, 1881.

Buttrick, David. *A Captive Voice: The Liberation of Preaching*. Louisville: Westminster John Knox, 1994.

———. *Homiletic: Moves and Structures*. Philadelphia: Fortress, 1987.

Campbell, Charles L. *Preaching Jesus: New Directions for Homiletics in Hans Frei's Postliberal Theology*. Grand Rapids: Eerdmans, 1997.

Chapell, Bryan. *Christ-Centered Preaching: Redeeming the Expository Sermon*. Grand Rapids: Baker, 1994.

Cherry, Conrad, ed. *Horace Bushnell: Sermons*. New York: Paulist, 1985.

Cleland, James T. *Preaching to Be Understood*. New York: Abingdon, 1965.

———. *The True and Lively Word*. New York: Scribner's, 1954.

Coleridge, Samuel Taylor. *Aids to Reflection*. From the 4th London ed. Edited by Henry Nelson Coleridge. Port Washington, NY: Kennikat, 1971.

———. *Biographia Literaria*. Edited by James Engell and W. Jackson Bate. Princeton: Princeton University Press, 1983.

Conyers, A. J. *God, Hope, and History: Jürgen Moltmann and the Christian Concept of History*. Macon, GA: Mercer University Press, 1988.

Craddock, Fred B. *As One without Authority*. Revised and with new sermons. St. Louis: Chalice, 2001.

———. *Preaching*. Nashville: Abingdon, 1985.

———. "When the Roll Is Called Down Here." *Preachingtoday.com* (2009). http://www.preachingtoday.com/sermons/sermons/2010/july/whentherolliscalleddownhere.html.
Crawford, Evans E., with Thomas H. Troeger. *The Hum: Call and Response in African American Preaching*. Nashville: Abingdon, 1995.
Davis, H. Grady. *Design for Preaching*. Philadelphia: Fortress, 1958.
Dorrien, Gary. "A Third Way in Theology? The Origins of Postliberalism." *Christian Century*, July 4–11, 2001, 16–21.
Duke, James O. *Horace Bushnell: On the Vitality of Biblical Language*. Chico, CA: Scholars, 1994.
Dulles, Avery. *Models of Revelation*. Garden City, NY: Doubleday, 1983.
Dunn, James D. G. *The Theology of Paul the Apostle*. Grand Rapids: Eerdmans, 1998.
Ebert, Roger. Review of *Romeo and Juliet*, directed by Franco Zeffirelli. September 17, 2000. http://www.rogerebert.com/reviews/great-movie-romeo-and-juliet-1968.
Edwards, O. C., Jr. *A History of Preaching*. Vol. 1. Nashville: Abingdon, 2004.
Edwards, Robert L. "Portrait of a People: Horace Bushnell's Hartford Congregation." In *Studies of the Church in History: Essays Honoring Robert S. Paul on His Sixty-Fifth Birthday*, edited by Horton Davies, 149–63. Allison Park, PA: Pickwick, 1983.
Ellingsen, Mark. *The Integrity of Biblical Narrative: Story in Theology and Proclamation*. Minneapolis: Fortress, 1990.
Elliott, Mark Barger. *Creative Styles of Preaching*. Louisville: Westminster John Knox, 2000.
Eslinger, Richard L. *Narrative and Imagination: Preaching the Worlds That Shape Us*. Minneapolis: Fortress, 1995.
———. *A New Hearing: Living Options in Homiletic Method*. Nashville: Abingdon, 1987.
———. *The Web of Preaching: New Options in Homiletic Method*. Nashville: Abingdon, 2002.
Farley, Edward. *Practicing Gospel: Unconventional Thoughts on the Church's Ministry*. Louisville: Westminster John Knox, 2003.
Farris, Stephen. *Preaching That Matters: The Bible and Our Lives*. Louisville: Westminster John Knox, 1998.
Fee, Gordon D. *The First Epistle to the Corinthians*. Grand Rapids: Eerdmans, 1987.
Fiske, John. *Introduction to Communication Studies*. London: Routledge, 1990.
Fosdick, Harry Emerson. *The Living of These Days: The Autobiography of Harry Emerson Fosdick*. New York: Harper Chapel, 1967.
Frei, Hans W. *The Eclipse of Biblical Narrative: A Study in Eighteenth and Nineteenth Century Hermeneutics*. New Haven: Yale University Press, 1974.
———. *The Identity of Jesus Christ*. 1975. Reprint, Eugene, OR: Wipf & Stock, 1997.
Geertz, Clifford. *The Interpretation of Cultures*. New York: Basic Books, 1973.
Grant, Robert M., and David Tracy. *A Short History of the Interpretation of the Bible*. 2nd ed., revised and enlarged. Philadelphia: Fortress, 1984.
Graves, Mike. *The Sermon as Symphony: Preaching and the Literary Forms of the New Testament*. Valley Forge, PA: Judson, 1997.
Green, Joel B., and Michael Pasquarello, eds. *Narrative Reading, Narrative Preaching: Reuniting New Testament Interpretation and Proclamation*. Grand Rapids: Baker, 2003.

Greene, Thomas M. *The Vulnerable Text: Essays on Renaissance Literature*. New York: Columbia University Press, 1986.

Greidanus, Sidney. *The Modern Preacher and the Ancient Text: Interpreting and Preaching Biblical Literature*. Grand Rapids: Eerdmans, 1988.

Hartt, Julian N. *A Christian Critique of American Culture: An Essay in Practical Theology*. New York: Harper & Row, 1967.

Hays, Richard B. *First Corinthians*. Louisville: Westminster John Knox, 1997.

———. *The Moral Vision of the New Testament: A Contemporary Introduction to New Testament Ethics*. San Francisco: HarperSanFrancisco, 1996.

Heyduck, Richard. *The Recovery of Doctrine in the Contemporary Church: An Essay in Philosophical Ecclesiology*. Waco: Baylor University Press, 2002.

Jacobsen, David Schnasa. "Homiletical Exegesis and Theologies of Revelation: Biblical Preaching from Text to Sermon in an Age of Methodological Pluralism." In *Systematisch Praktisch: Festschrift für Reiner Preul zum 65.Geburtstag*, edited by Wilfried Härle et al., 449–61. Marburg: Elwert, 2005.

———. *Preaching in the New Creation: The Promise of New Testament Apocalyptic Texts*. Louisville: Westminster John Knox, 1999.

Jensen, Richard A. *Telling the Story: Variety and Imagination in Preaching*. Minneapolis: Augsburg, 1980.

———. *Thinking in Story: Preaching in a Post-Literate Age*. Lima, OH: C.S.S. Publishing, 1993.

Jewett, Robert. *Saint Paul at the Movies*. Louisville: Westminster John Knox, 1993.

Johns, Cheryl Bridges. "Transcripts of the Trinity: Reading the Bible in the Presence of God." *Ex Auditu* 30 (2015) 155–64.

Johnston, A. F., ed. *The Mary Play*. http://www.chass.utoronto.ca/~ajohnsto/maryplay.html.

Johnston, Robert K., ed. *Reframing Theology and Film: New Focus for an Emerging Discipline*. Grand Rapids: Baker Academic, 2007.

Jones, Ilion T. *Principles and Practice of Preaching*. New York: Abingdon, 1956.

Jones, Larry Paul, and Jerry L. Sumney. *Preaching Apocalyptic Texts*. St. Louis: Chalice, 1999.

Kahrl, Stanley J., and Alexandra F. Johnston, eds. *The N-Town Plays: A Modernization*. http://homes.chass.utoronto.ca/~ajohnsto/frntmt.html.

Keener, Craig S. *The IVP Bible Background Commentary: New Testament*. Downers Grove, IL: IVP Academic, 1993.

Kolve, V. A. *The Play Called Corpus Christi*. Stanford: Stanford University Press, 1966.

Krentz, Edgar. *The Historical-Critical Method*. Philadelphia: Fortress, 1975.

Lash, Nicholas. "What Might Martyrdom Mean?" *Ex Auditu* 1 (1985) 14–24.

Lindbeck, George A. *The Nature of Doctrine: Religion and Theology in a Postliberal Age*. Louisville: Westminster John Knox, 1984.

Long, Thomas G. "The Life to Come: Preaching with Hope." *Concordia Journal* 22 (1996) 352–69.

———. "A Night at the Burlesque: Wanderings through the Pentecost Narrative." *Journal for Preachers* 14.4 (Pentecost, 1991) 25–31.

———. *Preaching and the Literary Forms of the Bible*. Philadelphia: Fortress, 1989.

———. "Preaching God's Future: The Eschatological Context of Christian Proclamation." In *Sharing Heaven's Music: The Heart of Christian Preaching*, edited by Barry L. Callen, 191–202. Nashville: Abingdon, 1995.

———. "The Significance of David Buttrick's Homiletic." *Homiletic* 12 (1987) 1–5.
Lose, David J. "Narrative and Proclamation in a Postliberal Homiletic." *Homiletic* 23 (1998) 1–14.
———. "Whither Hence, New Homiletic?" In Academy of Homiletics, *Papers of the Annual Meeting*, 35th Meeting (2000) 255–66.
Lowry, Eugene. *Doing Time in the Pulpit: The Relationship between Narrative and Preaching*. Nashville: Abingdon, 1985.
———. *The Homiletical Plot: The Sermon as Narrative Art Form*. Expanded ed. Louisville: Westminster John Knox, 2001.
———. *How to Preach a Parable: Designs for Narrative Sermons*. Nashville: Abingdon, 1989.
———. *The Sermon: Dancing the Edge of Mystery*. Nashville: Abingdon, 1997.
Luhrmann, Baz. *Behind the Red Curtain: Collector's Disc*. DVD: 20th Century Fox Home Entertainment, 2001.
McClain, William B. *Come Sunday: The Liturgy of Zion*. Nashville: Abingdon, 1990.
McClure, John S. *Other-wise Preaching: A Postmodern Ethic for Homiletics*. St. Louis: Chalice, 2001.
———. "Preaching, Eschatology and World View." *Journal for Preachers* 13.1 (Advent 1989) 2–10.
McGrath, Alister E. *The Genesis of Doctrine: A Study in the Foundations of Doctrinal Criticism*. Grand Rapids: Eerdmans, 1990.
McKee, Robert. *Story: Substance, Structure, Style, and the Principles of Screenwriting*. London: Methuen, 1999.
McKim, Donald K. *The Bible in Theology and Preaching: How Preachers Use Scripture*. Nashville: Abingdon, 1994.
Middleton, J. Richard, and Brian J. Walsh. *Truth Is Stranger than It Used to Be: Biblical Faith in a Postmodern Age*. London: SPCK, 1995.
Miles, Margaret R. *Seeing and Believing: Religion and Values in the Movies*. Boston: Beacon, 1996.
Mitchell, Henry. *Black Preaching: The Recovery of a Powerful Art*. Nashville: Abingdon, 1990.
———. *Celebration and Experience in Preaching*. Nashville: Abingdon, 1990.
———. *The Recovery of Preaching*. San Francisco: Harper & Row, 1977.
Moltmann, Jürgen. *The Coming of God: Christian Eschatology*. Translated by Margaret Kohl. Minneapolis: Fortress, 2004.
———. *The Future of Creation*. Translated by Margaret Kohl. London: SCM, 1979.
———. "Hope and History." *Theology Today* 25 (1968) 369–86.
———. "Theology as Eschatology." In *The Future of Hope: Theology as Eschatology*, edited by Frederick Herzog, 1–50. New York: Herder and Herder, 1970.
———. *Theology of Hope: On the Ground and the Implications of a Christian Eschatology*. Translated by James W. Leitch. 1967. Reprint, Minneapolis: Fortress, 1993.
———. *The Way of Jesus Christ: Christology in Messianic Dimensions*. Minneapolis: Fortress, 1993.
Nelson, Alan H. "'Sacred' and 'Secular' Currents in the Towneley Play of *Noah*." *Drama Survey* 3 (1964) 393–401.
Ollenburger, Ben C. "What Krister Stendahl 'Meant'—a Normative Critique of 'Descriptive Biblical Theology.'" *Horizons in Biblical Theology* 8 (1986) 61–98.

Ostwalt, Conrad. *Secular Steeples: Popular Culture and the Religious Imagination*. Harrisburg, PA: Trinity, 2003.

Overbye, Dennis. "Gravitational Waves Detected, Confirming Einstein's Theory." *New York Times*, February 27, 2016, http://www.nytimes.com/2016/02/12/science/ligo-gravitational-waves-black-holes-einstein.html.

Owst, G. R. *Literature and Pulpit in Medieval England*. Oxford: Blackwell, 1961.

———. *Preaching in Medieval England*. Cambridge: Cambridge University Press, 1926.

Pannenberg, Wolfhart. "The Revelation of God in Jesus of Nazareth." In *Theology as History*, edited by James M. Robinson and John B. Cobb Jr., 101–33. New York: Harper & Row, 1967.

Placher, William C. "Postliberal Theology." In *The Modern Theologians: An Introduction to Christian Theology in the Twentieth Century*, edited by David F. Ford, 343–56. Oxford: Blackwell, 1997.

Randolph, David James. *The Renewal of Preaching: A New Homiletic Based on the New Hermeneutic*. Philadelphia: Fortress, 1969.

Reid, Robert, Jeffery Bullock, and David Fleer. "Preaching as the Creation of an Experience: The Not-So-Rational Revolution of the New Homiletic." *Journal of Communication and Religion* 18 (1995) 1–9.

Robinson, Haddon. "The Church of God in Christ Chicken Restaurant." http://discovertheword.org/special-features/church-of-god-in-christ-chicken-restaurant/.

Romeo and Juliet. Directed by Franco Zeffirelli. Paramount, 1968. Blu Ray.

Rose, Lucy Atkinson. *Sharing the Word: Preaching and the Roundtable Church*. Louisville: Westminster John Knox, 1997.

Rushkoff, Douglas, and Liam Sharp. *Testament*. Vol. 1, *Akedah*. New York: DC Comics, 2006.

Sampley, J. Paul. *Walking between the Times: Paul's Moral Reasoning*. Minneapolis: Fortress, 1991.

Scholes, Robert. *Semiotics and Interpretation*. New Haven: Yale University Press, 1982.

Schüssler Fiorenza, Elisabeth. *Revelation: Vision of a Just World*. Minneapolis: Fortress, 1991.

Steimle, Edmund A., Morris J. Niedenthal, and Charles L. Rice, eds. *Preaching the Story*. Philadelphia: Fortress, 1980.

Stendahl, Krister. "Biblical Theology, Contemporary." In vol. 1 of *The Interpreter's Dictionary of the Bible: An Illustrated Encyclopedia*, edited by George Arthur Buttrick, 418–32. Nashville: Abingdon, 1962.

Stone, Bryan P. *Faith and Film: Theological Themes at the Cinema*. St. Louis: Chalice, 2000.

Stott, John R. W. *Between Two Worlds: The Art of Preaching in the Twentieth Century*. Grand Rapids: Eerdmans, 1982.

Taylor, Barbara Brown. *Home by Another Way*. Boston: Cowley, 1999.

Thiselton, Anthony C. *The First Epistle to the Corinthians: A Commentary on the Greek Text*. Grand Rapids: Eerdmans, 2000.

———. *The Two Horizons: New Testament Hermeneutics and Philosophical Description*. Grand Rapids: Eerdmans, 1980.

Thompson, James W. *Preaching Like Paul: Homiletical Wisdom for Today*. Louisville: Westminster John Knox, 2001.

Tolkein, J. R. R. "On Fairy-Stories." In *Tree and Leaf*, 1–81. London: HarperCollins, 2001.
Tombstone. Directed by George P. Cosmatos. Hollywood Pictures Home Video, 1993. Blu Ray.
Troeger, Thomas H. *Imagining a Sermon*. Nashville: Abingdon, 1990.
Vanhoozer, Kevin J. *Biblical Narrative in the Philosophy of Paul Ricoeur: A Study in Hermeneutics and Theology*. Cambridge: Cambridge University Press, 1990.
———. *The Drama of Doctrine: A Canonical Linguistic Approach to Christian Theology*. Louisville: Westminster John Knox, 2005.
Wells, David F. "The Debate over the Atonement in 19th-Century America, Part 1 (of 4 Parts): American Society as Seen from the 19th-Century Pulpit." *Bibliotheca Sacra* 144 (1987) 123–43.
Wells, Samuel. *Improvisation: The Drama of Christian Ethics*. London: SPCK, 2004.
White, Hayden. *Tropics of Discourse: Essays in Cultural Criticism*. Baltimore: Johns Hopkins University Press, 1986.
Wilder, Amos N. *Early Christian Rhetoric*. New York: Harper & Row, 1964.
———. *Theopoetic: Theology and the Religious Imagination*. Philadelphia: Fortress, 1976.
William Shakespeare's Romeo + Juliet. Directed by Baz Luhrmann. 20th Century Fox, 1996. Blu Ray.
Williams, Michael E. *Friends for Life: A Treasury of Stories for Worship and Other Gatherings*. Nashville: Abingdon, 1989.
———. "Preaching as Storytelling." In *Journeys toward Narrative Preaching*, edited by Wayne Bradley Robinson, 106–29. Cleveland: Pilgrim, 1990.
Willis, Wendell Lee. *Idol Meat in Corinth: The Pauline Argument in 1 Corinthians 8 and 10*. Chico, CA: Scholars Press, 1985.
Wilson, Paul Scott. *Broken Words: Reflections on the Craft of Preaching*. Nashville: Abingdon, 2004.
———. "Coherence in *Biographia Literaria*: God, Self, and Coleridge's Seminal Principle." *Philological Quarterly* 72 (1993) 451–69.
———. *A Concise History of Preaching*. Nashville: Abingdon, 1992.
———. *The Four Pages of the Sermon: A Guide to Biblical Preaching*. Nashville: Abingdon, 1999.
———. "Fusion." In *The New Interpreter's Handbook of Preaching*, edited by Paul Scott Wilson, 188–89. Nashville: Abingdon, 2008.
———. *Imagination of the Heart: New Understandings in Preaching*. Nashville: Abingdon: 1988.
———. *The Practice of Preaching*. Rev. ed. Nashville: Abingdon, 2007.
———. *Preaching and Homiletical Theory*. St. Louis: Chalice, 2004.
———. *Preaching as Poetry: Beauty, Goodness, and Truth in Every Sermon*. Nashville: Abingdon, 2014.
Wolterstorff, Nicholas. *Works and Worlds of Art*. Oxford: Clarendon, 1980.
Wright, N. T. "How Can the Bible Be Authoritative?" *Vox Evangelica* 21 (1991) 7–32.
———. *Jesus and the Victory of God*. Christian Origins and the Question of God 2. Minneapolis: Fortress, 1996.
———. *The New Testament and the People of God*. Christian Origins and the Question of God 1. Minneapolis: Fortress, 1992.

———. *The Resurrection of the Son of God*. Christian Origins and the Question of God 3. Minneapolis: Fortress, 2003.

Zhang, Longxi. *Allegoresis: Reading Canonical Literature East and West*. Ithaca: Cornell University Press, 2005.

www.ingramcontent.com/pod-product-compliance
Lightning Source LLC
Chambersburg PA
CBHW031807220426
43662CB00007B/563